THE WEEKEND WOODWORKER

Quick-and-Easy
PROJECTS

THE WEEKEND WOODWORKER

Quick-and-Easy
PROJECTS

Furniture and Accents, Plywood Projects, Toys, Kitchen Projects, Shelving and Storage

Selected and Written by William H. Hylton

Illustrations by Sally Onopa

Photographs by Mitch Mandel

Rodale Press, Emmaus, Pennsylvania

If you have any questions or comments concerning this book, please write:
Rodale Press
Book Reader Service
33 East Minor Street
Emmaus, PA 18098

The authors and editors who compiled this book have tried to make all of the contents as accurate and as correct as possible. Plans, illustrations, photographs, and text have all been carefully checked and cross-checked. However, due to the variability of local conditions, construction materials, personal skill, and so on, neither the author nor Rodale Press assumes any responsibility for any injuries suffered or for damages and other losses incurred that result from the material presented herein. All instructions and plans should be carefully studied and clearly understood before beginning construction.

Senior Woodworking Editor: Jeff Day
Editorial Assistance: Stacy Brobst and
    Karen Earl-Braymer
Copy Editor: Susan G. Berg
Cover Designer: Darlene Schneck
Cover Photographer: Mitch Mandel
Book Designer: Robert E. Ayers,
    PUBLICATION DESIGN
Illustrator: Sally Onopa

Library of Congress Cataloging-in-Publication Data

Hylton, William H.
    The weekend woodworker quick-and-easy projects : furniture and accents, plywood projects, toys, kitchen projects, shelving, and storage / selected and written by William H. Hylton ; illustrations by Sally Onopa ; photographs by Mitch Mandel.
        p.   cm.
    "Simultaneously published by Rodale Press as a book entitled The weekend woodworker annual, 1992"—T.p. verso.
    Includes bibliographical references.
    ISBN 0–87596–128–2 hardcover
    ISBN 0–87857–997–4 paperback
    1. Woodwork.   I. Title.
TT185.H92   1992
684'.08—dc20   91–33573
                                                        CIP

Distributed in the book trade by St. Martin's Press

2   4   6   8   10   9   7   5   3   1   hardcover
2   4   6   8   10   9   7   5   3   1   paperback

CONTENTS

PART THREE: Kitchen Projects

PART FOUR: Toy Projects

PART FIVE: Shelving and Storage Projects

INTRODUCTION

Here's a book being pitched as a collection of projects that can be built in a weekend or two. And over the riffling of pages, I can hear a lot of you saying, "Oh, yeah!?!" You're looking at the veneered piano bench-cabinet, the finger-jointed walnut lap desk, or the flashy painted blanket chest. Or maybe the wall-hung display cabinet.

Collecting projects, under any banner, is a risky proposition. For every woodworker snowed by a project, there's another who feels unchallenged by it. One's scared off, the other's too bored to continue. And that quickly, you as writer and editor have two less in your audience.

My goal in developing this book has been to present a practical collection of projects—a collection with some range, both in woodworking demands and in aesthetic offerings. So the book includes some traditional country-style furniture and accents, some sleek contemporary pieces, and a couple dozen cheap, quick, and easy projects. Practical things like the baker's cooling rack, the small chest, the folding tray tables, the notions box.

I do consider myself a "weekend woodworker." I've been writing and editing books on woodworking and woodworking projects for about 15 years now. Despite all the hours I spend immersed in woodworking, I don't get very much actual shop time. Rodale Press wants written words, and that's what I spend my working hours producing. At home,

there are always chores to do and kids to chauffeur; there are school activities to support, and there's neighborliness to maintain. And yes, I still spend a little time exclusively with my wife. Does this sound at all familiar? I bet it's the story of your life, too.

It's what turns a woodworker into a weekend woodworker.

The upshot is that when I do set time aside to actually work in the shop, I'm rusty. It's in my head, but not in my hands.

In writing up the directions, I've tried to explain to you what I'd like explained if I were the reader. My goal has been to save you time in the planning and execution, so that when you—like me—*do* manage to set aside time to spend in your wood shop, you can get right to work. So each project includes a cutting list and detailed drawings with lots of measurements listed in them. Because flat, one-dimensional drawings don't always make clear how parts fit together, there's at least one exploded view for each project. I talked to the woodworkers who made the pieces shown, learning their approach before writing the step-by-step directions. I always tried to find out from them exactly how they did particular steps, and why they did them that way. The shop tips scattered throughout the chapters emphasize safety and shortcuts. Reminders on tool setups are included right in the text. (Maybe *you* don't need to be reminded, but *I* don't lay out dovetails very often. When I do, I spend the first half hour reading up on how it's done.)

This is not to guarantee that there isn't another way, maybe even an easier way. But every effort has been made to convey accurate dimensions, a complete listing of parts, and a rational, safe, and doable approach.

Go ahead, though, and be sensibly skeptical. Compare the drawings and the cutting list. Read over the directions a few times. Compare them with what you know about woodworking. Is it all there?

Then get to work and make something. Challenge yourself. Build that veneered bench-cabinet or that dovetailed chest. It may take more than a weekend's work, but you *can* do it—and you'll have a good time in the bargain.

PART ONE

FURNITURE AND ACCENT PROJECTS

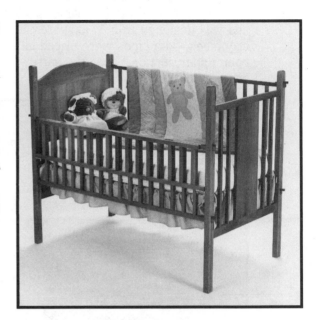

PIPE BOX

The original of this distinctive box dates from before the Revolutionary War and was designed to hold long-stemmed clay pipes. The pipes were placed in the open upper section, while the narrow drawer held tobacco.

The particular box shown was made several years ago by Michael Dunbar, a Portsmouth, New Hampshire, woodworker best known for his books and workshops on making Federal furniture and Windsor chairs. His copy hangs by his back door; each day, as he brings in the mail, he places any bills he's received in the box. That way, they are all in one spot when the time comes to pay them. He keeps stamps in the drawer.

The pipe box may seem unremarkable, but to Dunbar it isn't. To him it is "a sophisticated design." In part the sophistication stems from "the box's curvilinear upper edges that flow both forward and down in a three-dimensional cascade, moving from the top of the fishtail back to the deepest point of the cutout front," he says. "This unbroken movement amounts to $16\frac{7}{8}$ inches on each side, a distance more than four-fifths the box's height. Furthermore, the curves actually appear to wrap around corners. This illusion is accomplished by a distinctive rabbet joint produced by a narrow, low shoulder with a curved corner."

Dunbar points out that profiles of the sides and front duplicated molding profiles common in the eighteenth century. "The box's curves were shapes its owners and users certainly recognized," he explains, "for they were surrounded everywhere by them. No matter where this pipe box hung, one or more of the moldings used for the interior woodwork were the same shape as its cut-out edges."

Design sophistication aside, the box's construction is very simple.

EXPLODED VIEW

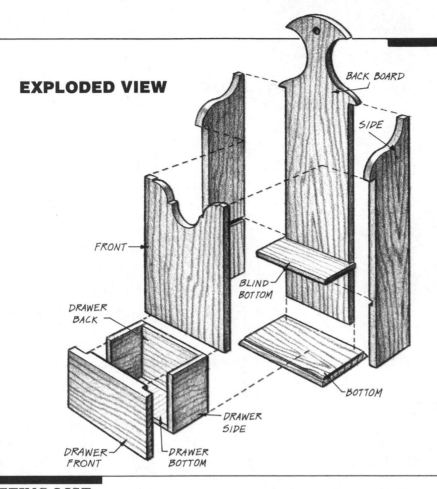

BACK BOARD

SIDE

FRONT

BLIND BOTTOM

DRAWER BACK

BOTTOM

DRAWER SIDE

DRAWER FRONT

DRAWER BOTTOM

CUTTING LIST

Part	Quantity	Dimensions	Material
Front	1	$\frac{3}{8}'' \times 5\frac{3}{4}'' \times 8\frac{1}{8}''$	Pine
Sides	2	$\frac{3}{8}'' \times 3'' \times 14\frac{3}{8}''$	Pine
Back board	1	$\frac{3}{8}'' \times 5\frac{3}{4}'' \times 19\frac{9}{16}''$	Pine
Blind bottom	1	$\frac{1}{4}'' \times 5\frac{1}{4}'' \times 2\frac{3}{4}''$	Pine
Bottom	1	$\frac{7}{16}'' \times 3\frac{7}{8}'' \times 7''$	Pine
Drawer sides	2	$\frac{1}{4}'' \times 3\frac{1}{4}'' \times 2\frac{7}{16}''$	Pine
Drawer bottom	1	$\frac{1}{4}'' \times 4\frac{3}{8}'' \times 2\frac{7}{16}''$	Pine
Drawer front	1	$\frac{11}{16}'' \times 3\frac{1}{4}'' \times 5\frac{3}{4}''$	Pine
Drawer back	1	$\frac{1}{4}'' \times 3'' \times 4\frac{3}{8}''$	Pine

Hardware

1 brass mushroom knob (optional)
1″ headless brads. Available from Tremont Nail Co., 8 Elm St., P.O. Box 111, Wareham, MA 02571.

PLAN VIEWS

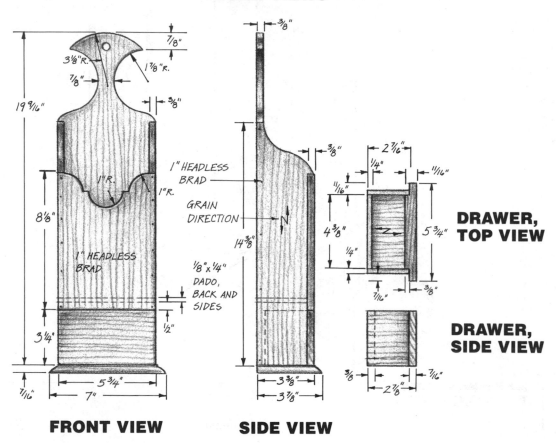

FRONT VIEW

SIDE VIEW

DRAWER, TOP VIEW

DRAWER, SIDE VIEW

1 Select the stock and cut the parts. The original box is made from pine, but almost any even-textured wood (hard or soft) will do. Dunbar made his replica from basswood.

Much of the stock is quite thin. You may want to resaw 4/4 (four-quarters) or 5/4 (five-quarters) stock on a band saw, then plane the stock to thickness. In any case, hand plane all surfaces to remove any machine marks. Cut, joint, and square the individual pieces.

2 Lay out and cut the front, sides, and back. The box's curvilinear upper edges flow both forward and down, from the top of the fishtail to the deepest point of the front cutout. These curves actually appear to wrap around the corners, an illusion created by the distinctive tabs that overlap the adjoining pieces.

Lay out the curved profiles on the front, sides, and back following the *Profile Patterns*. If you cut them on a band saw, use a narrow, fine-toothed blade. But you can cut the curves just as quickly with a coping saw. Clean up the edges with a drum sander or a combination of hand tools, including a spoke-shave, files, and sandpaper. Use a chisel to pare the fillets that separate the astragals and the cove in the front.

The blind bottom fits into dadoes cut in the sides and back. Cut them ¼ inch wide × ⅛ inch deep.

Finally, locate and drill a ¼-inch hole in the back. The hole should be centered on a line between the points of the fishtail.

3 **Make the bottom.** The bottom's edge has a shape called a thumbnail (the name's inspiration is clear if you look at your thumb's profile). Dunbar formed the edge profile with a specialized plane. To approximate the profile with a router, use a ¾-inch rounding-over bit, engaging only the outer segment of the cutter. (A smaller rounding-over bit will produce too blunt a profile.) Because the workpiece is small, do this on a table-mounted router. An alternative approach—slightly less refined but quite acceptable—is to bevel the edges with a block plane.

SHOP TIP:
The dadoes for the blind bottom are short, narrow, and shallow. They can be cut very quickly by hand. Try this: Lay them out with a try square and scratch awl. (The awl creates a very fine line and is therefore more accurate than a pencil.) Score the edges of the dadoes with a utility knife, and pare out the waste with a ¼-inch chisel.

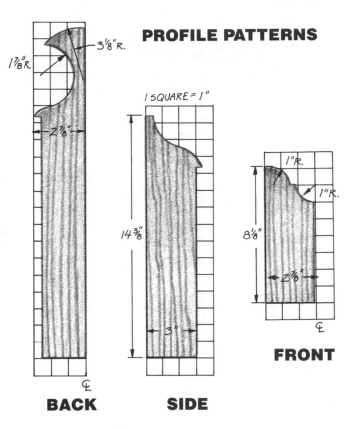

PROFILE PATTERNS

1 SQUARE = 1"

BACK   SIDE   FRONT

4 **Assemble the box.** The box is simply nailed together. Attach the sides to the back first, using 1-inch headless brads. Insert the blind bottom into its dadoes. Make sure its front edge is flush with the sides. Nail the front in place, then the bottom.

5 **Make the drawer.** Like the box itself, the drawer is simply nailed together with headless brads. The sides and bottom fit into rabbets cut in the front. The rabbets on the ends of the drawer front (these are for the sides) are $^{11}/_{16}$ inch wide × ¼ inch deep. The rabbet on the bottom is ¼ inch wide × ¼ inch deep. Cut these rabbets.

SHOP TIP: The drawer front is quite small, so the rabbets in it can be cut easily and quickly with a dovetail saw. Use a marking gauge and a try square to lay out the rabbets, then cut them with the saw. Clean up the saw cuts with a shoulder plane.

Assemble the drawer by nailing the two sides to the front with 1-inch headless brads. Fit the back between the two sides and nail it in place. Insert the bottom. If any adjustment needs to be done to make the bottom fit, use a block plane. Nail the bottom in place.

The original pipe box has no drawer pull; rather, it is opened by gripping the end edges. Over the years, repeated use has worn away the paint and even rounded the edges—a very charming effect. If, however, it's an effect that doesn't appeal to you, add a pull. A small brass mushroom knob would be appropriate. To install such a knob, locate the drawer front's center and make a pilot hole with a bradawl. Screw the knob into this hole.

EMMY'S FOOTSTOOL

In the old days a footstool was used to prop up your feet, the way we do these days with an ottoman. A footstool is more often used today for reaching high places. That's certainly the purpose of the footstool shown. Two-year-old Emmy Mandel needs a step up to reach the sink, which the stool provides.

Emmy's dad, woodworking photographer Mitch Mandel, built the stool in just a couple of hours. He used oak, since that's what he had on hand, but a lighter-weight material would definitely make it easier to carry. The splayed legs make the stool quite stable, and the generous overhang provides practical handles for Emmy, who needs two hands to manage the stool.

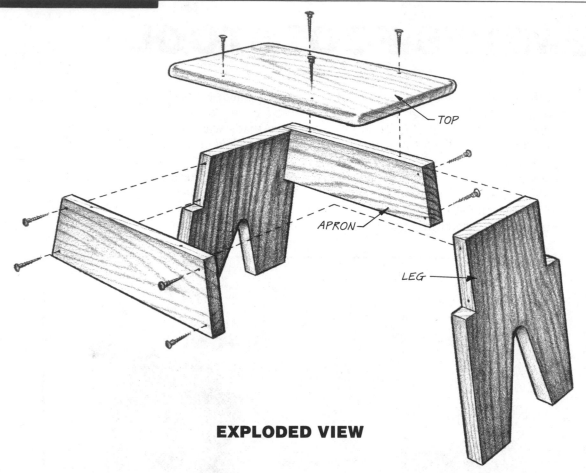

TOP

APRON

LEG

EXPLODED VIEW

1 **Select the stock and cut the parts.** You can make this footstool from almost any wood. The required pieces are few and small; you probably can find them in your shop's scrap bin, or you can work around defects in lower-grade material. The stool Mitch made for Emmy has all five parts cut from 4/4 (four-quarters) oak, which he had on hand for other projects. Because it is oak, the stool is fairly heavy.

After selecting your material, dress the wood if necessary. Mitch's oak had been dressed to a $13/16$-inch thickness, which accounts for the dimension in the Cutting List. To accommodate thicker or thinner stock, simply adjust the depth of the apron notches. Cut the parts to the sizes specified by the Cutting List.

2 **Cut the bevels and miters.** The legs of the stool are canted for stability. Their top and bottom edges are beveled, so that they rest squarely on the floor and against the top. Set your table saw to cut a 10-degree bevel, and trim both legs to length (make sure the bevels you cut on each leg are parallel, as opposed to converging).

To ensure that the miters on the ends of the aprons match the bevels, use a sliding T-bevel to capture the angle from the saw blade. Crank the blade as high as it will go, and press the sliding T-bevel against it (with the handle flat on the saw table, the tongue against the side of the blade). Return the saw blade to its perpendicular setting. Use the sliding T-bevel to set the angle of the miter gauge by holding the bevel's handle

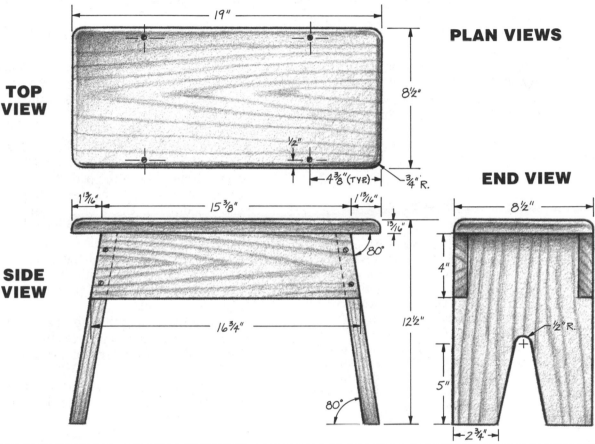

PLAN VIEWS

TOP VIEW

SIDE VIEW

END VIEW

CUTTING LIST

Part	Quantity	Dimension	Material
Legs	2	$^{13}/_{16}'' \times 8^{1}/_{2}'' \times 12''$	Oak
Aprons	2	$^{13}/_{16}'' \times 4'' \times 16^{3}/_{4}''$	Oak
Top	1	$^{13}/_{16}'' \times 8^{1}/_{2}'' \times 19''$	Oak

Hardware

12 drywall screws, #6 × 2″

against the saw blade and adjusting the gauge's fence parallel to the bevel's tongue.

Having done this, miter the ends of the aprons. These cuts should converge, as shown in the *Side View*. Leave the miter gauge set to use in the next step.

3 **Notch the legs for the aprons.** On each leg, lay out the apron notches as well as the V-shaped notch that forms the feet as indicated in the *End View*. Adjust the depth of cut of your table saw to match the thickness of the aprons. Stand the leg on edge in the miter gauge (still set to the angle at

SHOP TIP: Assembly of a project like this stool can be made easier if you have two drill-drivers. Chuck a pilot-hole bit in one, a screwdriver bit in the other. (The best pilot-hole bits have a tapered drill bit and an adjustable collar to control the counterbore depth.) While you hold two parts in alignment with one hand, drill the pilot hole with the other. Still holding the assembly, lay down the drill-driver, position a screw, pick up the other drill-driver (with the screwdriver bit), and set the screw.

which the aprons were mitered), and make the shoulder cut. Drill a 1-inch-diameter hole at the crotch of the V-shaped notch. Complete the notches with a saber saw.

4 **Complete the top.** Mark the corners to be rounded off with a compass. Using a saber saw, round them off. Finally, with a ¼-inch rounding-over bit in a router, machine the edges of the top.

5 **Assemble the stool.** The stool is assembled with glue and drywall screws. Counterbore the pilot holes, so that the screws can be concealed beneath wood plugs. Use a plug cutter to make plugs from scraps of the stock used in the stool. Apply glue to the hole with a cotton swab and set the plug, aligning the plug's grain with that of the stool. After the glue dries, pare off the plugs with a chisel.

Before attaching the top, use a router and rounding-over bit to radius the exposed edges of the leg-and-apron assembly.

After the stool is assembled and the plugs have been trimmed, sand the stool and apply a finish.

FOLDING TRAY TABLE

Here's the perfect occasional table: You can't accidentally collapse it, yet it easily folds flat. There are no loose parts to lose, and it even has an integral handle. The table is designed around a very nifty concept, one that's so simple it's confusing.

Each pair of legs is joined by a pivot and forms an X. The legs naturally tend to move in opposite directions around the pivot. Unfettered, the leg tops spread farther and farther apart until the assembly collapses. The design takes advantage of this tendency by linking halves of the tabletop to opposite halves of the legworks. When the tabletop

halves meet, they interlock, arresting the legs. The more downward force that's applied on the tabletop, the more the halves of the top press against each other, because the legs are trying to spread.

To collapse the table, you simply lift the outside edges of the top and pull the two halves away from one another. The legs close up and the tabletop halves swing down flush on either side.

I first saw the table's engineering in an upscale occasional table that a professional furniture maker had built. More recently, a colleague showed me a little stool—kind of a camping stool—built this

way. Then someone else showed me photos of a folding picnic table—same concept. For me, the little table shown is the ideal application. Though now that I think about it, an occasional shop or kitchen stool would be nice. . . .

At any rate, this table is a great weekend project. In fact, you ought to build a pair or a quartet. Depending on the state of your lumber and scrap supplies, you can build a couple of tables for less than $20 in lumber and hardware. A few afternoons or evenings in the shop is all the time needed to make them.

1 Select the stock and cut the parts. For the table shown, the tabletop was cut from old (late nineteenth century) pine stair treads, the handle from a birch dowel, and the remaining parts from mahogany 1 × 4 tongue-and-groove "porch flooring." The intent in selecting pine and mahogany stocks was to have contrast in wood color between the legworks and the tabletop. You can use almost any wood in making the table. Given the slender members in the project, you'll want to avoid boards with defects that will weaken the structure or

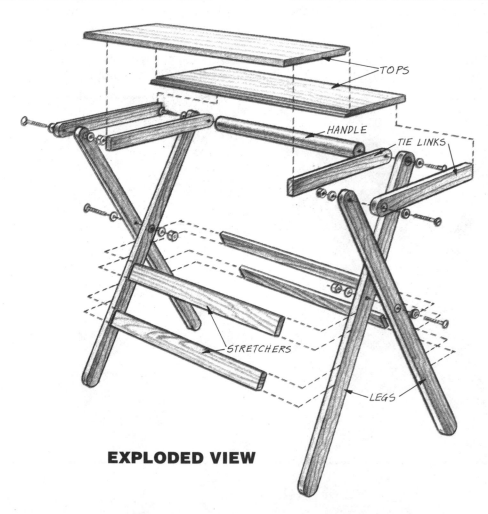

EXPLODED VIEW

CUTTING LIST

Part	Quantity	Dimensions	Material
Tops	2	$\frac{1}{2}'' \times 8'' \times 24''$	#2 pine
Handle	1	$1\frac{1}{8}''$ dia. $\times 16''$	Hardwood dowel
Legs	4	$\frac{3}{4}'' \times 1\frac{3}{8}'' \times 28\frac{1}{2}''$	Mahogany
Tie links	4	$\frac{3}{4}'' \times 1\frac{3}{8}'' \times 13''$	Mahogany
Stretchers	2	$\frac{5}{16}'' \times 1\frac{3}{8}'' \times 20\frac{1}{2}''$	Mahogany
Stretchers	2	$\frac{5}{16}'' \times 1\frac{3}{8}'' \times 19''$	Mahogany

Hardware

12 flathead wood screws, #4 $\times 1\frac{1}{4}''$	4 roundhead machine screws, $\frac{10}{32} \times 1\frac{1}{4}''$
16 flathead wood screws, #4 $\times 1''$	4 stop nuts, $\frac{10}{32}$
2 roundhead wood screws, #8 $\times 2''$	10 washers, #8

detract from the project's appearance. For the top, you might think about cabinet-grade plywood.

Cut the parts to the sizes specified by the Cutting List. If necessary, glue up stock to form the two tops.

It may be helpful to note that the dimensions of the mahogany I used gave rise to some of the part dimensions. For example, after ripping off the tongue and the groove, I could rip the mahogany in half and get two strips $1\frac{3}{8}$ inches wide—hence the width of the legs, tie links, and stretchers. I could resaw one $\frac{3}{4}$-inch-thick strip on the table saw to get two $\frac{5}{16}$-inch-thick stretchers. These dimensions allowed me to cut the legworks for two tables from 18 linear feet of mahogany.

2 **Make a template for the legs and tie links.** For the sake of appearance, the legs and tie links should be as uniform as possible. When the table is folded, the legs and links nest together, and profile variations become obvious.

To start with uniform layouts, make all of them from a single template. Lay out the shape and screw-hole locations on a piece of hardboard or $\frac{1}{4}$-inch plywood. Cut the template on the band saw or with a saber saw, and bore the holes.

3 **Make the legs and tie links.** Use the template to lay out four legs for each table. This is a matter of positioning the template on the leg blank, then marking the hole locations and scribing the arcs at the top and bottom. Since each tie link is a duplicate of the top segment of the leg, you can use the template to mark the screw-hole locations and the top shape on the tie links as well.

On the band saw or using a saber saw, round off the tops and bottoms of the parts, cutting to within $\frac{1}{16}$ inch of the layout marks.

Drill the holes using a $\frac{5}{16}$-inch-diameter bit, making sure that they are perpendicular. Some of these holes must be counterbored, so that the screwheads and nuts seat below the wood surface, allowing the assembly to fold properly. Counterbore the leg's pivot hole in one face, then roll the leg over to counterbore the top hole in the other face. Counterbore the holes in only two of the tie links.

Sand the curved ends of these parts to the layout lines, then break the edges with either a block plane or a router and ⅛-inch rounding-over bit. Sand the parts thoroughly.

4 **Ready the stretchers, handle, and tops for assembly.** There are several minor operations remaining before the table can be assembled.

Drill two pilot holes in each end of the stretchers for 1-inch wood screws. Position them uniformly for best appearance. Break the exposed edges with a block plane, then sand these parts.

Drill a pilot hole for a 2-inch wood screw into the center of each end of the handle. Sand the handle.

If you glued up stock for the top, remove the clamps and scrape away any dried glue. If necessary, trim the panels to the size specified by the Cutting List. Plane or sand them flat.

Next cut the rabbets that lock the two halves of the tabletop together when the completed table is set up. I cut them with a router and a ½-inch rabbeting bit. Set up as if you were cutting a half-lap, which is to say you want to cut away exactly one-half the thickness of the stock from each tabletop piece. Be sure you rabbet the top of one piece, the bottom of the other. When you are done, finish sand the tops.

5 **Assemble the table.** The first step in the assembly process is to fasten the tie links to the tops. To position the links, lay out the tops and links, using the legs and handle to provide the correct spacing. Orient the rounded ends of the outer links (the ones with the counterbores) opposite those of the inner links; the counterbores face out. Drill three countersunk pilot holes through each link into the top, and drive 1¼-inch wood screws to fasten the links to the top; the outer links are attached to one half of the top, the inner links to the other.

With the links screwed down, you can install the handle and legs. Drive a 2-inch wood screw through a leg and an inner link into each end of the handle. Connect the legs and outer links with machine screws and stop nuts. Then connect each pair of legs with a machine screw and stop nut, creating a pivot.

With the unit folded, install the stretchers using 1-inch wood screws. Attach the short stretchers to the inner legs, then turn the unit over and attach the long stretchers to the outer legs.

Test the folding action. If the several pivot points are too tight, the action will be unnecessarily stiff. The machine screws can be loose enough to permit easy knockdown and setup; the stop nuts won't loosen and fall off, even if they aren't tightened.

6 **Apply a finish.** I applied a penetrating oil finish, brushing it on the partially disassembled table. (I removed the machine screws at the leg pivot, giving me two elements.) Use whatever finish you favor, even paint.

PLAN VIEWS

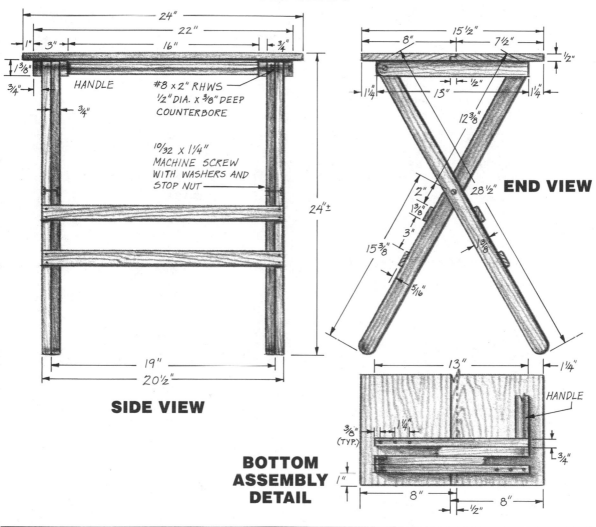

24"
22"
16"
1"
3"
3/4"
1 3/8"
3/4"
3/4"
HANDLE
#8 x 2" RHWS
1/2" DIA. x 3/8" DEEP
COUNTERBORE

10/32 x 1 1/4"
MACHINE SCREW
WITH WASHERS AND
STOP NUT

24"±

19"
20 1/2"

SIDE VIEW

15 1/2"
8"
7 1/2"
1/2"
1 1/4"
1/2"
1 1/4"
15"
12 3/8"
2"
1 3/8"
3"
15 3/8"
5/16"
3/8"
28 1/2"

END VIEW

13"
1 1/4"
HANDLE
3/8"
(TYP.)
1 1/4"
3/4"
1"
8"
1/2"
8"

BOTTOM ASSEMBLY DETAIL

FOLDING SEQUENCE

1. LIFT EDGES OF TOP SLIGHTLY AND PULL OUTWARD.

2. FOLD LEGS BY CONTINUING TO PULL TOP HALVES AWAY FROM EACH OTHER.

3. WITH LEGS FOLDED, LOWER TOPS.

4. COMPLETELY FOLDED

2 3/8"
28 1/2"
1/2"
1 3/8"

15

FOLDING STOOL

Want to make a folding stool?

This stool is built to use the same engineering as the folding tray table. It is constructed in the same sequence. The parts are slightly different dimensions, and the seat is slatted rather than solid. Use the stool whenever and wherever a lightweight, portable, space-efficient seat is felicitous. No need to burden you with the step-by-step instructions, but here's a cutting list and some plan views.

FOLDING STOOL, PLAN VIEWS

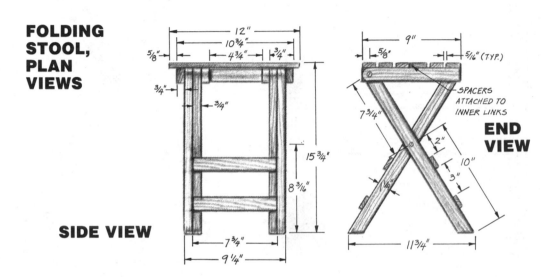

SIDE VIEW

END VIEW

SPACERS ATTACHED TO INNER LINKS

CUTTING LIST

Part	Quantity	Dimensions	Material
Top slats	6	$\frac{5}{16}'' \times 1\frac{1}{4}'' \times 12''$	Mahogany
Slat spacers	2	$\frac{5}{16}'' \times \frac{5}{16}'' \times 1\frac{1}{4}''$	Mahogany
Handle	1	$1''$ dia. $\times 4\frac{3}{4}''$	Hardwood dowel
Stool legs	4	$\frac{3}{4}'' \times 1\frac{1}{4}'' \times 18\frac{3}{8}''$	Mahogany
Tie links	4	$\frac{3}{4}'' \times 1\frac{1}{4}'' \times 9''$	Mahogany
Stretchers	2	$\frac{5}{16}'' \times 1\frac{1}{4}'' \times 9\frac{1}{4}''$	Mahogany
Stretchers	2	$\frac{5}{16}'' \times 1\frac{1}{4}'' \times 7\frac{3}{4}''$	Mahogany
Hardware			

12 flathead wood screws, #4 $\times 1\frac{1}{4}''$

16 flathead wood screws, #4 $\times 1''$

2 roundhead wood screws, #8 $\times 2''$

4 roundhead machine screws, $\frac{10}{32} \times 1\frac{1}{4}''$

4 stop nuts, $\frac{10}{32}$

10 washers, #8

SMALL CHEST

This small chest was originally built as a repository for placemats; its drawers are just the right size. It never saw much use as such, but it did spend a number of years in my office as a catch-all. Now it's serving as a bedside table.

Made from pine and spare in design, this chest is an excellent weekend project. The joinery is basic but sound. All the cuts and the dadoes and grooves can be produced on the table saw (or radial arm saw), so an extensively equipped shop isn't required. There's no special hardware to buy. Probably the only deterrent to completing it in a single weekend is the number of bar or pipe clamps you have. There are four panels that must be glued up from narrow boards; if you can do them all at once, you can complete the project by Sunday evening.

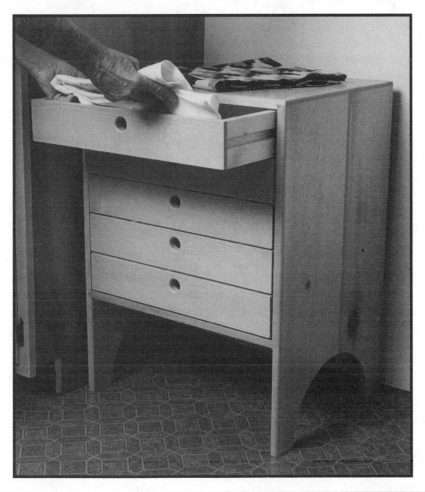

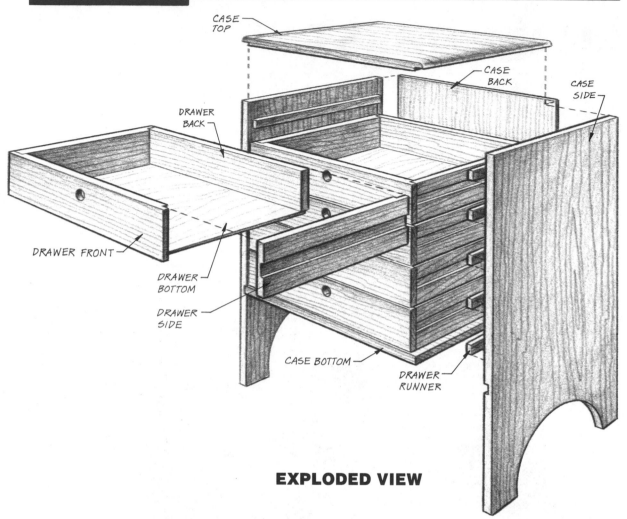

CASE
TOP

CASE
BACK

CASE
SIDE

DRAWER
BACK

DRAWER FRONT

DRAWER
BOTTOM

DRAWER
SIDE

CASE BOTTOM

DRAWER
RUNNER

EXPLODED VIEW

1 Select the stock and cut the parts. The chest shown is made from pine, but any number of woods would be suitable. We used commonplace 1-by stock rather than more pricey furniture-making stock. Regardless of your choice, make sure that they're flat, straight-grained boards, particularly for making up the case's panels. Some knots are acceptable, though you want to avoid loose ones.

Pine tends to cup. One way to minimize this is to make up the 17-inch-wide case panels from four or five narrow boards rather than only a couple of wide boards. And given the joinery, it's a good idea to alternate the direction of the growth rings, again to minimize cupping across the width of the panels.

Cut the case back and drawer bottoms from plywood. We used lauan plywood, an inexpensive variety faced with Philippine mahogany. It generally blends well with pine, especially if it is to be stained. And as used here, it is fairly well hidden.

18

CUTTING LIST

Part	Quantity	Dimensions	Material
Case sides	2	$\frac{3}{4}''$ × 17″ × $28\frac{5}{8}''$	Pine
Case top	1	$\frac{3}{4}''$ × 17″ × $21\frac{1}{8}''$	Pine
Case bottom	1	$\frac{3}{4}''$ × 17″ × $20\frac{3}{8}''$	Pine
Case back	1	$\frac{1}{4}''$ × $20\frac{3}{8}''$ × 19″	Lauan plywood
Drawer bottoms	5	$\frac{1}{4}''$ × $13\frac{5}{8}''$ × $18\frac{3}{4}''$	Lauan plywood
Drawer fronts	5	$\frac{3}{4}''$ × $3\frac{1}{2}''$ × $19\frac{1}{2}''$	Pine
Drawer sides	10	$\frac{3}{4}''$ × $3\frac{1}{2}''$ × 14″	Pine
Drawer backs	5	$\frac{3}{4}''$ × $3\frac{1}{2}''$ × $18\frac{3}{4}''$	Pine
Drawer runners	10	$\frac{3}{8}''$ × $\frac{23}{32}''$ × $16\frac{1}{8}''$	Pine

Hardware

6d finishing nails
$\frac{3}{4}''$ brads

2 **Cut the drawer joinery.** Work on the drawers can proceed while the glue in the case panels dries. Except for the bottoms, all the drawer parts must be grooved or rabbeted for assembly.

Cut a ¼-inch-wide × ¼-inch-deep groove in the front, sides, and back of each drawer for the bottom. The joinery allows these grooves to be plowed from end to end of each piece. Use your standard saw blade to make these grooves. Set the rip fence to locate the groove in relation to the bottom edge; make a pass through each piece. Move the fence slightly, and make a second pass to widen the groove. Match the thickness of the bottom as closely as possible, so that it doesn't rattle after assembly.

Groove the sides for the drawer runners next. Using a dado cutter, make these grooves ¾ inch wide × ⁵⁄₁₆ inch deep. Position these grooves as indicated in the *Drawer, Front View*.

With the dado cutter, cut the rab-

bets next. Leave the width of the cutter unchanged, but increase the depth of cut to ⅜ inch. Cut rabbets on both ends of the fronts, but only on the rear ends of the sides. As you rabbet the sides, be sure to make five matching pairs of sides rather than ten identical sides. When cutting the rabbets, use the rip fence to control the width of the cut, and guide the workpieces with the miter gauge.

3 **Drill the finger holes in the drawer fronts.** A 1-inch-diameter hole in the center of each drawer front serves as the pull. You can use a spade bit to bore these holes. To minimize tearout, don't drill completely through the pieces. Instead, flip each piece over when the center point breaks through, and complete the hole from the back.

Use a router and a ¼-inch rounding-over bit to radius the edges of the finger holes.

PLAN VIEWS

DRAWER DETAILS

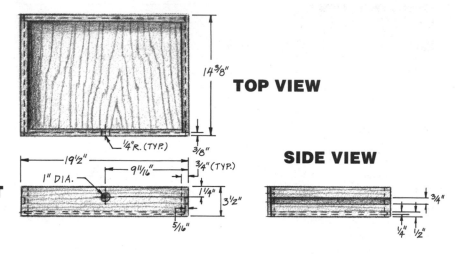

TOP VIEW

SIDE VIEW

FRONT VIEW

CASE DETAILS

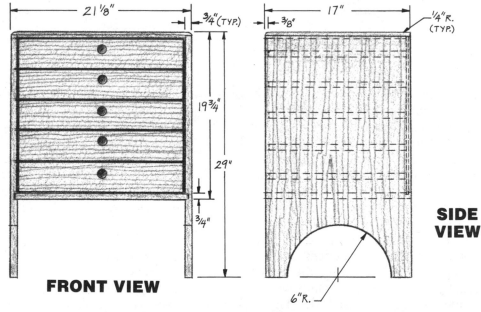

FRONT VIEW

SIDE VIEW

4 **Assemble the drawers.** Before assembling the drawers, finish sand all the parts. Use glue and 6d finishing nails to join each drawer. Because you are securing the glue joints with nails, you don't need to clamp.

To assemble each drawer, lay out a side and stand the bottom in its groove.

Don't glue the bottom in place. Add the front and back, then the second side. Drive nails through the second side into the front and back. Flip the drawer so that it is resting on the side that's been nailed, and finish nailing the drawer. The bottom *should* square up the drawer, but check with a try square.

Buckling is almost inevitable when edge-gluing several boards to create a broad panel for casework. As you tighten the clamps on your arrangement of four or five boards, the center of the assembly starts to bulge upward. You deal with the center seam, and the buckling shifts to another joint.

Alternating clamps from one face to the other is the common fix. But you can increase the likelihood of creating a flat panel by gluing only two boards at a time. Glue up the first two boards, and after the glue sets, add a third. Still later, add the fourth, and so on. Having only one seam to worry about takes a lot of vexation out of the clamping process.

5 **Cut the joinery in the case sides and top.** The sides join the top in rabbet joints. The bottom fits into dadoes in the sides. That's it.

You can cut the rabbets and the dadoes using a dado cutter on the table saw. But it may be easier to guide a router across the panels than to guide the panels over the table saw. If you use a router, clamp a straightedge to the panels to guide the tool. Make both the cuts ¾ inch wide × ⅜ inch deep.

Finally, cut the groove for the back. Do this on a table saw with its standard blade, as you grooved the drawers for their bottoms. The groove in the top and bottom can be cut from end to end, while the grooves in the sides must stop at the dado. You'll have to flatten the groove's bottom at the dado using a chisel.

6 **Cut the foot arch, and nail the drawer runners to the sides.** The arch that forms the chest's feet has a 6-inch radius, scribed from the midpoint of the sides' width. Use a string compass or trammel to lay out the arches, then cut them on the band saw or with a saber saw. Sand the cuts smooth.

Nail the drawer runners to the sides using ¾-inch brads. Don't glue the runners, since that will inhibit the sides' freedom to expand and contract with changes in the weather. Position the runners as shown in the *Case, Side View*. After tacking each runner with a couple of brads, you can test the spacing by standing the drawers on their sides and fitting them over the runners.

7 **Assemble the case.** The case is joined strictly with glue. Assemble the case without glue first, and if everything fits properly, repeat the process using glue. Before proceeding with the glue-up, sand all the parts. With one side laid out, stand the back in its groove, but don't glue it. Glue the bottom into the dado, then add the second side. Set the case on its feet, add the top, and apply clamps.

8 **Apply a finish.** After the glue has dried and the clamps are removed, radius the exposed edges of the case with a router and a ¼-inch rounding-over bit. Do any necessary sanding, and check the fit of the drawers in the case.

Apply two coats of whatever finish you prefer. The chest shown was finished with Deft, a polyurethane.

SPLAY-LEGGED TABLE

This table, a copy of a nearly 200-year-old piece, has been used around Michael Dunbar's house for some ten years. Since it's small, the table is most comfortable for two, though it will seat four. Made from pine, it's very lightweight. These qualities make it the ideal occasional table—useful for numerous light-duty, utilitarian tasks. In this way, it probably serves the Dunbars much as the original served its owners.

"We keep the table against a wall in the den and move it out when we want to eat in front of the television," says Dunbar. "It acts as a serving table when we have a large number of guests, a work table when I pay the monthly bills. And in the summer, it is easily carried outside when we are entertaining in the backyard."

The legs on this table are angled, or splayed, which gives the form its name. Though they are splayed at only 99 degrees, the legs' cant is exaggerated because just their two inside surfaces are tapered. This makes the angle formed

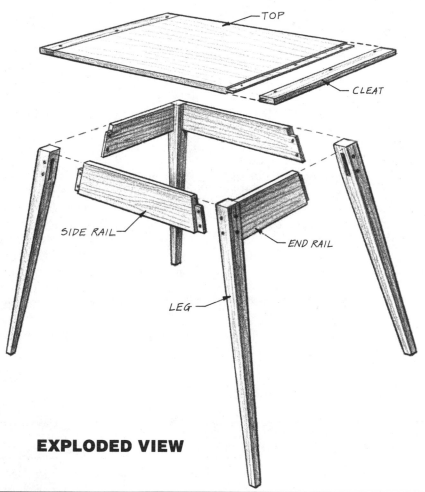

TOP

CLEAT

SIDE RAIL

END RAIL

LEG

EXPLODED VIEW

CUTTING LIST

Part	Quantity	Dimensions	Material
Top	1	$5/8'' \times 21\,3/4'' \times 32\,3/4''$	Pine
Cleats	2	$3/4'' \times 2'' \times 22\,3/4''$	Pine
Wooden pins	22	$1/4''$ dia.	Pine
Legs	4	$1\,1/2'' \times 1\,1/2'' \times 30\,1/2''$	Pine
Side rails	2	$11/16'' \times 4\,3/8'' \times 23\,7/8''$	Pine
End rails	2	$11/16'' \times 4\,3/8'' \times 13\,7/8''$	Pine

Hardware

4 cut finishing nails, 8d

between the bottom of the skirt and each leg's inner surface 101 degrees.

As a project for a class Dunbar once taught on basic hand tools, particularly the plane, the table shown was made using hand tools exclusively. However, you most likely will use some machinery in combination with hand tools. In doing so, don't completely surrender the details that portray the handmade character of the table. Among these are the whittled pins that secure the joints and the cut nails that attach the top to the leg assembly. "They may not seem very important," Dunbar points out, "but small details often make the piece."

1 Make the top panel. The table has what is known colloquially as a breadboard top. It has a cleat on either end to keep it from warping. The cleats

SHOP TIP: To counter a wide surface's tendency to warp, alternate the grain orientation of the boards composing the panel. If the first is heart side up, place the second heart side down, and so forth.

are joined to the top panel with a deep tongue-and-groove joint that is pinned in three places, which allows for seasonal movement. The top is 21¾ inches wide. Although it is possible to find boards that wide in some parts of the country, most woodworkers will have to glue up several narrower boards. To allow for truing and squaring the top, the boards' total width should be slightly more than the finished width. Joint the edges, glue, and clamp.

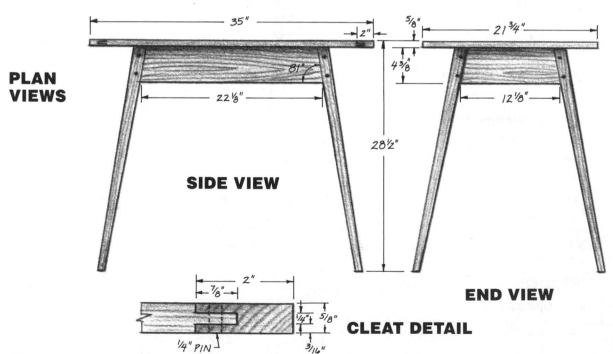

PLAN VIEWS

35"   2"   5/8"   21¾"

81°   4⅜"

22⅛"   12⅛"

28½"

SIDE VIEW

END VIEW

2"   7/8"   ¼"   5/8"

¼" PIN   3/16"

CLEAT DETAIL

After the glue has dried, plane or sand the top to achieve a truly flat surface with no irregularities. Then cut the top to size. Without the cleats, the length is 32¾ inches. Joint one edge to be sure it is straight and to remove any dents left by the bar clamps. Square the two ends with this edge. Cut the second edge parallel to the first.

Form the tongues next by cutting a ⅞-inch-wide × 3⁄16-inch-deep rabbet in each face of the top. Use a router with a straight bit to cut these wide rabbets.

2 **Make and attach the cleats.** Cut the cleats to length, width, and thickness. Rout the ¼-inch-wide × ⅞-inch-deep groove.

Because the grain in the cleats runs opposite to the top's, you may experience an interesting phenomenon. If you make the top in the summer when the humidity is high, it will shrink in the winter when your house is full of very dry air, becoming more narrow than the cleat is long. On the other hand, if you make the top in the winter, it will swell wider than the cleats in the summer. For this reason, you should fasten the cleats only with wooden pins, as shown in the *Cleat*

Detail. Do not glue these joints, as the top will tear itself apart if not allowed to move freely.

Slide each cleat over its tongue, and hold it tightly in place with a pair of bar clamps. Drill three ¼-inch holes that are centered on the tongue's width. Each end hole should be about 1¾ inches from the edge, while the third hole is centered on the top's width. Drill from the top side, so that any problems with tear-out will occur underneath.

Whittle a pin about the size of a pencil. Tap it through the hole with a light hammer until it stops moving. Cut it off with a backsaw, and pare it flush with a chisel. Repeat for all the holes.

LEG JOINERY DETAIL

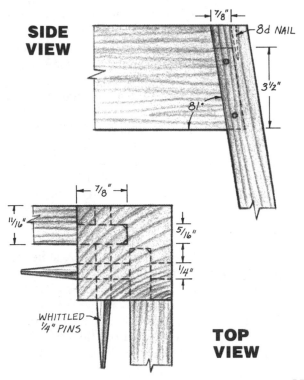

SIDE VIEW

⅞"

8d NAIL

3½"

81°

⅞"

11⁄16"

5⁄16"

¼"

WHITTLED ¼" PINS

TOP VIEW

3 **Make the legs.** Prepare the stock. Notice the length given for the legs by the Cutting List is 2 inches longer than in the drawing. This excess will be cut off when the joinery is complete. Plane the wood to thickness and joint one edge. Rip four legs to 1½ inches square, and hand plane all four surfaces to remove tool marks.

Lay out the mortises, leaving an inch of the leg's extra length above the skirt's upper edge. If you rout or drill the mortises, square their ends with a sharp chisel. At the same time, use the chisel to angle the mortise's lower edge toward the foot. This will accommodate the tenon's lower edge, which is not at a right angle to the shoulder.

4 **Make the skirts.** The tenons that join the skirts to the legs have only one shoulder and one haunch, a form traditionally used in table and chair construction. With no shoulder on the back surface, the front shoulder becomes deeper, resulting in a thicker mortise wall—important on a long-legged piece of furniture. While glue blocks usually back up this single-shoulder type of tenon, no glue blocks were used on the original table, and it has managed to survive almost 200 years. Remember, though, the table is intended only for light duty.

Start the skirts by planing the stock to thickness and ripping it to width. If you use a table saw, tilt the blade to rip one edge to 81 degrees. This will be the top edge. Cut the stock to length next, mitering the ends to 81 degrees. Now cut the tenons. Set a sliding T-bevel to 81 degrees and use it to mark the tenon shoulders, ⅞ inches from the ends of the skirts. (Leave the T-bevel set for

later use.) You can cut the tenons with a router or on a table saw. They are so simple you also can do them easily by hand. Each tenon has one haunch on its upper edge. Cut this with a backsaw.

5 **Fit the joints.** Fit each tenon into its corresponding mortise. Make any fine adjustments to the tenons with a shoulder plane. Bevel the edges of each tenon's end, as they are easier to start into a tight mortise. Before you take a joint apart, trace a line on the leg using the skirt's top edge as a guide. This line will help you when you have to trim the leg tops.

6 **Complete the legs.** Mold the edges first. This operation is optional, as the outside corners can be left square without seriously affecting the table's appearance. The molding can be done with a router, a shaper, a combination plane, or even a scratch tool.

Trim the tops of the legs, cutting at a compound angle, 81 degrees on each side. This will make the leg tops flush with the skirts and parallel to the tabletop's lower surface. Cut the legs by tilting your table saw blade to 9 degrees off vertical and setting the miter gauge to 81 degrees. Or you can use the sliding T-bevel to extend onto all four sides the lines you traced along the tops of the

SHOP TIP: As you take apart the mortise-and-tenon joints, number them in sequence from 1 to 8, marking both mortise and tenon with the joint number. This way you can quickly match the parts later.

LEG PROFILE

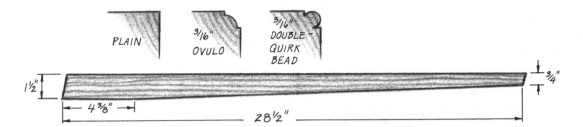

skirts. Then use a backsaw to cut on the pencil lines.

Cut the legs to length. Measure 28½ inches from the highest point on the leg's end and make a mark on the opposite edge. Use the sliding T-bevel to lay out the same compound angle as at the top of the leg. Each line at the foot must be parallel to its counterpart at the top. Cut on this line using either the table saw or a backsaw.

Finally, taper the legs. Taper only the two inside surfaces (those with the mortises). You can taper the legs on a table saw using a tapering jig. However, the job can be done just as quickly with a jointer plane. At the leg's bottom, measure and mark ¾ inch from each outside edge. Use a try square to make a line even with the bottom of the mortises. With a straightedge, draw a line connecting the two marks. Repeat for the second taper. Set your jointer plane to make a heavy cut, and plane to the line.

7 Join the legs and skirt. Before assembling the legs and skirts, cut two wedges to 9 degrees (the complement of 81 degrees) to act as shims for the bar clamps. Use 2-inch-thick scrap.

Now assemble the two sides of the

table base independently. Apply glue to the mortises and insert the tenons. Span the assembly with a bar clamp, with the two shims protecting the legs. Use the clamp to pull the assembly tightly together—until there is no gap showing between the leg and the tenon shoulder. Pin the joints next. Drill two ¼-inch holes that pierce each joint. Whittle a pin and drive it with a light hammer. Saw off the pin, whittle a new one, and repeat for all four holes.

Repeat the entire process for the other side.

The sides are then joined to the end pieces in one operation. Glue all four mortises and insert their tenons. Clamp and pin on one end, then repeat on the other. Be sure to stagger the pin holes so that those on the ends do not intersect with those for the sides.

Finally, trim the pins, shaving their ends flush with the legs.

8 Attach the top. The top on Dunbar's table is joined to the base in the same way as the original: nailed to the leg tops with square-headed nails. Use a cut nail for this, as its square head runs with the grain and is less obvious than a round head.

SHOP TIP: If you whittle the pins that secure the mortise-and-tenon joints as well as the top's tongue-and-groove joints, use scrap pine with a straight grain. Split it with a chisel into lengths about the thickness of a pencil. Dunbar whittles pins using a 35mm #3 sweep carving gouge. Hold the handle against your sternum, and pull the wood against the blade. Whittle the pins so that they have a pointed end, like a pencil, and make them longer than the leg is thick.

Tap them into place with a light hammer. The facets bite into the edges of the hole, ensuring that the pins will not later pull loose. No glue is necessary. Saw off the pins close to the leg's surface, and pare them flush with the same gouge used to whittle them.

If you want your table to resemble the original, don't cut off the pointed ends. They are well out of sight under the top, but they remain as evidence of your handwork and as an interesting surprise for the few people who care enough about furniture and woodworking to examine the table in detail.

Center the top by measuring the overhang. It should be equal on both ends and on both sides.

To nail the top, drill a pilot hole for one nail. The hole must pierce the top and enter the leg. Drive the nail in this location, but only about halfway. Do the same for the leg diagonally opposite. The top, now fixed at two points, cannot shift. Do the same at the other two locations. Finally, drive all four nails flush with the top.

9 Apply a finish. Dunbar painted his table with blue milk paint, then oiled it, turning the color a green-blue. The original had a scrubbed top, a feature collectors consider very desirable and for which they pay lots of money. A genuine scrubbed top results only after many years of frequent cleanings with harsh soaps (made of lye), which slowly wear away the finish and bleach the top to the color of an old bone. The process also rounds the edges and wears away the grain's softer late wood. As a result, the denser early wood stands slightly proud.

If you want to create a scrubbed top in far less time, apply finish to only the legs and skirt. Dilute liquid laundry bleach in water, about 3:1. Immerse a #3 steel wool pad, and without squeezing out any of the liquid, scrub the top vigorously. The steel wool, which is very coarse, gently rounds the soft pine edges and wears away the late wood. Meanwhile, the bleach whitens the surface.

WALNUT LAP DESK

This lap desk—believe it or not!—contributed to the survival of a woodworking business. When Kelly Mehler and his partner went into business more than a decade ago, they recognized pretty quickly that if their business was to survive, they would have to make items like quilt racks and boxes. They took their work to craft fairs, but people couldn't afford their trestle tables and chests of drawers. Peter Blunt, Mehler's partner, designed and built the prototype of the lap desk shown. A functional item, made from nicely finished, highly figured hardwood, it was very successful.

"People called them Shaker desks because of the simple design," Mehler says, "but Peter wasn't copying any style. These desks are an old idea, with many variations."

Mehler first described how to build the lap desk in an article published several years ago in *Fine Woodworking* magazine. (The construction directions that follow are derived from that article.) He and his partner continue to sell them in their Berea, Kentucky, gallery, called Tree Finery. The particular lap desk shown was purchased from Mehler in the early 1980s.

EXPLODED VIEW

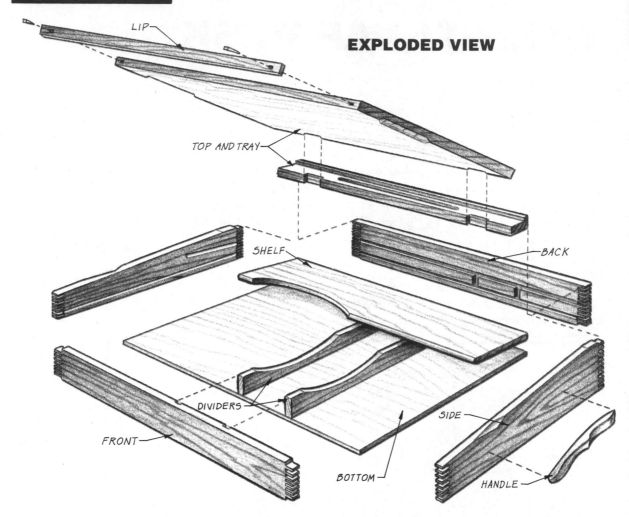

LIP

TOP AND TRAY

SHELF

BACK

DIVIDERS

FRONT

BOTTOM

SIDE

HANDLE

The lap desk is an ideal weekend project. It doesn't require much wood, so you can afford good walnut or cherry. The distinctive finger joints can be cut efficiently on the table saw, and all the grooves for the bottom and shelves are routed. In addition to being easy to cut, the fingers and slots in the joints interlock so snugly that the box virtually squares itself up during assembly. And the large glue surface offered by the interlocking components makes the joints incredibly strong.

1 Select the stock and cut the parts. Grain is an important design feature of a small object like this, so choose your stock carefully. Mehler cuts the stock for each desk body from a single plank, so that the continuity of grain and color will lead the eye around the piece. Because the top is the most closely scrutinized surface, he resaws the boards for it from a single plank. For the top, quartersawn lumber is better than plainsawn, both for figure and to avoid warping. Tips for resawing on the

CUTTING LIST

Part	Quantity	Dimensions	Material
Back	3	$3/8'' \times 3'' \times 17\,5/8''$	Walnut
Front	1	$3/8'' \times 1\,15/16'' \times 17\,5/8''$	Walnut
Sides	2	$3/8'' \times 3'' \times 14\,1/8''$	Walnut
Dividers	2	$3/8'' \times 1\,1/2'' \times 13\,3/4''$	Walnut
Shelf	1	$3/8'' \times 5\,7/16'' \times 17\,3/16''$	Walnut
Bottom	1	$1/4'' \times 13\,3/4'' \times 17\,1/4''$	Plywood
Tray and top	1	$3/4'' \times 14\,1/4'' \times 17\,5/8''$ *	Walnut
Lip	1	$5/8'' \times 1/8'' \times 17\,5/8''$	Walnut
Dowels	As needed	$1/8''$ dia.	Hardwood dowel
Handles	2	$3/4'' \times 3/4'' \times 5\,1/2''$	Walnut

Hardware

2 pairs brass butt hinges, $1\,1/2'' \times 1''$
$3/4''$ brads
Liquid hide glue

*Glued up as a single panel; the tray is ripped from the panel, and the top is planed to a $1/2$-inch thickness.
See Step 5.

band saw can be found under "Resawing" on page 174.

Begin with a plank about $1\,1/2$ inches thick and 4 inches wide. Resaw a 36-inch-long section for the body parts, producing full-width, $1/2$-inch-thick slices. Plane the pieces to $3/8$ inch thick. Cut the back, front, two sides, two dividers, and shelf to the sizes specified by the Cutting List. Rip the pieces to the proper width, then crosscut them to length.

To make the top (including the pencil tray), resaw a 2-inch-thick, $5\,1/2$-inch-wide plank into three pieces, each nearly $3/4$ inch thick and $18\,1/2$ inches long. Edge-glue the pieces. If possible, arrange the boards so that all the grain patterns run in the same direction to avoid tearout when the top is surfaced. Set this aside, so that the glue can cure while you make the desk body.

While the bottom can be made from solid wood, a plywood bottom will obviate problems with wood movement. Consider using a hardwood plywood with a face that matches the rest of the desk.

2 Cut the finger joints. The lap desk is assembled with finger joints, made by cutting equally spaced interlocking slots and fingers into the ends of mating pieces. For the pieces to interlock, one piece must begin with a finger, and the mating piece, with a slot.

Cutting the fingers requires a shop-made jig, which provides a guide for stepping off the fingers and slots as you move the stock through the blade. Details on making the jig, positioning it on the table saw's miter gauge, and using it are given in "Cutting Finger Joints" on

PLAN VIEWS

TOP VIEW

VIEW THROUGH TRAY AND TOP

FRONT VIEW

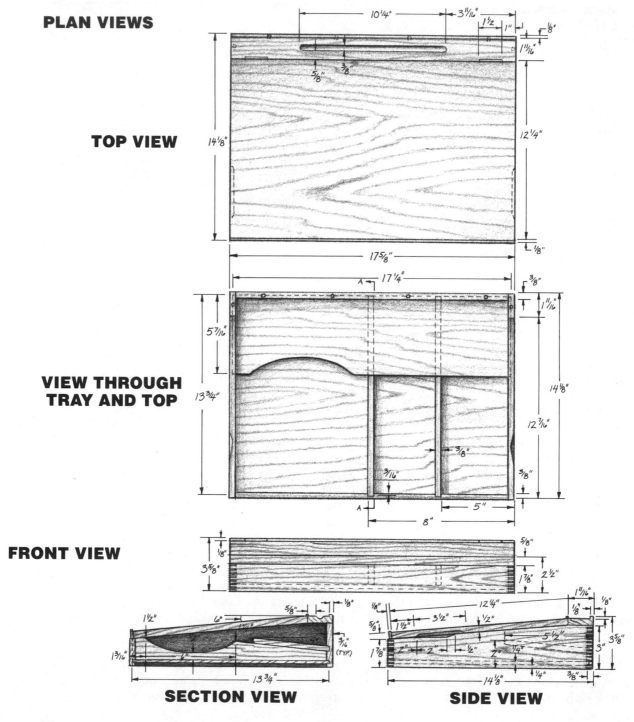

SECTION VIEW

SIDE VIEW

page 40. For the lap desk, the slot—and thus the thickness of the jig's key—is one kerf.

Ideally, each board should start and end with the same element, either a slot or a finger. While this isn't absolutely necessary, it does let you flip each piece end-for-end and cut both sides at the same time with the same setup. You can check this before you begin by dividing the board's width by the kerf's width. If you won't have full-width fingers or slots across the board, you have a little flexibility in the project's dimensions. You can trim the board to remove a partial slot or finger.

Always cut the first piece so that the joint begins with a finger. That way, you can butt the piece against the spline to position the first cut. After cutting the last slot on this first board, butt the mating board against it so that the last finger on the first board serves to position the first slot on the mating board.

3 **Taper the sides and cut the shelf and divider profiles.** After cutting all the joints, dry assemble the basic frame to check the fit. Mark the sides as left and right to avoid cutting the taper the wrong way.

Cut the 6-degree taper with the jig shown. The length of the jig isn't impor-

SHOP TIP: Because the margin of error for the lap desk's finger joints is so slim, you need to test your cutting setup thoroughly on scraps of the working stock before cutting the good pieces. The trick is to get the spline set exactly one kerf away from the blade. Even a slight error compounds across the width of a board to create a no-go situation. This is where your test pieces come in. Cut a few fingers on ends of scrap and see if they fit together. If they don't, keep fiddling with the setup.

tant, as long as it doesn't interfere with the fence. What is important is adjusting the fence so that the rip cut leaves the proper flat at the top and that the height of the sides matches the width of the front, as shown in the *Front View*. Mehler always tests the setup with scrap pieces, and you should, too.

The curved profiles of the shelf and the dividers are primarily decorative, although the cutouts do allow more hand room for picking up papers. Therefore, shape these cutouts to suit your taste. Mark a taper on the portion of each divider that will fit under the shelf. Cut these pieces on the band saw or with a saber saw, then round over the exposed edges with sandpaper.

TAPERING JIG

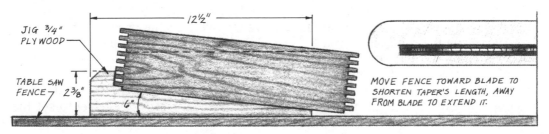

JIG ¾" PLYWOOD

12½"

TABLE SAW FENCE 2⅜"

6°

MOVE FENCE TOWARD BLADE TO SHORTEN TAPER'S LENGTH, AWAY FROM BLADE TO EXTEND IT.

4 **Groove the sides, front, and back for the shelf and dividers.** Mehler grooves the sides, front, and back with an overarm router. Few hobby woodworkers have this specialized tool, but a table-mounted router equipped with a fence and stops works well.

Cut the groove for the bottom first, making it ¼ inch wide × ³⁄₁₆ inch deep. Set the stops and groove both sides, then reset the stops and groove the front and back. It's easy to break off the fingers at the end of the cut, so work carefully.

Cut the angled grooves for the shelf next. Use a tapering jig, like that used to cut the sides, but this time make the angle of the taper 4 degrees. While the exact angle isn't critical, having both sides the same is. The shelf should be angled enough to keep pencils from rolling off. These grooves are ³⁄₈ inch wide × ³⁄₁₆ inch deep.

After cutting the angled grooves, mark where they meet the back, and plow the shelf groove in the back at that location. Finally, cut the ³⁄₈-inch-wide × ³⁄₁₆-inch-deep dadoes in the front and back for the dividers.

5 **Assemble the desk.** Test fit the parts before gluing them together. Mark and bevel the top edge of the front so that it matches the taper of the sides. Check the fit of the shelf and the dividers; if they are too long, they'll bow. Thoroughly scrape and sand any surfaces that'll be inside the desk, since you won't be able to do this after assembly.

Mehler assembles the finger joints with liquid hide glue because it is easy to clean up and slow to set up, offering plenty of time to tap all the little pieces

SHOP TIP: If, in grooving the desk parts, a finger does pop off, you can make one from the scraps used for test cutting and glue it in place. Finger joints are so strong, they won't be weakened significantly by the patch.

into place. Wipe off excess glue with a damp cloth as soon as it appears.

To assemble the parts, first join a side and the back to form a corner, then insert the bottom and shelf. The other side and the dividers are next. The front goes on last. Between the bottom and the tight-fitting finger joints, the box just about pulls itself square; but do check it with a framing square, and adjust it if necessary. Mehler generally doesn't clamp the desk unless he has a problem squaring it.

6 **Make the top and pencil tray.** As noted, the panel you glued up previously yields both the top and the pencil tray. True up the panel by planing it to ⅝ inch thick. Rip off a 1⅝-inch-wide strip for the tray, then plane the remaining part to about ½ inch thick.

For the ledge on the tray, make a single cut on the table saw to form a 1½-inch-wide × ⅛-inch-deep rabbet. Pop off the waste to create the ledge. The pencil groove is cut with a router and cove bit. The groove, which is a little longer than a new pencil, usually is located slightly past the middle of the tray toward the back.

Before hinging the tray and top together, use a sliding T-bevel to set the table saw blade to the same angle as the side taper. Rip a slight bevel on the upper edge of the top. This bevel allows the hinges between the tray and top to close properly. Mortise for the hinges and attach them, so that you can fit the tray and top to the box as a unit. Before attaching the top, however, rout the handholds visible on the edges of the top with a 60-degree chamfer bit. Each handhold is about four fingers wide.

7 **Attach the tray-and-top unit to the desk.** The first step is to fit the tray-and-top unit to the desk body. Drive several brads into the top edge of the back and the flats of the sides, leaving the brads proud of the surface. Clip off their heads. Center the tray-and-top assembly on the box and force it down, marking locations for 1/8-inch-diameter dowels. After removing the brads, bore holes, insert the dowels, spread glue on the mating edges, and clamp the tray down so that the joint is tight.

The next step is to sketch out a gently chamfered recess on each side, directly under the handholds in the top, and to shape it with chisels and sandpaper.

Finally, attach the lip to the front edge of the top with glue and little pegs, which are cut from the dowel.

8 **Make and attach the handles (optional).** Mehler doesn't put handles on the lap desks he makes these days. But our sample—made in 1981—has them. If you want to add them to your desk, here's how:

Enlarge the top and side patterns shown in the *Handle Detail*. Trace the patterns on the handle blanks, and cut the handles on the band saw. Cut the top

HANDLE DETAIL

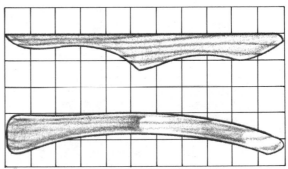

1 SQUARE = 1/2"

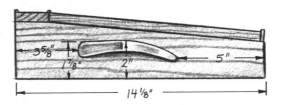

first. Save the waste and tape it back to the blank so that you can cut the side layout. Remember that you need a right handle and a left handle; they are mirror images of each other. To complete them, sand them thoroughly, rounding the exposed edges.

Attach the handles with glue, positioning them as indicated in the *Handle Detail*.

9 **Apply a finish.** After scraping and sanding the exterior, apply a finish. Mehler sprays the lap desks he makes with one coat of sealer and two coats of lacquer. Inside, he applies one coat of sealer and one coat of lacquer. The lacquer is durable and doesn't need to be maintained. Moreover, it sets off the walnut's gorgeous grain patterns.

NOTIONS BOX

Back when he was just learning the woodworking craft, Jeff Day, now a senior woodworking editor at Rodale Press, built this little notions box. Though it required little wood and took only a couple of evenings to complete, it provided ample practice at resawing and at cutting finger joints.

The box has two compartments with lids. One has a rack to store a couple dozen spools of thread, while the other accommodates needles, thimbles, pins, and packets of binding, elastic, and ribbon. Jeff made his notions box of mahogany. With today's concern about rain forest devastation, you may choose to use a less-threatened domestic species.

1 Select the stock and cut the parts. The obvious hitch in this project is the stock: It's only ⅜ inch thick. You can't buy it that way from the lumberyard; you have to make it. The best way is to resaw 4/4 (four-quarters) stock on a band saw. From each rough-sawn 4/4 board, you can get two dressed ⅜-inch-thick pieces. There are a number of legitimate approaches. Here's one:

Rough-cut the parts about ¼ inch greater than the widths and lengths specified by the Cutting List. Bear in mind that you can get both sides from a single 4 × 12-inch piece of 4/4 stock. Joint one face, then one edge of each piece. Using a marking gauge, or just a

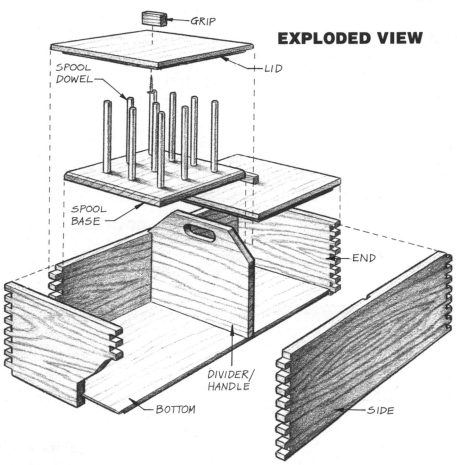

GRIP

EXPLODED VIEW

SPOOL DOWEL

LID

SPOOL BASE

END

DIVIDER/ HANDLE

BOTTOM

SIDE

CUTTING LIST

Part	Quantity	Dimension	Material
Sides	2	$3/8'' \times 4'' \times 12''$	Mahogany
Ends	2	$3/8'' \times 4'' \times 6''$	Mahogany
Bottom	1	$3/16'' \times 5\,5/8'' \times 11\,5/8''$	Mahogany
Divider/handle	1	$3/8'' \times 5\,5/8'' \times 5\,1/2''$	Mahogany
Lids	2	$3/8'' \times 5\,3/4'' \times 6''$	Mahogany
Grips	2	$1/4'' \times 1/2'' \times 1''$	Mahogany
Spool base	1	$3/8'' \times 5\,1/8'' \times 5\,5/16''$	Mahogany
Spool dowels	10	$1/4''$ dia. $\times 3\,1/2''$	Hardwood dowel

Hardware

2 brass roundhead wood screws, #6 $\times 3/4''$

37

PLAN VIEWS

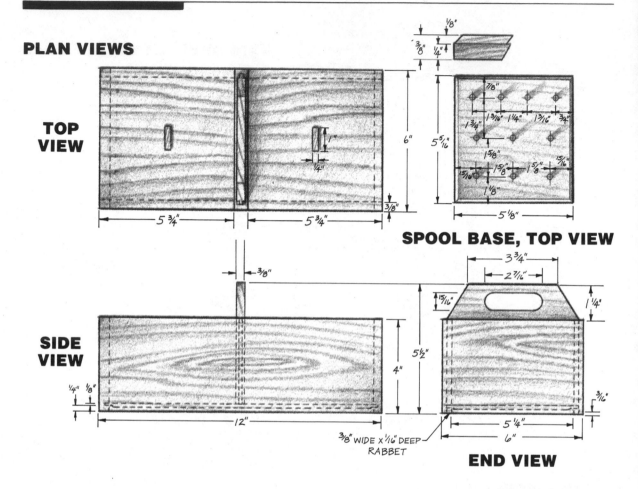

TOP VIEW

SIDE VIEW

SPOOL BASE, TOP VIEW

3/8" WIDE x 1/16" DEEP RABBET

END VIEW

pencil and rule, mark a cutting line on the unjointed edge of each piece to be resawed. At the band saw, stand the piece on edge and saw it in half along the line. (Also see "Resawing" on page 174.) Plane the sawed surfaces smooth and flat. Now trim the pieces to their final specified dimensions.

2 **Cut the finger joints.** The sides and ends of the box are joined with finger joints. The thickness and length of the fingers, of course, are dictated by the 3/8-inch thickness of the working stock. The finger width is not critical; I'd

suggest making them 1/4 inch, a measure that yields eight fingers and eight slots on each end of a piece.

Cut the fingers with a table saw and dado cutter, as explained in "Cutting Finger Joints" on page 40.

3 **Dado and groove the sides and ends.** The bottom of the box is housed in a groove cut in the sides and ends. The divider/handle is housed in dadoes cut in the sides. Cut both joints on a table-mounted router, using a 1/8-inch straight bit.

Plow the grooves first, centering

them $\frac{5}{16}$ inch from the bottom edge of the workpiece and cutting them $\frac{3}{16}$ inch deep. On the end pieces, the groove aligns with a finger and must to stopped so that it doesn't show when the box is assembled. Clamp two stop blocks to the router table's fence, each $5\frac{9}{16}$ inches from the center of the bit. With the router running, tip the workpiece against the fence and the near stop block, then lower it onto the cutter. Push it forward until it hits the far stop block, then tip the end up off the cutter. The groove in the side aligns with a slot and can be plowed straight through.

The dado in each side is centered equidistant from the ends and stopped at the groove. Cut it in the same fashion that you cut the stopped groove in each end.

4 **Make the bottom.** The bottom is made from a piece of $\frac{3}{16}$-inch-thick stock. Form a $\frac{3}{8}$-inch-wide $\times$ $\frac{1}{16}$-inch-deep rabbet around the edge of the bottom using the table-mounted router with a piloted rabbeting bit. Switch to a $\frac{1}{4}$-inch core box bit, and guiding the workpiece along the router table's fence, round the shoulder of the rabbet.

5 **Make the divider/handle.** Lay out the handle hole and the curved edges. Before cutting them, form a tongue along each edge (to fit into the dadoes in the sides) by cutting a $\frac{3}{16}$-inch-wide $\times$ $\frac{1}{8}$-inch-deep rabbet into opposing faces. Drill a $\frac{15}{16}$-inch-diameter hole at each end of the handle hole, then cut out the waste between them with a saber saw. Use the saw to curve the edges, too.

ROUTING A STOPPED DADO

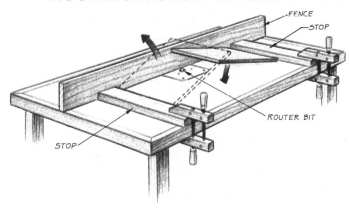

6 **Assemble the box.** Assemble the box without glue to test how the joints fit. If you are satisfied, lightly sand all the parts, then glue up the box.

7 **Make and assemble the lids.** With a piloted rabbeting bit in the table-mounted router, machine a $\frac{7}{16}$-inch-wide $\times$ $\frac{3}{16}$-inch-deep rabbet around each lid. Glue and screw a grip to each lid, orienting it across the grain so that it will be parallel with the divider. Use a #6 $\times$ $\frac{3}{4}$-inch brass roundhead screw.

8 **Make the spool rack.** Lay out the holes for the spool dowels as shown in the *Spool Base, Top View.* Dress up the edge of the base by machining a chamfer around the top edge. Use a piloted chamfering bit in the table-mounted router. Drill the holes, then glue a $3\frac{1}{2}$-inch-long piece of $\frac{1}{4}$-inch-diameter dowel in each.

9 **Finish the box.** Touch-up sand the entire project, then apply two coats of the finish of your choice.

CUTTING FINGER JOINTS

The finger joint is sort of a square-cut through dovetail. The easiest way to cut the slots is on a table saw with a dado cutter. You need to make a little jig to attach to the miter gauge, but once that's done, it is strictly repetitive cutting.

To make the jig, select from your scrap pile a piece of ¾-inch-thick plywood, roughly 3 × 12 inches, and a 3- to 4-inch-long strip of hardwood. Decide how wide and deep the slots between the fingers will be. (The depth should be governed by the thickness of the working stock.)

• With the dado cutter mounted in the saw and set at the width you desire for the slots (and consequently for the fingers), hold the plywood on edge in the miter gauge and cut a slot about 4 inches from the end.

• Next fashion a "key" from the hardwood, making it the same width and thickness as the slot; it should fit snugly into the slot.

• With the saw turned off, hold the key against the dado cutter's side and line up the plywood with it so that the next cut will produce a slot that is exactly the key's width away from the first. Make the cut.

• Attach the plywood to the miter gauge with screws. With the saw still turned off, fit the second slot over the dado cutter, slide the miter gauge against it, then drive the screws.

• Glue the key into the first slot.

To use the jig, stand the workpiece in the miter gauge, its edge snug against the key. Cut a slot. Move the workpiece, fitting the slot over the key. Cut another slot. Repeat the process until all the fingers are formed.

The mating workpiece must begin with a slot rather than a finger. For the first cut, position the piece so that it just covers the slot in the jig. Otherwise, the process is the same.

CUTTING A FINGER JOINT

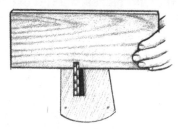

1.) CUT SLOT OF DESIRED WIDTH AND DEPTH IN PLYWOOD.

2.) USE "KEY" HELD AGAINST DADO CUTTER TO LOCATE POSITION OF SECOND SLOT IN PLYWOOD.

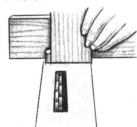

3.) POSITION FIRST SLOT IN WORKPIECE BY BUTTING IT AGAINST THE KEY NOW GLUED IN PLACE.

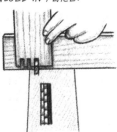

4.) FIT SLOT OVER KEY TO POSITION NEXT ONE.

EARLY AMERICAN SETTLE TABLE

How many times have you built something because you wanted to try a material (or piece of hardware) that was new to you? Sounds a bit thin as an excuse for kicking up some sawdust, but I bet it's done more often than it's admitted to. That's how this project started.

Kenneth Burton, Sr., wanted to try out some glued-up pine panels that the local lumberyard had just put on sale. He just wanted to experiment—see if they would save time and money or make a project come together a bit faster.

The project he fixed on was this bench-table. While it mimics no particular piece, its form is rooted in medieval times (though we Americans like to focus on the form's colonial revival). A settle is a wooden bench with arms, a high, solid back, and an enclosed base that can

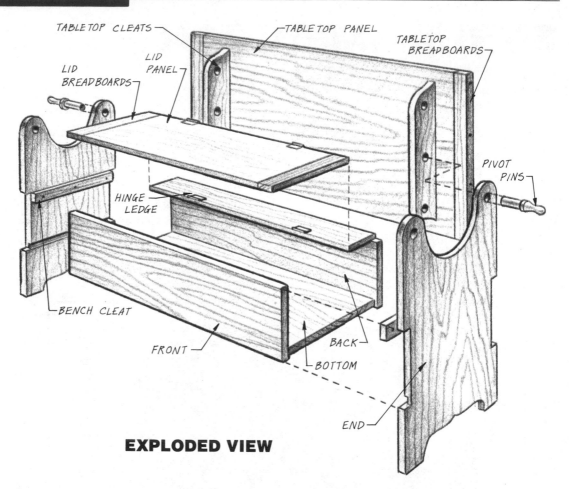

TABLETOP CLEATS

TABLETOP PANEL

TABLETOP BREADBOARDS

LID PANEL

LID BREADBOARDS

HINGE LEDGE

PIVOT PINS

BENCH CLEAT

FRONT

BACK

BOTTOM

END

EXPLODED VIEW

be used as a chest—a versatile form. But it becomes even more versatile when the back can drop onto the arms to become a tabletop. Call it a settle table.

In Burton's version, the tabletop is hinged to the bench with two removable pivot pins. You align holes in the tabletop cleats with holes in the bench ends and slip the pins into place, linking the two elements together. Looking at the photo, you can see the piece is most comfortable as a settle if the center holes in the cleats are used; even though the tabletop is folded back, its center of gravity is lower, making it unlikely to tip inadvertently. If the piece is used primarily as a table, put the pins in the rear holes, so that you can tip the top up to access the bench's storage area.

Burton's settle table was dimensioned so that it would fit at the foot of a double bed, although these days it spends its time as a hallway bench. The glued-up panels were used for the tabletop, bench lid, and bottom (he had to glue up the ends himself). To finish the exposed ends of the panels, he attached breadboards, which was a common approach in colonial days. The joinery is uncomplicated, but the piece is as solid

CUTTING LIST

Part	Quantity	Dimensions	Material
Ends	2	1¹⁄₁₆″ × 16½″ × 27¼″	Pine
Bottom	1	¾″ × 15″ × 36½″	Pine
Lid panel	1	¾″ × 13″ × 31¼″	Pine
Tabletop panel	1	¾″ × 23¼″ × 47¼″	Pine
Bench cleats	2	1¹⁄₁₆″ × 1″ × 15″	Pine
Front/back	2	¾″ × 8⅞″ × 37⅝″	Pine
Lid breadboards	2	¾″ × 2″ × 13″	Pine
Breadboard pins	16	⅜″ dia. × 3″	Hardwood dowel
Hinge ledge	1	¾″ × 4⅜″ × 35½″	Pine
Tabletop breadboards	2	¾″ × 1¹³⁄₁₆″ × 23¼″	Pine
Tabletop cleats	2	1¹⁄₁₆″ × 4″ × 20″	Pine
Cleat pins	8	⅜″ dia. × 2″	Hardwood dowel
Pivot pins	2	1½″ × 1½″ × 5½″	Hardwood

Hardware

6 flathead wood screws, #8 × 1½″
2 pairs black antiqued surface hinges, 2″ long
8d cut nails

and tight as when it was built nearly 20 years ago.

Although the completed project has been a part of the Burton family's household furnishings for two decades, Ken never again used the panels that launched it. They turned out to be fractionally undersized in thickness, which meant that integrating them with full-thickness components was problematic.

1 Select the stock and cut the parts. Ken Burton built his settle table from #2 pine. As he used the material, its knots are displayed for visual effect, but none impair its sturdiness. Imperfections in the wood are characteristic of this genre of furniture. They reduce the cost of the material, too.

Whatever stock you choose, select straight-grained boards. You need 4/4 (four-quarters) and 5/4 (five-quarters) stock. Unless the boards are dried specifically for furniture-making purposes, give them time to acclimate to the temperature and humidity conditions of your home.

Cut the parts to the sizes specified by the Cutting List. To achieve the widths necessary for some of the parts, you will have to join narrow boards edge-to-edge (unless, like Burton, you discover a supply of glued-up panels at the lumberyard). The obvious panels are the ends, tabletop, bench lid, and bottom. But wide pine boards tend to cup noticeably, so you may do well to glue up some narrow boards to form the front and back, too.

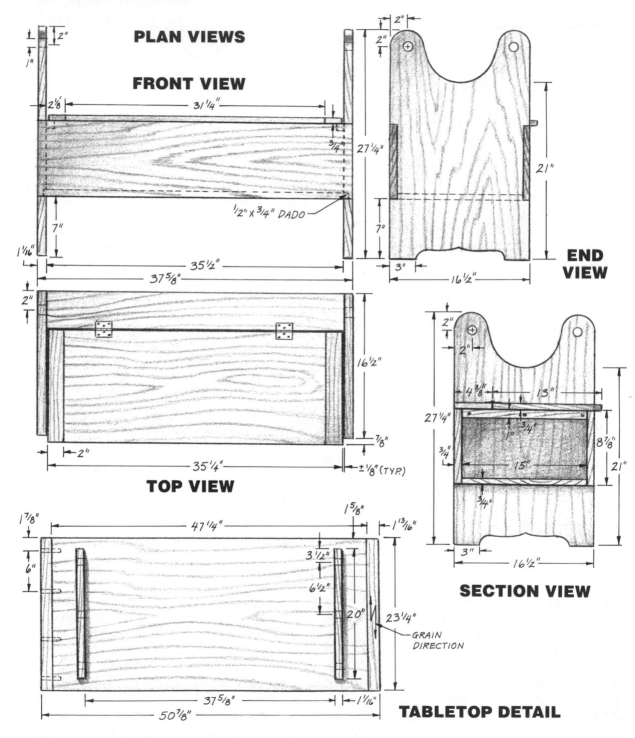

PLAN VIEWS

FRONT VIEW

2"

1"

2⅛"

31¼"

¾"

27¼"

7"

½" X ¾" DADO

1 1/16"

7"

35½"

37⅝"

END VIEW

2"

2"

21"

7"

3"

16½"

2"

35½"

2"

16½"

⅞"

2"

35¼"

±⅛" (TYP.)

TOP VIEW

SECTION VIEW

2"

2"

4⅜"

13"

27¼"

1"

¾"

8⅞"

¾"

15"

21"

¾"

3"

16½"

1⅞"

1⅝"

47¼"

1 13/16"

6"

3½"

6½"

20"

23¼"

GRAIN DIRECTION

37⅝"

1 1/16"

50⅞"

TABLETOP DETAIL

2 Glue up the ends and panels.
Unless you have a great many clamps, you probably won't glue up all the panels at one time. Rather, you'll probably do them in the order in which you need them: ends first, then the bottom and lid panel, and finally the tabletop panel.

After gluing up the ends, remove any dried squeeze-out with a scraper. True up the surfaces and square the end blanks, trimming them to size.

SHOP TIP: To avoid a regimented look in the glued-up panels, Burton usually rips his stock to random widths before jointing the boards and gluing them up.

3 Make the ends. The ends must be dadoed for the bottom, drilled for the pivot pins, and cut to their final shape. Because it is easier to position the dadoes accurately before the contour is cut, machine them first. Use a dado cutter or router, positioning the ¾-inch-wide × ½-inch-deep dadoes as shown in the *End View.*

Lay out the profile of the ends next. This task includes marking the cutout that forms the feet, the notches for the front and back, as well as the saddle at the top and centers of the pivot-pin holes. Enlarge the patterns provided and make a cardboard template. Trace around the template onto the ends. Drill the 1-inch-diameter holes for the pivot pins, then cut out the profile on the band saw or with a saber saw.

Finish your work on the ends by sanding their edges. Burton worked a

PATTERNS

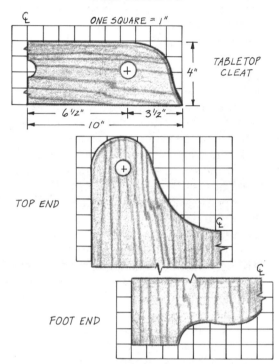

ONE SQUARE = 1"

TABLETOP CLEAT

4"

6½" — 3½"

10"

TOP END

FOOT END

low crown onto the 1¹⁄₁₆-inch-wide upper edges but left the vertical edges square. Although you can do this work with a belt sander, you may want to try a pneumatic drum sander chucked in an electric drill.

4 Assemble the bench. Start by screwing the bench cleats in place. Because the cleat's grain is perpendicular to that of the end, you have to accommodate the seasonal expansion and contraction of the end. Burton did this by driving each of the three screws into slightly oversized pilot holes, which give the screws a little room to move.

Assemble the remaining parts with cut nails, driving them into drilled holes.

Nail through the front and back into the bottom and ends, through the ends into bottom, and through the hinge ledge into the back and cleats.

5 **Make the bench lid.** The lid is constructed with so-called bread-board ends—narrow strips that are attached to the ends of the broad panel, concealing the end grain. The problem with this construction, as you may know, lies in the expansion and contraction of wood across the grain. The length of the breadboard will remain constant, while the width of the lid will vary with long-term humidity changes. The joinery has to allow this movement. Rather than struggle with the traditional mortise-and-tenon joinery, Burton secured the breadboards with dowels driven through them into the end of the lid panel. It's an unorthodox approach, but it has worked.

Drill holes for the dowels through the breadboards. After clamping the breadboards to the lid panel (use no glue), extend the holes for the dowels into the panel, using the holes in the breadboards as guides. Cut a dowel pin for each hole, slather it with glue, and drive it into place. Trim the pins flush after the glue sets.

6 **Install the lid.** Set the lid in place, resting it on the front and the cleats. Before installing the hinges, test the lid's fit; you should be able to open and close it easily. If the fit is too tight, plane one or both breadboards.

The lid is hinged with surface-mounted units. Position each pair about 6 inches from the end. Drill pilot holes and drive the screws supplied with the hinges.

7 **Make the tabletop.** The construction of the tabletop duplicates that of the bench lid. Bore dowel holes into the breadboards, as you did the lid breadboards. Clamp the breadboards to the tabletop panel without glue, extend the dowel holes into the panel, then glue a dowel pin into each hole. Trim the pins flush after the glue sets.

8 **Make and install the tabletop cleats.** The tabletop is attached to the bench with removable pivot pins, which fit through holes in the tabletop cleats into holes in the bench ends. Each end already has two holes, and each cleat gets three.

The cleats are made from the 5/4 stock. Enlarge the pattern, which is for half the cleat, and transfer it onto the two cleat blanks. Drill the pivot pin holes. Cut the shape on the band saw. Sand the exposed edges of the cleats, as you did the edges of the ends.

The cleats are attached to the tabletop with dowels, just like the breadboards. While the cleats *should* be positioned as shown in the *Tabletop Detail*, you ought to measure your bench and use the spacing that fits. Clamp the cleats in place, bore holes for the dowels, and glue a dowel into each hole. Trim the dowels flush after the glue dries.

9 **Turn the pivot pins.** Turning is a freehand operation, and producing duplicate pieces is not always easy. In this case, having the pivot pins be duplicates is hardly necessary.

After you have mounted a turning square on the lathe, round it from end to end, reducing it to the largest diameter specified anywhere along the pin. Transfer the locations and diameters of the profile's features to the spindle. Use a parting tool to groove the spindle at each feature, marking the starting and stopping points for that feature and also delineating the maximum depth of cut. Mark the groove bottoms with a pencil; as you turn the profile, be careful not to cut away the marks.

When the turning is completed, finish sand the pin before dismounting it from the lathe.

10 **Apply the finish.** Finish sand all the surfaces of the settle table, then apply whatever finish you prefer.

PIVOT PIN DETAIL

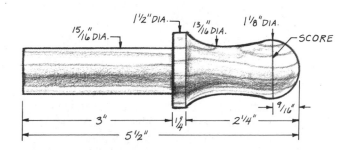

Burton finished his settle table with two coats of Waterlox, a tung-oil varnish. Twenty years after the finish was applied, it is still sound.

BEDSIDE TABLE

Fishermen talk about the size of "the one that got away." Woodworkers talk about The Board they once worked. This little table has such talk in it.

Built in the mid-1960s by Kenneth Burton, Sr., it was designed, and is still used, as a bedside table. In general, it is one of an almost endless variety of occasional tables: aprons joined to square legs in mortise-and-tenon joints, a square top, a single drawer. The specifics of this table evolved from its intended use,

from the builder's aesthetic, and from the materials.

Burton wanted bedside tables to use with the master bedroom's four-poster, so the height of that bed dictated the height of these tables. He knew he wanted turned—not square or tapered—legs. (After all, he was teaching high-school shop with Palmer Sharpless, a well-known Pennsylvania turner.) In planning the legs, Burton incorporated a design feature he had seen on an antique. When he saw the old piece, he remarked on the extent of the "drop," the stretch of unturned (or untapered) leg below the apron. Usually, the drop is about an inch; he made the drop nearly 3 inches on this table. Only the table's length and width remained unsettled.

The material he chose was African mahogany—"This was back when you could get mahogany for about 50 cents a board foot." As he inspected the mahogany available for the project, The Board settled the last dimensions. It was 18 inches across.

Although Burton didn't need to glue up stock to get the nearly 18-inch-square top, you undoubtedly will have to. Were he to build the table today, Burton says he would increase either the length or the width "to make it easier to get a vaccuum cleaner between the legs."

1 Select the stock and cut the parts. To build this project, you should use attractive, straight-grained stock. Burton was as impressed by the grain patterns in the mahogany board he selected for the top as he was by its

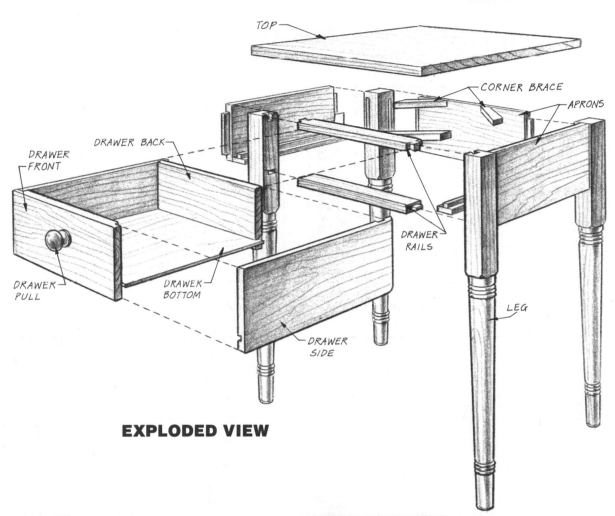

TOP

CORNER BRACE

APRONS

DRAWER BACK

DRAWER FRONT

DRAWER RAILS

DRAWER PULL

DRAWER BOTTOM

LEG

DRAWER SIDE

EXPLODED VIEW

width. The top is the showy component, so reserve for it the showiest boards. You need 4/4 (four-quarters) stock for most of the table parts, 8/4 (eight-quarters) stock for the legs.

Although the project is made from mahogany, the sides and back of the drawer are made from poplar, and the bottom is a piece of ¼-inch lauan plywood.

With your stock planed and jointed, cut all the table parts to the sizes specified by the Cutting List.

SHOP TIP: You can save if you purchase 2 × 2-inch table-leg turning squares. Many lumberyards stock such an item. Buying these will eliminate the need to cut and plane 10/4 (ten-quarters) stock to the required dimensions.

2 **Cut the dovetails in the upper drawer rail.** The upper drawer rail is joined to the legs by dovetail tenons. The usual procedure is to cut the mor-

PLAN VIEWS

DOVETAIL TENON DETAIL

VIEW THROUGH TOP

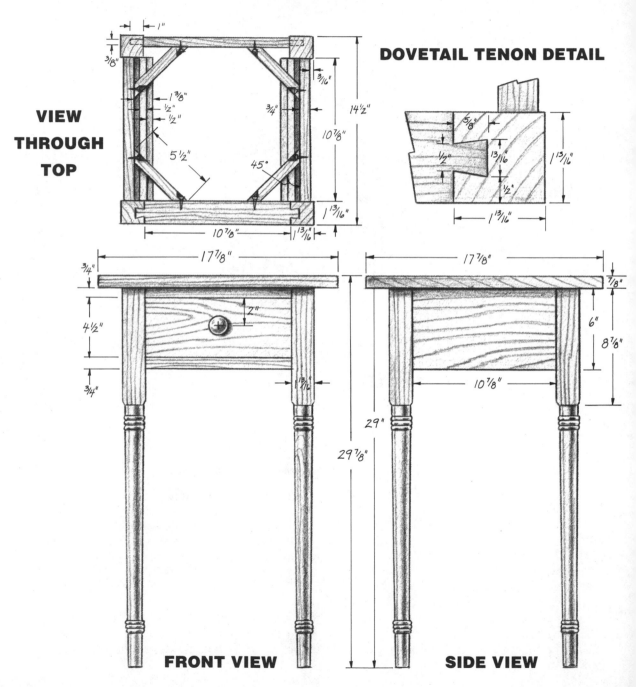

FRONT VIEW

SIDE VIEW

CUTTING LIST

Part	Quantity	Dimensions	Material
Drawer rails	2	$\frac{3}{4}'' \times 1\frac{13}{16}'' \times 12\frac{1}{8}''$	Mahogany
Legs	4	$1\frac{13}{16}'' \times 1\frac{13}{16}'' \times 29''$	Mahogany
Aprons	3	$\frac{3}{4}'' \times 6'' \times 12\frac{7}{8}''$	Mahogany
Drawer pull	1	$1\frac{1}{4}'' \times 1\frac{1}{4}'' \times 1''$	Mahogany
Top	1	$\frac{7}{8}'' \times 17\frac{7}{8}'' \times 17\frac{7}{8}''$	Mahogany
Drawer runners	2	$\frac{3}{4}'' \times 1\frac{3}{8}'' \times 10\frac{13}{16}''$	Mahogany
Drawer guides	2	$\frac{3}{8}'' \times \frac{1}{2}'' \times 10\frac{13}{16}''$	Mahogany
Corner braces	4	$\frac{3}{4}'' \times \frac{7}{8}'' \times 5\frac{1}{2}''$	Mahogany
Drawer front	1	$\frac{3}{4}'' \times 4\frac{3}{8}'' \times 10\frac{3}{4}''$	Mahogany
Drawer sides	2	$\frac{1}{2}'' \times 4\frac{3}{8}'' \times 13\frac{1}{8}''$	Poplar
Drawer back	1	$\frac{1}{2}'' \times 4\frac{1}{4}'' \times 10\frac{1}{4}''$	Poplar
Drawer bottom	1	$\frac{1}{4}'' \times 10\frac{1}{4}'' \times 12\frac{5}{8}''$	Lauan plywood

Hardware

12 flathead screws, #10 × 1¼″
1 roundhead screw, #8 × 1½″
4d finishing nails

tises and fit the tenons to them; but in this case, you should cut the tenons first, so that you can use them as templates to lay out the mortises. Lay out the dovetails and cut them on the band saw.

3 **Mortise the legs.** The legs and aprons are joined with mortise-and-tenon joints. Before turning the legs, lay out and cut all the mortises in them. Follow the *Apron-to-Leg Joinery* in laying out the mortises. Remember to make two front legs and two back legs.

The dovetail mortises in the front legs can be traced from the dovetail tenons in the upper drawer rail. The bottom drawer rail joins the legs in horizontal mortises. The aprons join the legs in vertical mortises.

After laying out the mortises, use a ⅜-inch-diameter bit to drill out most of the waste. Square up the mortises with a chisel.

SHOP TIP: A couple of layout tricks can speed the work while simultaneously improving accuracy. Line up the leg blanks and scribe across all of them at one time, marking the mortises' tops and bottoms. Use a marking gauge to scribe the verticals, marking one vertical on each leg, then resetting the gauge and marking the second.

4 **Tenon the aprons and the bottom drawer rail.** Both the apron tenons and the bottom rail tenons can be cut with the same basic setup. Cutting the tenons is easiest on the table saw. Use a dado cutter. Position the rip fence

APRON-TO-LEG JOINERY

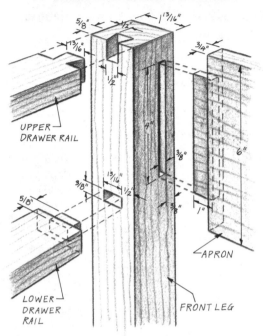

UPPER DRAWER RAIL

LOWER DRAWER RAIL

APRON

FRONT LEG

to serve as a stop governing tenon length. Use the miter gauge to guide the workpiece over the cutter. Use a backsaw to trim the tenons to the widths specified in the *Apron-to-Leg Joinery*.

After roughing out all the tenons, assemble the legs, rails, and aprons. Pare the tenons with a chisel, if necessary, to get them to fit into the mortises. Mark the mortises and tenons that go together, so that, at assembly time, you'll know which tenon was fitted to which mortise.

5 Turn the legs. After all the mortises and tenons are cut and fitted, turn the legs. Burton's design is shown in the *Turning Detail.* You can design your own turning pattern, or you can eschew turning altogether, choosing instead to taper the legs.

Turning is a freehand operation, and producing duplicate pieces is not always easy. Burton says he enjoys the challenge of producing duplicates "by eye" and points out that slight variations, obvious when the legs are laid side by side, become less obvious when the legs are moved apart.

If you are a less confident turner than Burton, a template can be a help. Enlarge the profile and sketch it on a strip of ¼-inch plywood. Cut along the layout line, keeping the "negative" element so that you can touch it to the side of the turning periodically to gauge your progress. On the template, mark the diameters of the various beads, tapers, and other shapes shown in the *Turning Detail.*

After you have mounted a turning square on the lathe, round the segment of the leg that is to be turned, reducing it to the largest diameter specified anywhere along the leg. Transfer the locations and diameters of the profile's features to the spindle. Use a parting tool to groove the spindle at each feature, marking the starting and stopping points for that feature and delineating the maximum depth of cut. Mark the groove bottoms with a pencil; as you turn the profile, be careful not to cut away the marks.

SHOP TIP: To turn a spindle to a predetermined diameter, preset calipers to that diameter. Lightly hold them to the spindle as you turn, working with the appropriate cutting tool in one hand, the calipers in the other. When the desired diameter is reached, the calipers will slip over the spindle. Stop cutting.

As the leg takes shape, compare it periodically to the template. Turn off the lathe and touch the template to the leg. When the template nestles into the leg perfectly, the turning is completed. Before dismounting the leg, finish sand the turned segment.

6 **Turn the drawer pull.** While you're working at the lathe, make the pull. This is a faceplate turning, so you must glue the turning block to a scrap of ¾-inch-thick wood. Be sure the turning block's grain is oriented parallel to the turning axis; if it isn't, you'll find the block next to impossible to turn satisfactorily. Mount the scrap on the faceplate and turn the pull. Then separate the pull from the scrap, and drill a pilot hole for the mounting screw.

7 **Assemble the table.** Before actually assembling the table, finish sand all of the parts that will show—top, legs (the unturned segments), aprons, and rails.

Before gluing up the legs, aprons, and rails, you'll want to assemble them without glue, both to confirm that all the joints fit properly and to practice applying the clamps. Adjust the fit of individual parts as necessary. A sound procedure is to glue up and clamp an apron between a front leg and a rear leg. When the glue dries, join those subassemblies with the remaining apron and the two drawer rails.

With the basic frame assembled, glue and clamp the runners to the appropriate aprons. After the glue has dried, glue and clamp the guides in place. At each corner of the leg-and-apron assembly, attach a corner brace with two flat-

TURNING DETAIL

head screws, positioning the brace flush with the top of the assembly.

The top is attached to the leg-and-apron assembly with flathead screws driven through the braces into the top. The shank holes in the braces should be slightly larger than the screw shanks, so that the top can expand and contract slightly, as wood is wont to do.

8 **Build the drawer.** With the table assembled, you can build the drawer to fit. Put the drawer front and sides into the drawer opening; if they are noticeably tight or dramatically loose, you can trim or recut them. No sense building a drawer that won't fit because the parts are missized.

As Burton constructed it, the drawer front is rabbeted for the sides, the sides are dadoed for the back, and the front, sides, and back are grooved for the bottom. You can cut the groove for the bottom on the table saw, taking a couple of passes over your standard rip blade. The groove is ¼ inch deep, ⁵⁄₁₆ inch from the bottom edges of the drawer. Cut the groove to accommodate your lauan plywood, which is not a full ¼ inch in thickness. The rabbets and dadoes can be cut on the table saw with a dado cutter or with a router.

Dry assemble the drawer to check the fit of the parts. If the unit is satisfactory, reassemble the front and one side with glue and 4d finishing nails. Fit the bottom into its groove (*without* glue),

then add the back and the second side, attaching them with glue and nails. (Yes, the back is narrower than the sides and thus will be shy of the sides' top edges.) The bottom should square up the assembly, but check it with a try square and adjust it if necessary. Make sure the drawer sits flat.

Sand the drawer, then attach the pull by driving the roundhead screw through the drawer front and into the pull. Test the drawer's fit in the table.

9 **Finish the completed table.** Remove the drawer from the table. Do any necessary touch-up sanding to the surfaces that still need it, then apply a finish to the project. Be certain to apply as many coats of finish to the underside of the tabletop as you do to the top side—this will help prevent warping. Burton used Waterlox, a tung-oil varnish, to finish the table shown.

DRAWER, PLAN VIEWS

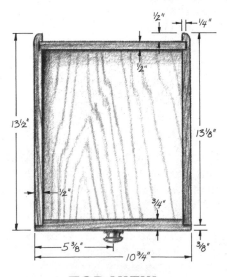

TOP VIEW

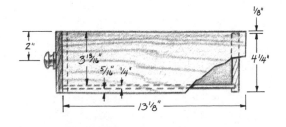

SIDE VIEW

NED'S CRIB

This is my contribution to family "heirloomdom," a crib I made for our third child, who turned out to be Ned. My wife and I had given away all the baby furniture we had—crib, playpen, changing table—after two children. Seven or eight years later, when we decided that we *wanted* a third child, I made this crib.

With the exception of the plywood deck of the mattress platform and the walnut wedges, the entire crib is made from cherry. In keeping with "heirloomhood," some of the cherry came from logs my father-in-law and I felled on his property. It was sawed at a local mill and air-dried for several years.

The interesting feature of this crib, I think, is the legs. I didn't have any cherry thicker than 5/4 (five-quarters), and I didn't want to buy any. I had read about a knockdown dovetail tenon I wanted to try, though I was less than confident about cutting it by hand (no drill press in my shop). Laminating the legs allowed me to use the wood I had to create the 1⅜ × 1¾-inch legs and, simultaneously, the necessary mortises.

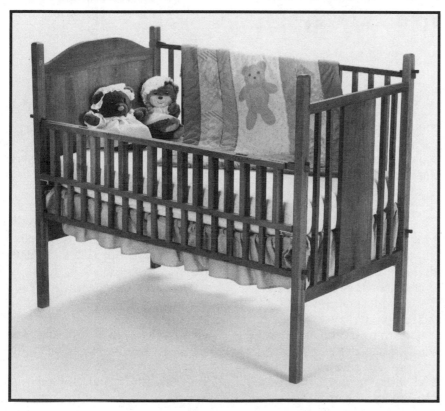

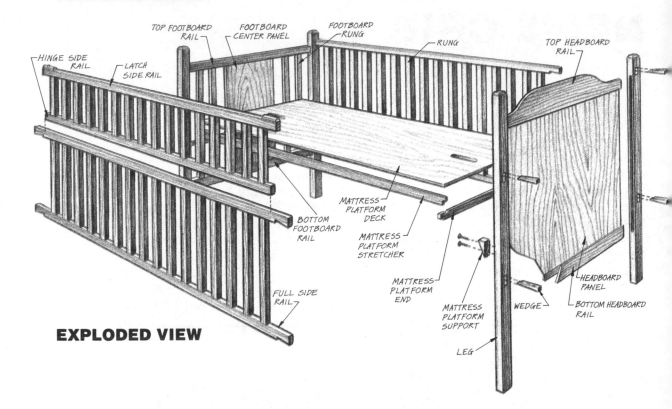

TOP FOOTBOARD RAIL
FOOTBOARD CENTER PANEL
FOOTBOARD RUNG
RUNG
TOP HEADBOARD RAIL
HINGE SIDE RAIL
LATCH SIDE RAIL
BOTTOM FOOTBOARD RAIL
MATTRESS PLATFORM DECK
MATTRESS PLATFORM STRETCHER
MATTRESS PLATFORM END
MATTRESS PLATFORM SUPPORT
WEDGE
HEADBOARD PANEL
BOTTOM HEADBOARD RAIL
FULL SIDE RAIL
LEG

EXPLODED VIEW

Although this isn't a project that the average hobby woodworker will complete in a single weekend, it is a set of discrete subassemblies, each of which *can* be completed in a single weekend.

1 Select the stock and cut the parts. Use a clear, straight-grained hardwood for this project. You don't need an enormous amount of wood, and none needs to be thicker than 5/4. As noted, the crib shown is constructed from cherry (except for the walnut wedges and the birch plywood deck of the mattress platform). The large panel in the headboard and the small one in the footboard do provide an opportunity to display wood with a showy figure or to book-match. But for the most part, you

want wood that is free of defects and straight-grained.

Mill the wood to the necessary thicknesses, and cut all the parts to the dimensions specified by the Cutting List. It usually is helpful to label the parts as they emerge from the saw; this is particularly true for all the rungs—there are four different lengths required.

To save time later on, glue up the panels for the headboard and footboard now. While the glue cures, you can be working on the side assemblies.

2 Make the side rails. There are two key tasks in making the side rails: tenoning the ends of the principal rails, and drilling all of them for their respective rungs. Before starting these

CUTTING LIST

Part	Quantity	Dimensions	Material
Sides			
Hinge rail	1	$^{13}/_{16}$" × 1" × 48¾"	Cherry
Latch rail	1	$^{13}/_{16}$" × 1" × 52"	Cherry
Full rails	4	$^{13}/_{16}$" × 1" × 56"	Cherry
Rungs	16	¾" × ¾" × 26"	Cherry
Rungs	16	¾" × ¾" × 16"	Cherry
Rungs	16	¾" × ¾" × 9"	Cherry
Headboard			
Panel	1	¾" × 28½" × 27"	Cherry
Top rail	1	1" × 5" × 29½"	Cherry
Bottom rail	1	1" × 2½" × 29½"	Cherry
Footboard			
Center panel	1	¾" × 10¼" × 27"	Cherry
Rungs	4	¾" × ¾" × 27"	Cherry
Top rail	1	¾" × 1½" × 29½"	Cherry
Bottom rail	1	¾" × 2" × 29½"	Cherry
Leg laminations			
Outer	8	⅝" × 1⅜" × 46"	Cherry
Center inner	2	½" × 1⅜" × 25"	Cherry
Bottom inner	4	½" × 1⅜" × 16¼"	Cherry
Center inner	2	½" × 1⅜" × 15"	Cherry
Top inner	2	½" × 1⅜" × 12⅝"	Cherry
Top inner	2	½" × 1⅜" × 2¾"	Cherry
Mattress platform supports	4	1" × 6" × 8" *	Cherry
Wedges	8	½" × ½" × 3½"	Walnut
Mattress platform			
Stretchers	2	¾" × 1½" × 51¾"	Cherry
Ends	2	¾" × 1" × 28¾"	Cherry
Deck	2	½" × 25⅞" × 26"	Birch plywood

Hardware

4 flathead wood screws, #6 × 1¾"
4 flathead wood screws, #6 × 1½"
2 brass surface bolts, 2"

2 pairs brass butt hinges, 2"
¾" brads

* To make the four mattress platform supports, it is safest to start with a scrap block at least this size, even though only a fraction of the stock is actually used. See Step 10.

procedures, however, give the long surfaces of each rail a lick or two with a smoothing plane to remove milling marks.

The hinge and latch rails, of course, are not tenoned, so set those aside for now. Lay out the tenons on the four full rails as shown in the *Half-Dovetail Tenon*

PLAN VIEWS

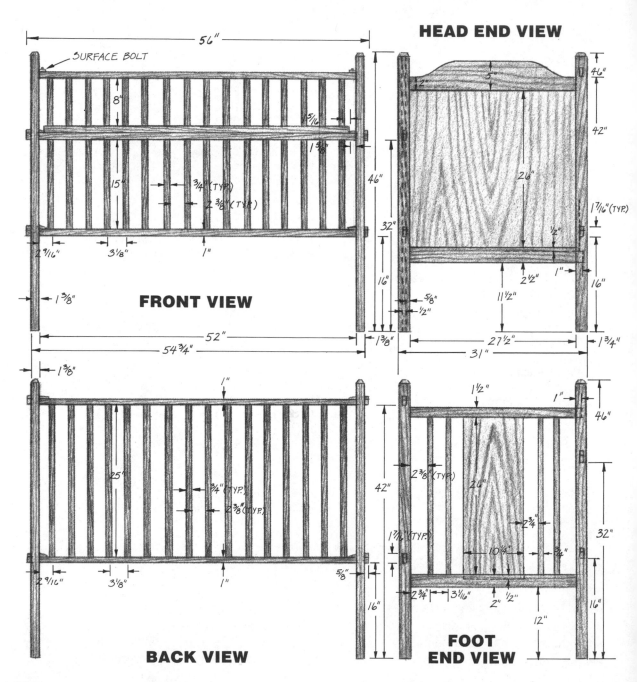

HEAD END VIEW

FRONT VIEW

BACK VIEW

FOOT END VIEW

Detail. You can group the rails together and cut the tenons with a straight bit in a router, or you can cut the tenons with a backsaw, as I did, paring the cheeks clean with a sharp chisel. Cut the dovetail-like notch with the backsaw, too.

Drill the ⅜-inch-diameter holes for the rung tenons next. Of course, all six rails must be drilled. Federal law stipulates that the space between rungs be no more than 2⅜ inches, so that an infant's head can't become wedged between them. Following the *Front View* and *Back View*, mark the location of the first rung, measuring from the shoulder of the tenon on the full rails and from the butt end on the latch rail and the hinge rail. The remaining rungs are positioned 3⅛ inches on center. Remember to lay out the full rails in pairs; the top rail must be drilled with the dovetail notch up, the bottom rail with the dovetail notch down.

You can bore the holes with a hand-

HALF-DOVETAIL TENON DETAIL

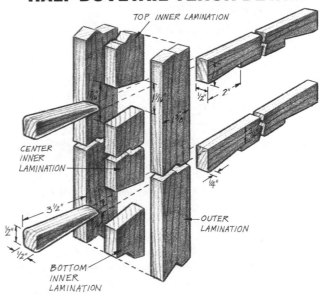

held drill guided by a doweling jig, though you are likely to do a more precision job using a drill press.

SHOP TIP:
A scrap of wood and a 2-inch-long piece of ⅜-inch-diameter dowel can save you a lot of layout time if you are boring the rung mortises on a drill press. Clamp a fence—one slightly taller than the rail—to the drill press table to position the hole across the width of the rail. To the top of the fence, screw a scrap of wood as shown in the *Drill Press Stop.* Lay out and drill the first hole, then slip the dowel into the hole. Slide the rail along the fence until the dowel hits the stop, and drill a second hole. Fit the dowel into the new hole, move the rail, and drill again. Repeat the process until all the holes are completed.

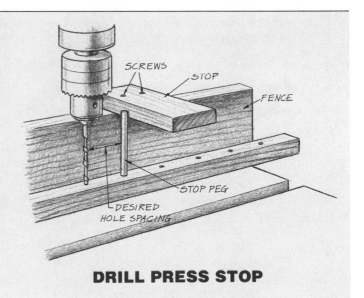

DRILL PRESS STOP

3 Tenon the rungs. In woodworking, anyway, you *can* force a square peg into a round hole, provided they are close in size. That's pretty much what I did to assemble the crib sides.

On a table saw, cut ⅜ × ⅜ × ½-inch tenons on each end of all the rungs. With a utility knife, trim off the four corners of the tenons, forming each into a rough octagon. These can be forced into the round mortises in the rails.

As you do this work, keep the various batches of rungs segregated. Be sure to tenon the rungs for the footboard while you have the table saw set up.

4 Assemble the sides. There are three side units, all of which are assembled in the same way. Do them one at a time.

Lay out the parts. With a cotton swab, apply glue to the round mortises and to the tenons. Fit all the rungs into one rail, then add the second rail. Apply pipe or bar clamps, using cauls to protect the rails from damage by the metal clamp jaws. Make sure each assembly is flat and square.

SHOP TIP: Cleaning up
glue squeeze-out during assembly is easy, and it obviates the need to do it later with a chisel or scraper. Use a saturated rag to remove the glue, then wipe the joint with a dry rag. A rag that's merely *damp* tends to smear the glue rather than remove it.

5 Prepare the panels for the head and foot. By now, the panels should be ready to be worked.

The headboard panel has a ⅜-inch-thick × ½-inch-long tongue around its edge that fits into grooves cut in the legs and rails. Cut the tongue on the table saw or with a router.

The footboard panel has a ⅜-inch-thick × ½-inch-long tenon on each end to join it to the rails. The tenon extends the width of the panel; since it has the same dimensions as the tongue on the headboard panel, it can be cut using the same setup.

6 Make the rails for the head and foot. Despite their different widths, all the head and foot rails have similar tenons on their ends: ⅜ inch thick × 1 inch long and extending the width of the piece. These tenons can be cut on a table saw or with a router.

After tenoning all four rails, set aside those for the footboard while you complete those for the headboard. Both of the head rails must be grooved for the panel. It is easiest to cut this groove with a dado cutter in a table saw (although it can be done using a router). The groove should be ⅜ inch wide × ½ inch deep and centered across the thickness of the rail. Plow the groove in the top edge of the bottom rail and in the bottom edge of the top rail.

To complete the top rail, you must lay out and cut the profile on the top. Enlarge the pattern for the top profile (note that the pattern is for half the profile), and make a template of cardboard or thin plywood. It is easiest to ensure the profile is symmetrical if you scribe both halves of the piece from the same template. Make a center line across the face of the rail, line up the template with it, and scribe. Turn the template as you

TOP HEADBOARD RAIL PATTERN

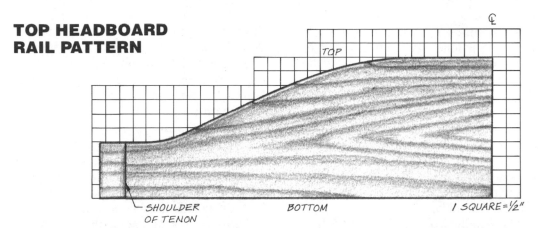

TOP

℄

SHOULDER OF TENON

BOTTOM

1 SQUARE = ½"

would turn the page of a book, lining it up on the other side of the center line, and scribe.

Cut the profile on a band saw or with a saber saw. Sand the newly cut edge with a drum sander in a drill (or in a drill press), or smooth it with a spokeshave followed by a scraper.

Each of the footboard rails needs four holes for the rung tenons and a mortise for the panel tenon. Lay these out as indicated in the *Foot End View*. Bore the round mortises for the rungs with a ⅜-inch bit, then use the same bit to rough out the panel mortise. With a chisel, square up each panel mortise and trim it to accommodate its respective tenon.

7 **Glue up the legs.** As noted earlier, the legs are formed by laminating three layers of stock. The ½-inch-thick inner layer is made up of three separate pieces, so that the half-dovetail mortises are formed during the lamination rather than being chopped out later. This allows you to perfectly fit the shape of each mortise to its respective tenon and the locations of the mortises to the assembled sides.

Trim the inner-layer elements to fit, then lay them atop an outer-layer strip. Lay the assembled side in place to confirm that the mortises will be properly sized and positioned, then mark the positions of the inner pieces on the outer strip. Apply glue to both mating surfaces and return the inner pieces to their marks. Drive a ¾-inch brad through each inner piece into the outer piece to prevent shifting as the clamps are applied. Spread glue on the exposed surface and on a second outer layer, mate them, and apply clamps.

Repeat this process to glue up three more legs. Make two with the half-dovetail mortises 26 inches apart (center-to-center) and two with the mortises 16 inches apart.

8 **Mortise and groove the legs.** The legs must next be mortised for the head and/or foot rails. As you lay out these mortises, keep your head about you: There's only one way to pair and orient the legs. Take the legs with the 26-inch mortise spacing and lay them out foot-to-foot, with their inner faces up (the inner face is the one with the smaller mortise opening). Beside them, lay out the other legs, also foot-to-foot and with their inner faces up. Label one side-by-side pair the headboard legs, the other pair the footboard legs. On the adjoining faces of each pair of legs, lay out the mortises to be cut next.

Mark the locations and dimensions of the mortises. Drill out the majority of the waste, then square and trim the mortises with a chisel to fit their respective tenons. The footboard legs are now ready for assembly.

The headboard legs still need to be grooved for the headboard panel. Using a router equipped with an edge guide, plow the ⅜-inch-wide × ½-inch-deep groove from mortise to mortise, centering it across the thickness of the leg.

SHOP TIP: You can

make an edge guide for your router very easily if you don't already have one. With the appropriate bit chucked in the router, measure and mark on the router's base plate the location of the guide that is necessary for the cut you are making. Remove the base plate from the router, drill a couple of holes for mounting screws, and screw a strip of hardwood to the plate, aligning it with the marks. Reinstall the plate on the router.

9 Assemble the head and foot. Both end units are put together in like manner. Make one as follows, then repeat the process for the other.

First assemble the unit without glue to ensure that all the parts go together. Trim if you must, and even remake parts to get correct fits. When everything is ready, apply glue to the mating surfaces and join them. With the footboard, push

the rungs and the panel into one rail, then fit the second rail onto the tenons. Next insert the assembly into the mortise of one leg, then add the second leg. Now apply pipe or bar clamps, aligning them with the rails. Clean up any glue squeeze-out with a wet rag.

Note that the panels are captured by the assemblies and don't *need* to be glued in place. However, applying glue to a short section in the middle of them can fix their positions while leaving them free to "breathe," accommodating seasonal expansion and contraction.

10 Make and install the mattress platform supports. The approach is to form a wedge-shaped blank, then to rip it into four supports. Although the individual supports are small, it is best—and safest—to begin with a piece of stock at least the size specified by the Cutting List.

Tilt the table saw blade to 20 degrees, *away* from the fence; this probably requires moving the fence from its usual position to the opposite side of the blade. Stand the stock on end, and support it with a tenoning jig as you cut a chamfer across the width of the stock as indicated in the *Support Detail*. Keeping the blade at the same angle, use the miter gauge as a guide to bevel-crosscut the support blank from the bulk of the stock.

To rip the individual supports from the wedge you now have, use the miter gauge with a scrap-wood extension attached to guide the workpiece. As you cut each piece, cut through the extension as well. I made my supports ⅝ inch wide. Sand each support, rounding the edges.

The supports are fastened to the inner edges of the legs with screws, so that they can be moved as your baby grows. The usual routine is to set the newborn's mattress fairly high in the crib's "cage," then to lower it as the baby grows and learns to stand. I used a 1¾-inch screw near the top of the wedge-shaped supports, a 1¼-inch screw near the bottom.

11 **Set up the crib and install the hardware.** To ensure that the sides join the head and foot ends properly, set up the crib. It will stay together without the wedges.

Cut the wedges that lock the half-dovetails, shaping them as indicated in the *Half-Dovetail Tenon Detail*. Fitting the individual wedges is a trial-and-error process; when the crib is in use, you do want to tap them tight with a mallet. I made the wedges from scraps of walnut to contrast with the cherry crib.

With the crib still set up, clamp the hinge rail to its mating side rail to lay out the hinge mortises. Cut the mortises with a chisel, then install the hinges. Swing the side into its closed position; if necessary, trim the ends of the latch rail. Install the surface bolts. On the legs, mark where the bolts themselves make contact. Excavate a mortise for the bolt, and install the plate on the leg.

12 **Make the mattress platform.** The platform is a plywood deck, stiffened by stretchers and end pieces. The ends rest on the platform supports. Build this element while the crib is set up to ensure that it fits *before* you glue it together.

Make the stretchers first. Start by

SUPPORT DETAIL

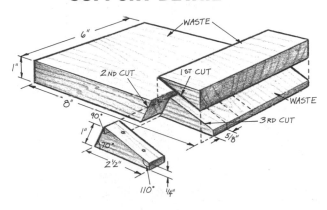

making sure they'll fit comfortably between the head and foot. Cut a ¼-inch-wide × ½-inch-deep rabbet in the top inner edge, extending from end to end. Next cut a ¾ × ¾-inch notch into the bottom of each end, and trim the little bit of wood between the rabbet and the notch, leaving a ½-inch-wide × ¾-inch-high stub at each end of the stretchers.

Turn to the end pieces. Across the bottom edge at each end, cut a ⅝-inch-wide × ⅛-inch-deep rabbet, which will fit over the platform supports. Test the fit. Across the top edge, ⅞ inch from the end, cut a ½-inch-wide × ¼-inch-deep dado for the stretcher stub.

Glue the platform frame together. Cut and glue the deck in place. I cut the plywood so that the grain of the face plies would parallel the ends rather than the stretchers, making the deck slightly more stiff. Of course, doing this requires you to make up the deck from two pieces. For ease of setting up, cut two or three hand-holes in the deck. For each, drill a couple of 1-inch-diameter holes about 4 inches apart, then cut away the plywood between them.

MATTRESS PLATFORM

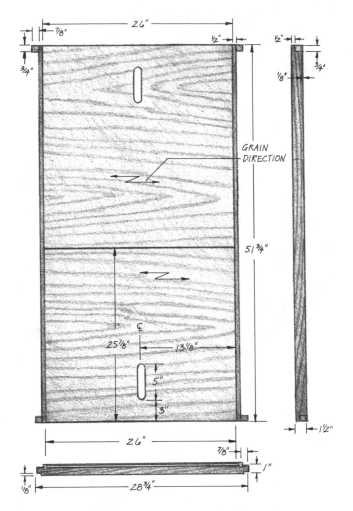

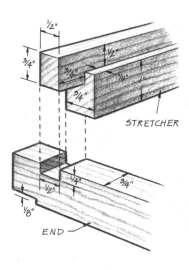

STRETCHER

END

repeating this process a couple of times. Then I rubbed off the surface excess with soft rags. It looked great eight years ago, and still looks pretty good. The joints are as tight today as when I made them.

Of course, you can apply whatever finish you prefer. Be very sure the finish you use will not sicken a child who chooses to teethe on a rung or rail.

13 **Apply a finish.** Having done all this, remove the hardware to apply a finish.

Watco's Natural Oil is what I used as a finish. Following the manufacturer's instructions, I brushed it on liberally and let the various assemblies soak. After a few minutes, I recoated the dry spots,

14 **Reinstall the hardware and set up the crib.** Once the finish is dry, set up the crib again. Reinstall the hinges, the surface bolts, and the mattress platform supports. Drop the platform into position and lay the mattress on it, and the crib is ready for baby.

BUNK BEDS

An uncomplicated project that even a beginner can build in a weekend or two, this bunk bed ensemble includes three distinct elements: the beds themselves, a ladder to provide access to the top bunk, and two storage drawers that reside beneath the lower bunk.

The ensemble was made several years ago by Rodale Press staff woodworker Phil Gehret. The clean, simple design is almost timeless. It's a practical project, too, since bunk beds are a time-honored way to fit two youngsters into a single bedroom.

The bunks are neither difficult nor time-consuming to complete. No fancy joinery is required—most of the bed parts simply bolt together—and all the materials can be obtained easily at ordinary lumberyards and hardware stores. The beds are sized for standard single mattresses: 30 × 75 inches. The design provides safety, with extra rails around the mattresses to prevent the sleepers from falling out of bed. As shown in the photo, you have access to the lower bunk from the side, to the upper bunk from the end. You can easily modify the

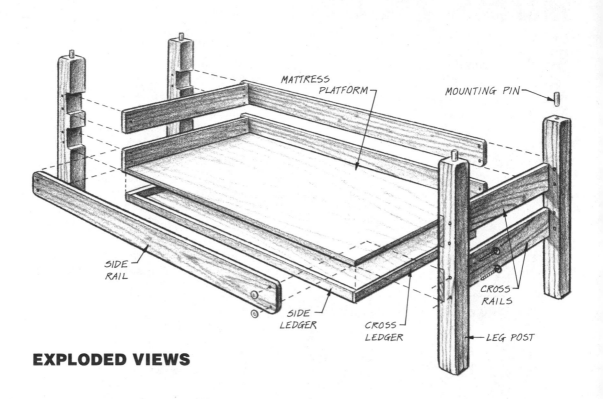

MATTRESS PLATFORM

MOUNTING PIN

SIDE RAIL

SIDE LEDGER

CROSS LEDGER

CROSS RAILS

LEG POST

EXPLODED VIEWS

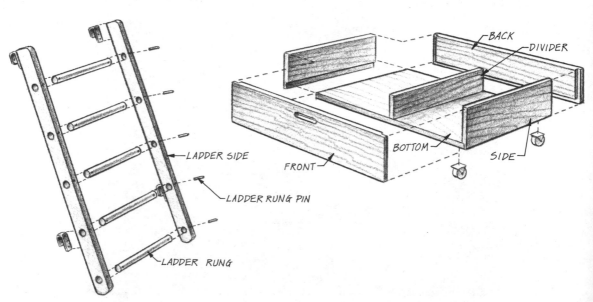

LADDER SIDE

LADDER RUNG PIN

LADDER RUNG

BACK

DIVIDER

FRONT

BOTTOM

SIDE

CUTTING LIST

Part	Quantity	Dimensions	Material
Beds			
Leg posts	8	$3\frac{1}{2}'' \times 3\frac{1}{2}'' \times 36''$	Cedar
Cross rails	7	$\frac{3}{4}'' \times 5\frac{1}{2}'' \times 31''$	Cedar
Side rails	7	$\frac{3}{4}'' \times 5\frac{1}{2}'' \times 82\frac{1}{2}''$	Cedar
Mattress platforms	2	$\frac{3}{4}'' \times 31'' \times 76''$	Plywood
Cross ledgers	4	$\frac{3}{4}'' \times 1\frac{1}{2}'' \times 31''$	#2 pine
Side ledgers	4	$\frac{3}{4}'' \times 1\frac{1}{2}'' \times 74\frac{1}{2}''$	#2 pine
Mounting pins	4	$1''$ dia. $\times 4''$	Hardwood dowel
Ladder			
Sides	2	$\frac{3}{4}'' \times 2\frac{1}{2}'' \times 49''$	Cedar
Rungs	5	$1''$ dia. $\times 14''$	Hardwood dowel
Rung pins	10	$\frac{3}{16}''$ dia. $\times 2''$	Hardwood dowel
Storage drawers			
Fronts and backs	4	$\frac{3}{4}'' \times 8\frac{1}{4}'' \times 37\frac{1}{4}''$	Plywood
Sides	4	$\frac{3}{4}'' \times 8\frac{1}{4}'' \times 19\frac{7}{8}''$	Plywood
Bottoms	2	$\frac{3}{4}'' \times 19\frac{7}{8}'' \times 36\frac{1}{2}''$	Plywood
Dividers	2	$\frac{3}{4}'' \times 5'' \times 19\frac{1}{8}''$	Plywood

Hardware

8 flathead wood screws, #10 $\times$ $2\frac{1}{2}''$ (beds)
34 flathead wood screws, #10 $\times$ $1\frac{1}{2}''$ (beds)
28 flathead wood screws, #10 $\times$ $1''$ (beds)
28 carriage bolts, $4\frac{1}{2}''$ $\times$ $\frac{5}{16}''$ dia. with brass washers and brass acorn nuts (beds)
6 flathead wood screws, #6 $\times$ $1\frac{1}{4}''$ (ladder)

8 flathead wood screws, #6 $\times$ $\frac{3}{4}''$ (ladder)
4 corner brackets, $\frac{1}{8}''$ $\times$ $\frac{3}{4}''$ $\times$ $3\frac{1}{2}''$ $\times$ $3\frac{1}{2}''$ (ladder)
Self-adhesive felt (ladder)
8 casters, $1\frac{1}{4}''$ dia. (drawers)
4d finishing nails (drawers)

plans to provide side access to both bunks, if you want.

The ladder has been designed to mount securely at either the side or the end of the beds. Strong yet light in weight, it is made from 1-inch-diameter hardwood dowels glued and pinned into cedar side rails, which match the beds. The ladder is suspended by means of four ordinary metal corner brackets (angle irons) that are bent to hook over the cedar bed rails. Self-adhesive felt covers the metal to protect the rails. Because the ladder hangs securely from the brackets, it does not take up floor space, nor will it slide or fall down.

The storage drawers are optional—they make use of plywood left over from the platforms that support each mattress—and are mounted on casters. The drawers roll in and out on the floor rather than slide from bed-mounted fixtures.

With this project, care has been taken to round over all corners and projections that might cause injury.

PLYWOOD CUTTING DIAGRAM

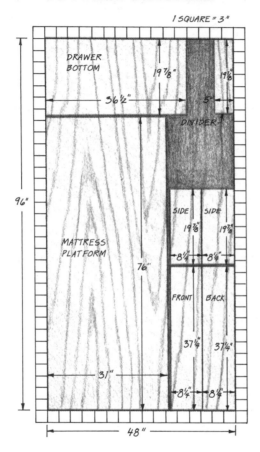

1 SQUARE = 3"

DRAWER BOTTOM

19⅞"

19⅞"

36½"

5"

DIVIDER

96"

SIDE   SIDE

19⅞"   19⅞"

8¼"   8¼"

MATTRESS PLATFORM

76"

FRONT   BACK

37¼"   37¼"

31"

8¼"   8¼"

48"

1 **Cut the parts for the two bunk beds.** The bunks shown are made from cedar, a commonly available construction timber chosen primarily because it's attractive when treated with a clear finish and it's light in weight. The legs are made from 4 × 4 posts, the rails from 1 × 6 boards. Cedar's drawbacks are its extra expense—it costs more than other types of construction stock—and its softness and tendency to split when worked. Pine is just as good

for this project, as would be any variety of lumber commonly used in building construction.

The mattress platforms are made from common construction plywood with one good side. You need a full sheet for each platform; the leftovers are used in building the storage drawers. Note the cutting scheme suggested in the *Plywood Cutting Diagram.*

Cut the parts to the sizes specified by the Cutting List. Use a circular saw for the posts; you need to make passes on both sides of each post to cut through it. Label four posts as uppers and four as lowers.

2 **Cut the joinery in the leg posts.** To begin, use a router and a ½-inch rounding-over bit to radius all the edges of the leg posts, including the ends.

Lay out and cut dadoes in the legs for the cross rails. Two dadoes are cut into all four legs of the lower bunk and into two legs the upper bunk. As indicated in the *Bunk Bed, End View,* the lower dado is 12 inches from the leg bottom, and the upper one, 9 inches from the leg top. The remaining two upper bunk legs have only one dado apiece— the lower one. Each dado is 5½ inches wide × ¾ inch deep, and all are cut into the inside face of the legs.

SHOP TIP: The router is primarily a trimming tool. It's easy to overburden the motor and overstress the bit in making too deep a cut. To excavate these ¾-inch-deep dadoes, make a series of passes, lowering the bit about ⅛ to ¼ inch further with each pass.

BUNK BED, PLAN VIEWS

¾" (TYP.)

3 ½"

TOP VIEW

¼" R. ALL
EXPOSED
EDGES

24"

31"

32 ½"

3 ½"

¾" (TYP.)

¼"

82 ½"

¼"

END VIEW

83"

3 ½"

3 ½"

THIS SIDE RAIL
ON TOP BUNK ONLY

76"

SIDE RAIL FAR SIDE
ONLY (BOTTOM BUNK),
BOTH SIDES (TOP BUNK)

FHWS
W/ PLUG
(FAR SIDE ; TYP.)

4"

2"

9"

5 ½"

1 ⅛"

36"

4"

5 ½"

1 ⅛" R. (TYP.)

1 ⅛"

½" R. (TYP. ALL EDGES OF LEG POSTS)

1 ⅛" (TYP.)

12"

1 ⅜" (TYP.)

5/16" x 4 ½" CARRIAGE
BOLT W/ BRASS
WASHER AND ACORN
NUT (TYP.)

2 ⅛"

(TYP.)

SIDE VIEW

Because the legs are fairly bulky, it is easiest to use a router and straight bit to cut the dadoes. Line up the legs, clamp them together, and lay out the dado locations on all at the same time. Clamp a pair of straightedges to the legs to guide the router. Cut the lower dado in all eight legs, then the upper dado in the appropriate six legs.

Next drill holes for the pins that lock the upper bunk in position atop the lower one. The 1-inch-diameter × 2-inch-deep holes should be centered in the butt ends of the legs. Drill into the

SHOP TIP: If securing the legs to drill the mounting-pin holes has you stumped, try this. Tighten a large hand screw onto the leg so that it projects at a right angle. Rest the hand screw on your workbench, and the leg will be suspended perpendicular to the work surface. Use a second hand screw to clamp the first to the bench.

tops of the four lower bunk legs and into the bottoms of the four upper bunk legs. The holes must be aligned perfectly.

3 **Make the cross rails.** The two bunks share seven cross rails. Four of the rails—two per bunk—have ledgers attached that help support the mattress platform. The other rails serve as guards to prevent the sleeper from tumbling out of bed.

Glue and clamp the cross ledgers flush against the bottom inside edges of four of the cross rails. With a #10 pilot-hole bit, bore and counterbore two pilot holes through the ledger and into the cross rail, about 10 inches from the ends. (You counterbore these holes so that you can glue in wood plugs to conceal the screwheads.) Drive 1-inch screws into these holes to reinforce the glue joint.

Test fit all the cross rails into their respective dadoes in the legs. Mark the cross rails where they intersect the legs, then radius their exposed edges—in other words, radius from mark to mark—with a router and a ¼-inch rounding-over bit.

4 **Assemble the end frames.** Glue the cross rails into their dadoes. Drill and counterbore three pilot holes in both ends of each rail. Where the hole passes through the ledger and the cross rail, use a 2½-inch screw. Otherwise, use 1½-inch screws.

With a rasp or file, work a ½-inch radius on the ends of each cross rail to match the radius on legs.

5 **Make the side rails.** The side rails, like the cross rails, serve either to help support the mattress or to prevent the sleeper from falling out of bed. The rails with the former function must have ledgers attached to them.

Position these ledgers flush along the inside bottom edge of four side rails, 4 inches shy of the rail ends. Glue each ledger in place, then drive five equally spaced 1-inch screws through it into the side rail to reinforce the joint. Counterbore the pilot holes for the screws, so that they can be covered later with wood plugs.

With a router and a ¼-inch rounding-over bit, work a radius on all edges of each side rail.

6 **Drill bolt holes into the legs and rails.** The side rails are attached to the end frames with bolts.

Drill ⁵⁄₁₆-inch-diameter holes into each leg as indicated in the *Bunk Bed, Side View*. The holes are adjacent to each cross rail against which a side rail will be attached. Remember that cedar is fragile, so you need to back up the wood with a scrap to prevent tearout and splintering as the bit emerges. "Hang" the end frames on the side or end of your workbench—turn the frame sideways and rest one leg on the bench top, with the other leg dangling parallel to the floor. Place a scrap board between the leg and the bench top.

Drill matching holes into the side rails.

7 **Apply a finish to the bed parts.** If you are a perfectionist, you can enhance the appearance of the bunks by covering all the screws with wood plugs. If you want the plugs to contrast somewhat with the cedar, slice them from a dowel of the appropriate diameter. If you want to truly conceal the screws, use a plug cutter to make plugs from scraps of the working stock.

SHOP TIP:

Save yourself precious minutes and, at the same time, position the bolt holes more accurately by using the little drilling jig shown. The body of the jig is the same width as the side rails. One fence strip fixes the holes in relation to the edge of the leg, while the other does the same in relation to the end of the rail.

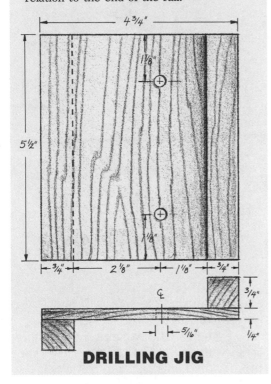

DRILLING JIG

In either case, glue the plugs into place, then use a backsaw or chisel to trim them flush. If you saw off the excess, protect the surface of the wood with a thin scrap.

Sand all of the components of each bunk until they are smooth, then apply a finish. We used two coats of brush-on lacquer.

8 Assemble the beds. Now it is time to bolt the beds together and to stack one atop the other.

Fasten the side rails to the legs with 4½-inch-long carriage bolts, using brass washers and brass acorn nuts. Insert the bolts from the inside of the leg posts, so that the more decorative brass nuts are exposed.

Drop the mattress platforms into place.

Before lifting the upper bunk into place, chamfer the ends of each mounting pin (to ease insertion), and fit one into each hole in the lower bunk's leg tops. Gluing the dowels is unnecessary. Lift the upper bunk above the lower one, and carefully set it down so that the dowels enter the holes in the bottoms of the legs.

9 Cut the parts for the ladder. With the bunks completed, you need to make a ladder, so that a child can climb up to the top bunk. This one has five rungs and hangs on the cross rails of the bunks by metal hooks cobbled from corner brackets.

Cut the sides from cedar, the rungs from any 1-inch-diameter hardwood dowel, and the rung pins (which lock the rungs in place and prevent them from spinning) from ³⁄₁₆-inch-diameter hardwood dowel. Make these parts the sizes specified by the Cutting List.

10 Make the hangers. As noted, the ladder hangs on four shop-made brackets. For reasons that will become apparent, you should make the hangers now.

To form the hangers, bend the corner brackets as indicated in the *Hanger*

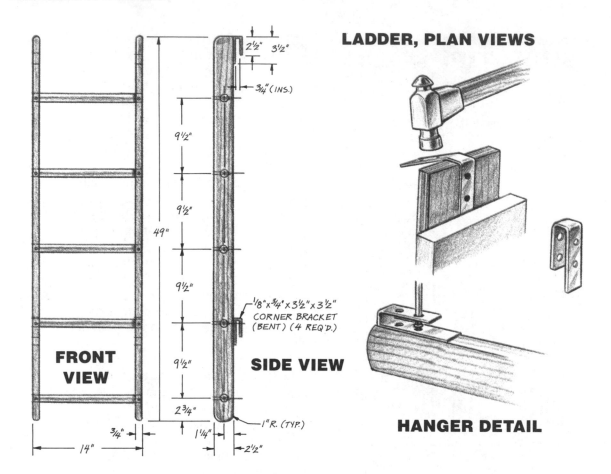

FRONT VIEW

49"

9½"

9½"

9½"

9½"

2¾"

14"

¾"

SIDE VIEW

2½"   3½"

¾" (INS.)

⅛" x ¾" x 3½" x 3½"
CORNER BRACKET
(BENT) (4 REQ'D.)

1" R. (TYP.)

1¼"

2½"

LADDER, PLAN VIEWS

HANGER DETAIL

Detail. Use a scrap of ¾-inch plywood as a form. Rest one leg of the bracket against the plywood's face, the other against the plywood's edge. Clamp the plywood and the tip of the bracket in a vise. Hammer the leg that extends beyond the plywood edge, working gradually to form the U shape.

Although each hanger has some holes in it, you probably need to drill additional ones—in the right spots—so that you can mount it on the ladder. Drill pairs of ¼-inch-diameter holes, penetrating both legs of the hangers; one hole in each pair is for the screwdriver that is needed to drive the screw through the other hole and into the ladder.

Complete the hangers by covering them with self-adhesive felt, which will protect the bed rails from scratches.

11 **Make the ladder sides.** Lay out one side as shown in the *Ladder, Side View.* Mark three corners to be rounded off; indicate the centers of the five holes for the rungs. Stack the two sides—with the markings exposed on top—and tape them together with masking tape.

Using a saber saw or a band saw,

cut the 1-inch radius on both corners of the bottom ends and on the outside corner of the top ends. Next drill 1-inch-diameter holes for the rungs.

Before radiusing the edges of the sides, mark the locations of the hangers. Hook hangers over the top and bottom cross rails of the now-set-up bunk beds. In turn, hold the ladder sides up to the hangers, and mark their edges where the hangers will be located. Now machine all the edges of the sides, *except* where the hangers will attach, using a router and a ¼-inch rounding-over bit.

12 **Install the rungs.** Glue the rungs into place. Start with one ladder side, applying glue to the insides of the holes (with a cotton-tipped swab) as well as to one end of the rungs. Press a rung into each hole. Apply glue to the holes in the second side and to the other end of the rungs, then fit the second side into place, driving it onto the rungs.

After the glue dries, drill a ³⁄₁₆-inch-diameter × 2-inch-deep hole through the sides into each rung. Apply glue to the rung pins, then drive one into each hole.

13 **Apply a finish to the ladder.** Sand the ladder as necessary, then apply the same finish you used for the bunks. When the finish is dry, install the hangers. Remember that you must use a narrow-tipped screwdriver, so that it can fit through the hole in one leg to drive the screw into the hole in the other leg. Use the shorter (¾-inch) screws in the upper holes of the lower brackets, which are even with the second rung from the bottom.

14 **Cut the parts for the storage drawers.** While the storage drawers aren't an essential part of the bunk bed ensemble, they do use up the plywood left from making the mattress platforms. The kids can use them for toys, or you can stow extra blankets and linens in them.

If you *are* going to make the drawers, cut all the parts to the sizes specified by the Cutting List. As you cut the parts, label them, and designate the plywood's "good" side as being the outside of the drawer.

15 **Cut the joinery.** With a router or a dado cutter, cut a ¾-inch-wide × ⅜-inch-deep rabbet in the front, back, and sides for the bottom. Cut the same dimension rabbet in both ends of the front and back for the sides.

Lay out and cut a 1-inch-wide × 5-inch-long hand-hole in the front of each drawer, locating it as shown in the *Storage Drawer, Front View.* Drill a 1-inch-diameter hole at each end of the hand-hole, then cut away the waste with a saber saw. Round over the inside and outside edges of the hole with a router and a ¼-inch rounding-over bit.

16 **Assemble the drawers.** Assemble the drawers with glue and finishing nails. Join the sides to the front and back, then set the bottom into its rabbet. Add the divider last. To secure the divider, drive nails into it through the front, back, and bottom of the drawer.

17 **Paint the drawers and install the casters.** Although the rest of the bunk bed ensemble has a natural

STORAGE DRAWER, PLAN VIEWS

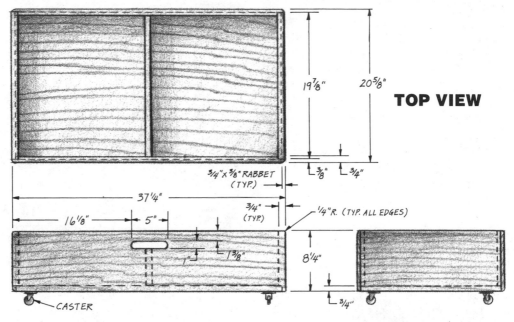

TOP VIEW

FRONT VIEW

SIDE VIEW

finish, the plywood's appearance hardly equals that of the cedar. It's better if you paint the drawers.

First sand the drawers and radius their exposed edges with a router and a ¼-inch rounding-over bit. Then brush on a good latex primer, followed by two coats of a semigloss latex enamel.

After the paint dries, turn the drawers over and install the casters.

PART TWO

PLYWOOD PROJECTS

YOUTH CHAIR

There is a stage in every child's life—a fairly protracted one, I might add—when he or she is too big for a high chair, yet a little small for a regular chair. The youth chair has long been a mealtime favorite of youngsters. They can eat at the table with everyone else, without teetering precariously on books or other boosters or sitting with their chins being just at tabletop level.

Brad Smith built this wonderful contemporary youth chair for a very practical reason: His child needed it. His design is marvelous in its simplicity. Its wide footing makes it very stable, and its footrest and side cutouts offer the youthful user several options for clambering up to the seat. Made from cabinet-grade birch plywood and poplar, it is assembled with truss-head screws. The most difficult part of its construction may well be laying out the sides. Excluding finishing, this is easily a one-day project.

Having designed and built the youth chair, Smith, owner of Bradford Woodworking in Worcester, Pennsylvania, adapted its construction concept to other childhood furniture needs. He developed complementary pieces that his children put to use—and that he put into limited production.

1 **Select the plywood and cut the parts.** Smith used the best-quality birch plywood he could in building his youth chair. You want a cabinet-grade material, commonly stocked only by lumberyards that serve commercial cabinet and furniture makers. Shop for a ½-inch plywood that has seven plies and is free of voids. Cut the plywood parts to the sizes specified by the Cutting List.

2 **Lay out the sides.** Lightly draw horizontal lines across the inside surfaces of the sides to locate the bottoms of the stretcher, footrest, seat, and

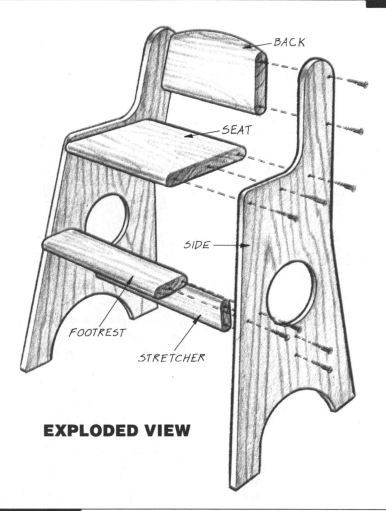

BACK

SEAT

SIDE

FOOTREST

STRETCHER

EXPLODED VIEW

CUTTING LIST

Part	Quantity	Dimensions	Material
Sides	2	½″ × 15¾″ × 29″	Birch plywood
Stretcher	1	1″ × 2¾″ × 13⅝″	Poplar
Footrest	1	1″ × 4″ × 12½″	Poplar
Seat	1	1″ × 9½″ × 11″	Poplar
Back	1	1″ × 6″ × 10½″	Poplar

Hardware

#10 × 2½″ truss-head wood screws. Available from Equality Screw Company, P.O. Box 1645, El Cajon, CA 92022, and from Bruss Fasteners, P.O. Box 88307, Grand Rapids, MI 49518.

PLAN VIEWS

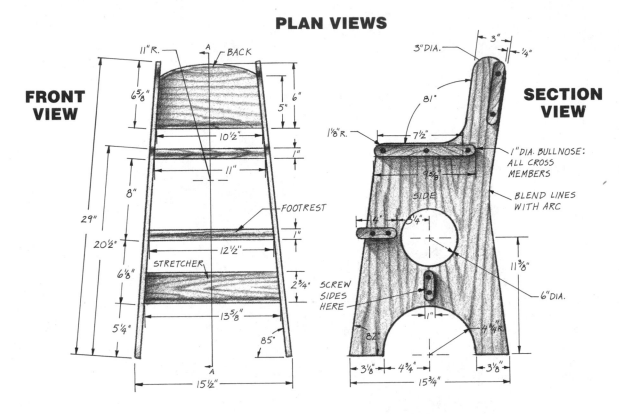

FRONT VIEW

SECTION VIEW

back. Lay out the shape of the sides as shown in the *Side Layout.* Here's how:

On the outside surface of a side blank, lightly draw a centerline from top to bottom. Along this centerline, locate centers for the circular cutout and the bottom arc. Draw these features with a compass. Next draw a horizontal line across each piece, 20½ inches from the bottom; this is the seat line. Draw the side lines next; starting at the bottom, extend lines at 82 degrees from the corners to the seat line. From the point at which the front side line meets the seat line, measure back along the seat line, and make marks at 7½ inches and 10⅝ inches. From these marks draw lines up and back at 81 degrees. Connect these

two lines at the top with a 3-inch-diameter arc, tangent to the top of the board. Blend the lines that form the back edge of the side with a shallow curve. Finally, draw in the various rounded corners.

SHOP TIP: When you have to make multiples of a part that's time-consuming (or tricky) to lay out, you can save time and good wood by laying out the part on posterboard. If the layout work goes badly, you've wasted only a 30-cent piece of cardboard. If you are satisfied with your work, you have a template from which you can lay out dozens of the same part.

3 Cut out the sides. Locate and mark the screw hole locations indicated in the *Side Layout.* Drill each with a ³⁄₁₆-inch drill bit.

Cut out the sides using a saber saw or band saw. If you use the latter, you can stack the two sides and cut both at the same time. The circular cutouts can be rounded to perfection with a router and a trammel jig. (See the *Trammel Jig Plan* on page 96.) Clean up the rough edges with scrapers and sandpaper.

SHOP TIP: A sanding drum is an excellent tool for removing saw marks from the plywood edges, especially those inside curves. Chuck the drum in a drill press, then lower it and lock it at table height. By resting the workpiece on the table as you feed its edge against the drum, you can ensure that the edge is square to the face. If you don't have a drill press, you can still make use of the sanding drum. Simply chuck the drum in a portable drill, secure the workpiece in a vise, and go to work.

4 Make the crosspieces. All the horizontal parts in the high chair shown are made from poplar. You can use other woods, including pine. Having made your choice, joint, plane, and saw the stretcher, footrest, seat, and back to the sizes specified by the Cutting List.

Cut the angles next. Set the table saw's miter gauge at 85 degrees to the blade, and miter the angle on both ends of the stretcher and back. Set the miter gauge square with the blade, and tilt the blade to 85 degrees (5 degrees off verti-

SIDE LAYOUT

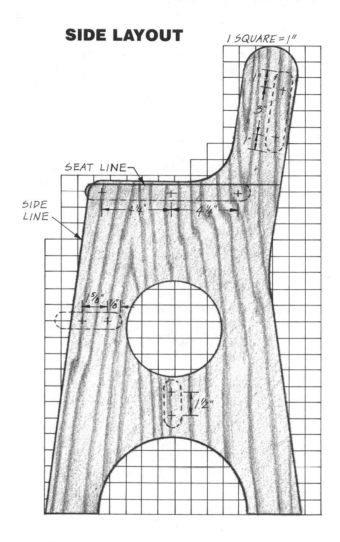

cal). Crosscut the angle on both ends of the seat and footrest.

Now lay out and cut the curve of the back. Draw a centerline from top to bottom on the back. Draw a reference line on the workbench or on a scrap of plywood. Carefully align the centerline on the back with the reference line on the bench. Measure 5 inches along the reference line, away from the bottom of the back, and make a mark. From this mark draw an 11-inch-radius arc across the top of the back. Cut the back along this line, then clean up the cut with a scraper or spokeshave.

Finally, shape the edges of the crosspieces. This is done most quickly using a router and a 1-inch bullnose cutter (part #765 from MLCS Ltd., P.O. Box 4053 C4, Rydal, PA 19046), since a single pass shapes the full edge. Alternatively, a ½-inch rounding-over bit can be used; you'll have to make two passes for each edge.

SHOP TIP: To ensure that the joints between the various crosspieces and the sides are tight, the bevels on the seat and footrest must duplicate the miters on the back and stretcher. Use a protractor to set a sliding T-bevel to 85 degrees. Then use the sliding T-bevel to set both the miter gauge for the miter cuts and the tilt of the blade for the bevel cuts. Using the same bevel setting helps to make all the angles identical. Leave the T-bevel set in case the pieces have to be trimmed upon assembly.

5 Drill pilot holes for the assembly screws. One at a time, hold the crosspieces in position against the sides. Through the holes already bored into the sides, drill ³⁄₃₂-inch pilot holes into the ends of the crosspieces.

Test how the parts fit. Screw the chair together with #10 × 2½-inch truss-head screws. Recut any of the pieces that do not fit well.

6 Apply a finish. When everything fits properly, take the chair apart and mark all the joints for reassembly. Finish sand all the parts.

As with the other items in this collection, the sides of the chair are painted in bright colors, while its crosspieces are coated with a natural finish. Paint the sides with one coat of latex primer and two coats of semigloss latex enamel. Finish the crosspieces with your favorite clear wood finish.

7 Complete the assembly. When the various finishes are dry, reattach the sides to the crosspieces with the truss-head screws.

PLAYROOM BOOKCASE

This simple yet elegant shelf unit would be a welcome addition to any child's room. It is perfect for holding books, small toys, models, or other treasures. While the bookcase was designed to complement the other pieces in Brad Smith's line of children's furniture, it is not so juvenile that it will be outgrown quickly.

The cleverness of Smith's design is subtle. Although it is shown hanging, and it does lend itself to that, it actually was designed to be a floor-standing unit. The cutouts on the bottom of the sides do two things: They provide clearance for baseboards, and they keep the bookcase against the wall. The idea is to stand the bookcase on the floor, pushed up against the wall. No need to secure it—it won't tip over or slide.

The construction is very straightforward. The unit consists of two plywood sides joined to solid poplar shelves with truss-head screws.

The prototype shown also demonstrates the reverse of the line's usual two-tone finish scheme. The sides have a natural finish, the shelves are painted.

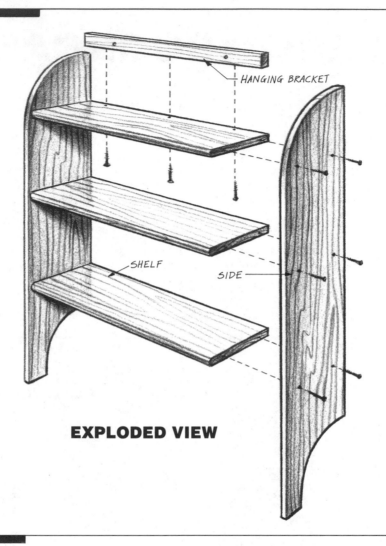

HANGING BRACKET

SHELF

SIDE

EXPLODED VIEW

CUTTING LIST

Part	Quantity	Dimension	Material
Sides	2	$\frac{1}{2}'' \times 7\frac{7}{8}'' \times 36''$	Birch plywood
Shelves	3	$\frac{3}{4}'' \times 7\frac{5}{8}'' \times 23''$	Poplar
Hanging bracket	1	$1'' \times 1\frac{1}{2}'' \times 23''$	Poplar

Hardware

#10 × 2½″ truss-head wood screws. Available from Equality Screw Company, P.O. Box 1645, El Cajon, CA 92022, and from Bruss Fasteners, P.O. Box 88307, Grand Rapids, MI 49518. 1¾″ drywall screws

PLAN VIEWS

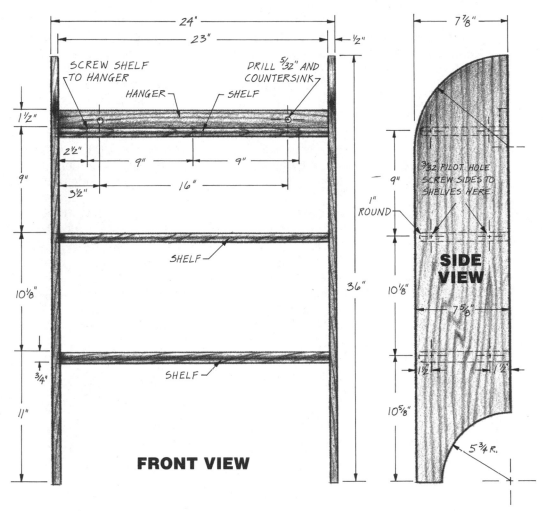

FRONT VIEW

SIDE VIEW

SCREW SHELF TO HANGER

DRILL ⁵/₃₂" AND COUNTERSINK

HANGER

SHELF

SHELF

SHELF

³/₃₂ PILOT HOLE SCREW SIDES TO SHELVES HERE

1" ROUND

5¾ R.

1 **Make the sides.** The two sides are made from cabinet-grade birch plywood. Cut them to the size specified by the Cutting List. Lay out the shelf locations on the inside surfaces as shown in the *Front View* and *Side View*. Mark off the screw locations according to the measurements given in the *Side View*. Drill a ³/₁₆-inch clearance hole for each screw.

Lay out and cut the profile of the sides. Using a compass and following the *Side View*, lay out the arcs on each side piece. Cut these curves with a saber saw or on the band saw. Carefully sand the cuts to remove ridges left by the saw blade, then sand all the faces and edges of the sides to prepare them for painting.

2 **Make the shelves.** The shelves are poplar. Mill the stock, then cut the shelves to the size specified by the Cutting List.

Round over the front edge of each shelf. With a 1-inch-diameter bullnose cutter in a router, you can do each shelf with a single pass. (Such a bit, part #765, is available from MLCS Ltd., P.O. Box 4053 C4, Rydal, PA 19046.) An alternative approach is to use a ⅜-inch rounding-over bit, which would require two passes to complete each shelf.

Complete the shelves by finish sanding them on all sides.

3 **Add the hanging bracket.** Joint, plane, and cut the hanging bracket to the size specified by the Cutting List. Drill and countersink ³⁄₁₆-inch holes through the bracket for hanging the assembled bookcase, as shown in the *Front View*. Finish sand the bracket, then glue and screw it to the top shelf using 1¾-inch drywall screws. Make sure the bracket is flush with the shelf along the back and at both ends.

4 **Assemble the unit.** On a flat surface, assemble the bookcase on its back, with all the pieces in their relative positions. Clamp the shelves and sides together, or have a helper hold the pieces in position, and drill a ³⁄₃₂-inch pilot hole for each screw. Label all the parts on their mating surfaces, so that you can return them to these positions for the final assembly.

Since the sides get a different finish than the shelves, it is easier to finish everything before the unit is assembled. The shelves get a coat of primer followed by two coats of semigloss latex enamel. You can use your favorite clear wood finish for the sides. Allow plenty of time for everything to dry.

Finally, screw the bookcase together using #10 × 2½-inch truss-head wood screws. A little wax or soap on their threads will make the screws easier to drive.

CHILD'S STOOL

To give a small child a boost, build this project. The stool can be used to lift youngsters to kitchen-counter height for making cookies or washing dishes. It provides a place on which to sit, a place from which to jump. The cant of the sides eliminates wobbliness, and the circular cutouts serve as handles.

As with the other pieces in this line, the construction is simple and straightforward. Plywood sides are cut out and screwed to poplar crosspieces with truss-head screws. The sides are brightly colored, while the seat and stretchers have a natural finish.

A critical component of the stool—and of most other pieces in this line—is the truss-head screw. End grain doesn't offer good "footing" for screws. The stool's builder, Brad Smith, nevertheless elected to screw the parts together, but used truss-head screws. These have a deep, coarse thread that bites sharply into the grain, and their heads are broad enough to act as their own washers. Although they are rare, the screws—available only in the #10 × 2½-inch size—can be purchased through the mail from the sources mentioned in the Cutting List.

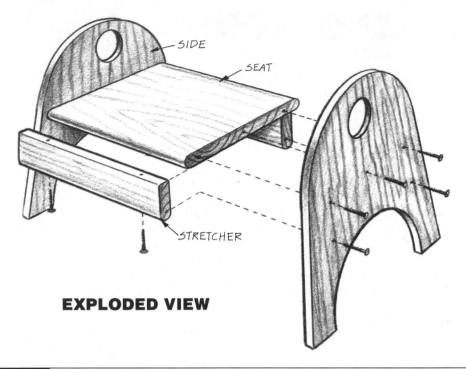

SIDE

SEAT

STRETCHER

EXPLODED VIEW

CUTTING LIST

Part	Quantity	Dimension	Material
Sides	2	½″ × 12″ × 12″	Birch plywood
Seat	1	1″ × 9⅞″ × 11½″	Poplar
Stretchers	2	1″ × 2½″ × 12″	Poplar

Hardware

1½″ drywall screws

#10 × 2½″ truss-head wood screws. Available from Equality Screw Company, P.O. Box 1645, El Cajun, CA 92022, and from Bruss Fasteners, P.O. Box 88307, Grand Rapids, MI 49518.

1 **Make the sides.** The sides are made from ½-inch cabinet-grade birch plywood. Cut the plywood for the sides to the dimensions specified by the Cutting List.

Across the inside surface of each piece, lightly draw a line 4 inches from the bottom. This marks where the bot-

tom of the stretchers are to go. On the outside of each piece, lightly draw a centerline from top to bottom. Mark the center points for the two arcs and the handle hole along this centerline, using the dimensions in the *End View*. Draw the arcs with a compass. Draw lines tangent to the top arc and through the bottom corners to lay out the sloped sides. Mark the screw locations according to the dimensions in the *End View*.

Cut out the sides on the band saw or with a saber saw. The handle cutouts can be made with a saber saw, a router fitted with a trammel jig (see the *Trammel Jig Plan* on page 96), or a hole saw chucked in a drill. Shape both edges of the handle holes with a ¼-inch rounding-over bit in the router. Smooth the cut edges with a drum sander chucked in a drill. Finally, at each location marked for a screw, drill a ³⁄₁₆-inch hole.

2 **Make the crosspieces.** Joint, plane, and cut the seat and stretchers to the sizes specified by the Cutting List. You may have to edge-glue boards to have a piece wide enough for the seat.

Next, miter and bevel these pieces. Set the table saw's miter gauge at 85 degrees to the blade, and cut both ends of each stretcher at this angle. As you do this, make sure the stretchers are the same length. Reset the miter gauge to be square with the blade, and tilt the blade to 85 degrees (5 degrees off vertical). Crosscut both ends of the seat at this setting. Make sure the length of the seat along its bottom matches the length of the stretchers along their tops.

Drill pilot holes into the stretchers for the screws that join them to the seat. Mark the locations of the holes on

PLAN VIEWS

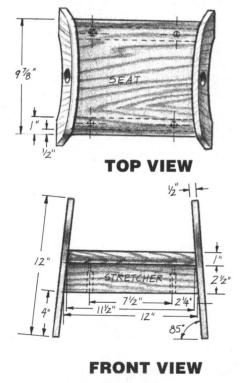

TOP VIEW

FRONT VIEW

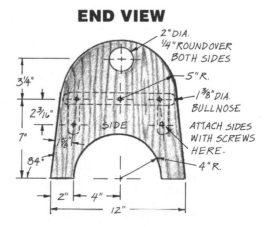

END VIEW

the bottom edge, using the dimensions given in the *Front View*. At each location, drill a ⅜-inch-diameter counterbore 1¾ inches deep and a ³⁄₁₆-inch clearance hole all the way through the stretcher.

Finally, shape both the exposed edges of the seat and the bottom edges of the stretchers using a 1⅜-inch bullnose bit in a router. (The bit, part #C1035, is available from Cascade Tools, Inc., Box 3110, Bellingham, WA 98227.) Alternatively, a ½-inch rounding-over bit could be used.

SHOP TIP: An extension fence screwed to your miter gauge can aid in making repetitive crosscuts. From a piece of straight scrap, make a fence 24 to 30 inches long and 3 inches high. To use it, clamp a stop block to the fence to establish the length of the workpiece as it is cut.

3 Assemble the stool. Join the stretchers to the seat first. Gently clamp the stretchers against the underside of the seat, ½ inch in from its

edges and flush with its ends. Screw the stretchers to the seat with 1½-inch drywall screws. No pilot holes are necessary in the seat if a relatively soft wood, like poplar, is being used. Otherwise, drill a ³⁄₃₂-inch pilot hole ¾ inch deep before screwing the pieces together.

Drill pilot holes for the truss-head screws next. Align the bottoms of the stretchers with the lines drawn previously on the insides of the sides. Make sure the seat is centered from front to back. Through the holes already bored into the sides, drill ³⁄₃₂-inch pilot holes into the seat assembly.

4 Apply the finish. Finish sand all the parts. Be careful not to eliminate any marks made to expedite assembly. Finish the seat assembly with a clear wood finish. Finish the sides with a coat of latex primer and two coats of semigloss latex enamel.

After the finish dries, align the pieces in their respective positions, and screw the stool together using the truss-head screws.

CHILD'S COATRACK

This small coatrack provides a special place for children to keep their clothing. Hang it at an appropriate height in the bedroom for bathrobes and pajamas, or near the back door for outdoor coats, hats, and mittens.

The construction is similar to the other pieces in this line—plywood sides joined to solid wood crosspieces with screws.

It's interesting that the design literally grew out of woodworker Brad Smith's scrap bin. Each time he made a stool or a set of chairs (see these projects on pages 85 and 98), he'd toss more semicircular pieces of good ply-

wood in the scrap. He challenged himself to come up with an addition to his line of children's furniture that would make use of those scraps. And this is it.

So if you want to make this coatrack, make the stool first; the scraps cut from the stool sides are used as the coatrack sides.

1 Cut the shelf, back, and pegs to size. As with the other pieces in this line, the coatrack's horizontal members are solid wood. While poplar was used in the unit shown, you can use whatever solid wood you like, including

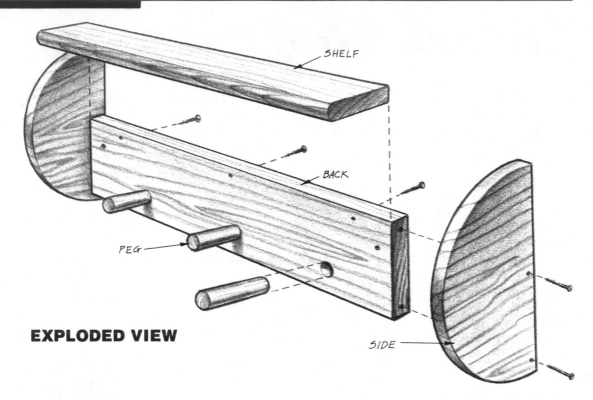

EXPLODED VIEW

SHELF

BACK

PEG

SIDE

CUTTING LIST

Part	Quantity	Dimensions	Material
Shelf	1	¾" × 3⅛" × 17¾"	Poplar
Back	1	1" × 3¼" × 17¾"	Poplar
Pegs	3	¾" dia. × 3"	Hardwood dowel
Sides	2	½" × 4⅜" × 7¾"	Plywood

Hardware

2" drywall screws
1½" drywall screws

pine. Mill the wood, if necessary, and cut the shelf and back to the sizes specified by the Cutting List.

Shape the front edge of the shelf. Using a 1-inch bullnose cutter in a router allows you to round the edge in a single pass. (Such a bit—part #765—is available from MLCS Ltd., P.O. Box 4053 C4, Rydal, PA 19046.) You also could use a rounding-over bit, ⅜ to ½ inch in size.

Cut the pegs to size, then sand and chamfer one end of each.

2 **Drill the back.** The back gets three sets of holes drilled into it.

The first set consists of three countersunk $\frac{3}{16}$-inch holes drilled from the back, $\frac{3}{8}$ inch down from the top. These holes will be used to screw the back to the shelf.

The second is a pair of countersunk $\frac{3}{16}$-inch holes drilled from the front, $1\frac{1}{4}$ inches down from the top. These are the holes used in mounting the coatrack to the wall.

SHOP TIP: Drilling a number of holes at a fixed distance from an edge can be accomplished easily by clamping a fence across the drill press table. Clamp the fence back from the center of the drill bit at the measurement required.

The final set of holes comprises three $\frac{3}{4}$-inch holes drilled from the front at a 14-degree angle, $\frac{3}{4}$ inch deep. These holes should be bored with a Forstner bit, which produces a flat-bottomed hole. Although the exact degree of the angle isn't vital, it should be the same for each hole; the rack won't look right if each peg is at a different angle. To maintain the angle on a drill press, simply cut a wedge to rest the workpiece on.

3 **Assemble the shelf and back.** Align the shelf with the ends and top edge of the back, and drill $\frac{3}{32}$-inch pilot holes into the shelf through the holes drilled previously into the back. Spread glue on the joint, and screw the two pieces together with 2-inch drywall screws. Glue the pegs into the angled holes; their chamfered ends are exposed.

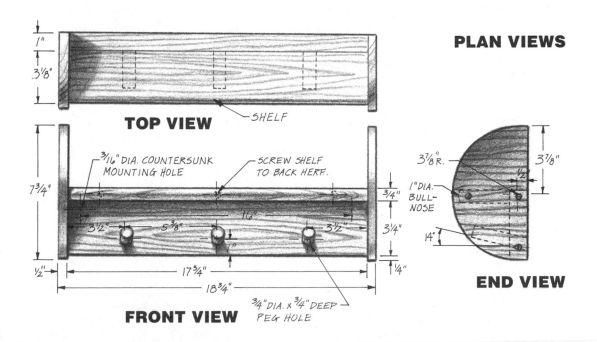

PLAN VIEWS

TOP VIEW

SHELF

$\frac{3}{16}$" DIA. COUNTERSUNK MOUNTING HOLE

SCREW SHELF TO BACK HERE.

$3\frac{7}{8}$" R.

$3\frac{1}{8}$"

1" DIA. BULL-NOSE

$7\frac{3}{4}$"

$3\frac{1}{2}$" $5\frac{3}{8}$"   16" $3\frac{1}{2}$"

$\frac{3}{4}$"

$3\frac{1}{4}$"

14°

$\frac{1}{2}$" $17\frac{3}{4}$" $\frac{1}{4}$"

$18\frac{3}{4}$"

$\frac{3}{4}$" DIA. x $\frac{3}{4}$" DEEP PEG HOLE

FRONT VIEW

END VIEW

1"

$3\frac{1}{8}$"

4 **Cut out the sides.** As I mentioned, the sides of the prototype coatrack shown are the cutouts from the sides of either a stool or a chair. Assuming you've made a stool or a chair or two, you only have to sand the sawed edges of the appropriate scraps from those projects.

If, however, you are starting from scratch, cut the plywood to the size specified by the Cutting List. On each piece, locate the arc's center point and draw the arc with a compass. Cut the sides with a saber saw or on the band saw. Clean up the sawed edge with sandpaper.

5 **Assemble the project.** Mark for the shelf on the inside surface of each side, 4¼ inches from the bottom.

This indicates the top of the shelf unit.

Drill and countersink ³⁄₁₆-inch pilot holes into the sides as shown in the *End View*. Align the shelf unit with the marks on the sides, and through the just-drilled holes bore ³⁄₃₂-inch pilot holes into the ends of the shelf unit.

6 **Apply a finish.** Since the sides are finished differently from the shelf unit, it is easiest to finish the pieces before they are assembled. Paint the sides with one coat of primer and two coats of semigloss latex enamel. Finish the shelf unit with a clear wood finish.

After the finish dries, carefully align the shelf unit with the sides and screw them together using 1½-inch drywall screws.

TOY CHEST

Toys! Your kids can't live without them, but you can't live with them—especially when they're scattered around the house. To children, toys are fun, entertainment, escape, occasionally the very focus of life. To moms and dads, they are vexing clutter.

In the Worcester, Pennsylvania, home of the Brad Smith family, the solution to the conflict is this toy chest. After a day's entertaining, all the toys go into the chest. They remain easily accessible to the Smith youngsters, yet they're off the floor and out of sight—all in one place.

The chest is of simple, sturdy construction and has just enough emphasis on style to make it an attractive addition to most rooms. Made entirely from cabinet-grade birch plywood, it is joined with truss-head screws. The sides are painted, while the crosspieces are given a clear finish. The handle openings dip below the lid to prevent pinches to little fingers. It should provide a home to many generations' worth of playthings.

1 **Select the plywood and cut the parts.** Cut the plywood parts to the sizes specified by the Cutting List.

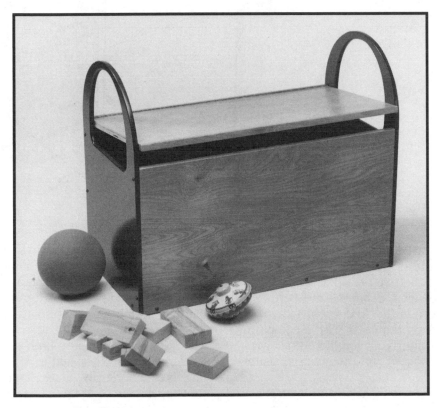

EXPLODED VIEW

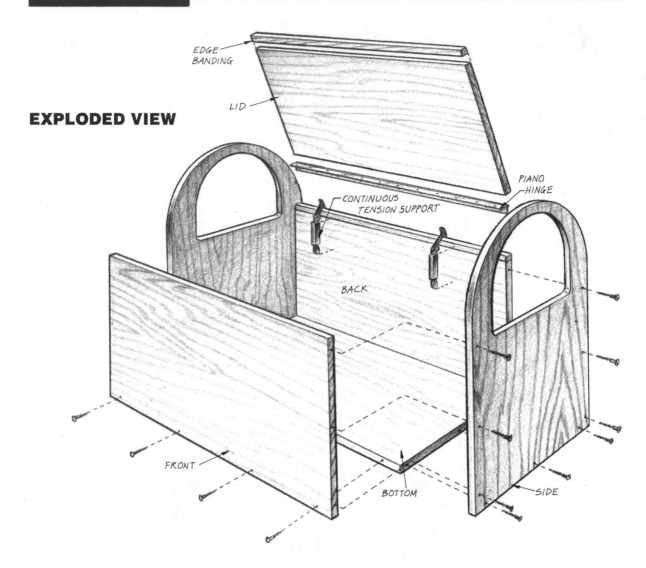

EDGE BANDING

LID

PIANO HINGE

CONTINUOUS TENSION SUPPORT

BACK

FRONT

BOTTOM

SIDE

2 **Lay out and cut the shape of the sides.** Locate and mark the centers of the two arcs that make up the top of the sides, using the measurements given in the *End View*. Draw these arcs on the sides with a compass. Complete the layout for the cutout with a framing square and the given measurements.

Cutting the curves can be accom-plished several different ways. The most expedient method is to use a band saw to cut the outside curve and a saber saw to cut the inside curve. After you finish cutting, refine the curves with sandpaper and scrapers.

Rout the edges on both sides of the cutout with a router and a ¼-inch round-ing-over bit. Finally, finish sand all edges to prepare for painting.

CUTTING LIST

Part	Quantity	Dimensions	Material
Sides	2	$\frac{1}{2}'' \times 16'' \times 24\frac{3}{4}''$	Birch plywood
Front	1	$\frac{3}{4}'' \times 15\frac{3}{4}'' \times 29''$	Birch plywood
Back	1	$\frac{3}{4}'' \times 15\frac{3}{4}'' \times 29''$	Birch plywood
Bottom	1	$\frac{3}{4}'' \times 14\frac{1}{4}'' \times 29''$	Birch plywood
Lid	1	$\frac{3}{4}'' \times 14\frac{3}{4}'' \times 28\frac{7}{8}''$	Birch plywood
Edge banding	2	$\frac{7}{8}'' \times \frac{3}{4}'' \times 29\frac{1}{2}''$	Birch

Hardware

#10 $\times$ 2½ truss-head wood screws. Available from Equality Screw Company, P.O. Box 1645, El Cajon, CA 92022, and from Brass Fasteners, P.O. Box 88307, Grand Rapids, MI 49518.

2 continuous tension supports. Available from The Woodworkers' Store, 21801 Industrial Blvd., Rogers, MN 55374.

1 piano hinge, $\frac{3}{4}'' \times 36''$ *

* Cut to required length with a hacksaw.

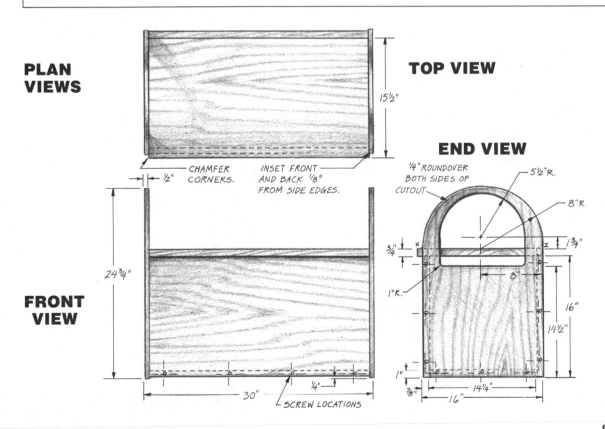

PLAN VIEWS

TOP VIEW

15½"

CHAMFER CORNERS. INSET FRONT AND BACK ⅛" FROM SIDE EDGES.

½"

END VIEW

¼" ROUNDOVER BOTH SIDES OF CUTOUT

5½"R.

8"R.

1¾"

8"

1"R.

FRONT VIEW

24¾"

16"

14½"

30" ¼"

SCREW LOCATIONS

1"

⅜"

14¼"

16"

SHOP TIP:

A trammel jig allows you to cut very accurate curves with a router.

First drill a ¼-inch hole at the center of each arc. Set the jig's pivot in the center hole for the outside arc. Adjust the router so that the inside edge of the cutter is in line with the arc. Cut the arc by pivoting the jig with the router running and the bit extended into the workpiece. Be careful not to cut beyond points X and Z as shown in the *End View*. Make two or three passes to complete the cut.

The inside curve is cut in the same fashion. This time, however, use the center point for the inner arc, and line up the outside edge of the cutter on the arc. Stopping the cut is not as critical on the inside, as the router will only be cutting into the waste part of the stock if you happen to overcut. Finish the cutout with a saber saw or router and an edge guide.

TRAMMEL JIG PLAN

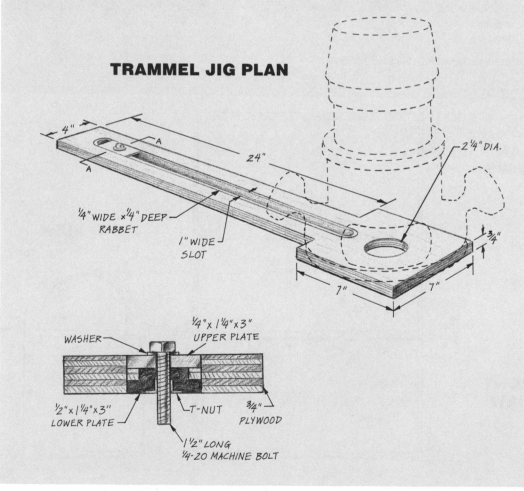

4"

24"

2¼" DIA.

¼" WIDE × ¼" DEEP RABBET

1" WIDE SLOT

¾"

7"

7"

WASHER

¼" × 1¼" × 3" UPPER PLATE

½" × 1¼" × 3" LOWER PLATE

T-NUT

¾" PLYWOOD

1½" LONG ¼-20 MACHINE BOLT

3 Edge-band the back and the lid. To cover the raw edge of the plywood—giving the toy chest a neater, more durable finished appearance—apply edge banding to the top edge of the back and to the front edge of the lid. Use birch for this.

Cut two pieces of birch to the size specified by the Cutting List. The bands are sized to allow for some slippage during glue-up; you trim them later. Glue the edge banding to the appropriate edges with wood glue. Place a ¾-inch scrap block between the clamps and the edge banding to prevent damage during glue-up. Space the clamps no more than 12 inches apart for adequate pressure.

When the glue dries, trim the edge banding to length with a hand saw. Then scrape and sand it flush with the faces of the plywood.

4 Drill holes for the assembly screws. As noted, the toy chest parts are joined with truss-head screws. Mark the screw locations on the sides, front, and back as shown in the various plan views. Drill ³⁄₁₆-inch-diameter clearance holes for the screws.

Align the bottom between the front and back. Make sure that it is flush at the ends and along the bottom edges. Drill ³⁄₃₂-inch-diameter pilot holes into the bottom, using the clearance holes previously drilled into the front and back as drill guides. Screw the front and back to the bottom.

Set this assembly on end, and align one of the sides on it. Note that the front and back are recessed ⅛ inch from the edges of the sides; the bottom is recessed ¼ inch. Drill ³⁄₃₂-inch-diameter pilot holes through each of the clearance holes. Mark the side for reassembly and set it aside. Invert the front-back-bottom subassembly, and repeat with the other side.

5 Apply a finish. As with the other items in this collection, the sides are painted in bright colors, and the remaining parts are coated with a natural finish. To prepare the parts for finishing, sand them carefully.

Paint the sides with one coat of latex primer and two coats of semigloss latex enamel. Finish the front, back, bottom, and lid with your favorite clear wood finish.

6 Complete the assembly. When the finishes are dry, attach the sides to the front-back-bottom subassembly with truss-head screws. Install the supports and hinge on the lid and back, following the manufacturer's instructions.

PLAYROOM TABLE AND CHAIRS

This small-scale table and four chairs is perfect for the playroom. Kids can play games, color and draw, have snacks, all at a level comfortable for them. And the family woodworker can provide a custom-made ensemble without weeks of work.

Created by Brad Smith, who designed and built all the projects in this section, the chair is a natural extension of the youth chair, his first project in the line. It has the same plywood sides sand-wiching a poplar seat and back. The sides cant, providing a wide-set, stable base. Although the profile of the chair appears to duplicate the top portion of the youth chair, it is slightly different in several key dimensions.

The table is scaled to complement the chairs. Its brightly colored finish, as much as its style, ties it to the chairs as well as to the other projects in the line. The construction approach is consistent with the other pieces, too.

EXPLODED VIEWS

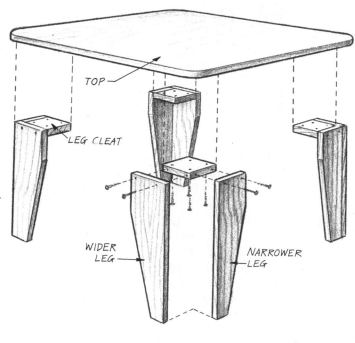

TOP

LEG CLEAT

WIDER LEG

NARROWER LEG

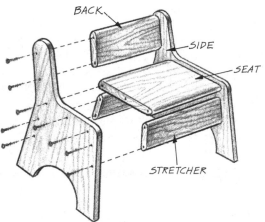

BACK

SIDE

SEAT

STRETCHER

CUTTING LIST

Part	Quantity	Dimensions	Material
Table			
Top	1	$\frac{3}{4}'' \times 32'' \times 32''$	Medium-density fiberboard
Legs	4	$\frac{1}{2}'' \times 4\frac{5}{8}'' \times 16\frac{3}{4}''$	Birch plywood
Legs	4	$\frac{1}{2}'' \times 4\frac{1}{8}'' \times 16\frac{3}{4}''$	Birch plywood
Leg cleats	4	$\frac{3}{4}'' \times 4\frac{1}{8}'' \times 4\frac{1}{8}''$	Birch plywood
Each chair			
Sides	2	$\frac{1}{2}'' \times 14'' \times 17\frac{3}{8}''$	Birch plywood
Stretchers	2	$1'' \times 3'' \times 11\frac{13}{16}''$	Poplar
Seat	1	$1'' \times 9\frac{1}{4}'' \times 10\frac{13}{16}''$	Poplar
Back	1	$\frac{3}{4}'' \times 5\frac{3}{8}'' \times 9\frac{7}{8}''$	Poplar

Hardware

#10 × 2½″ truss-head wood screws. Available from Equality Screw Company, P.O. Box 1645, El Cajun, CA 92022, and from Bruss Fasteners, P.O. Box 88307, Grand Rapids, MI 49518.
1¾″ drywall screws
1¼″ drywall screws

TABLE

1 **Make the top.** From medium-density fiberboard, cut the top to the dimensions specified by the Cutting List. Lay out the rounded corners and cut them on the band saw or with a saber saw. Sand the edges and break the corners slightly to prepare for finishing.

2 **Make the legs.** The legs are made from ½-inch cabinet-grade birch plywood. Cut the plywood for the legs to the dimensions specified by the Cutting List. Drill and countersink two ³⁄₁₆-inch

holes at the top of each leg piece as shown in the *Table, Side View*. Glue the leg pairs along one edge, with the two pieces at 90 degrees to one another. In each pair, make sure the wider piece overlaps the narrower one.

When the glue has dried, scrape off any squeeze-out, then cut the tapers on each side with the aid of the jig shown. Using the width of the jig as a guide, set the rip fence. With the jig butted against the fence, position a leg assembly in the jig's notch. Push the works through the saw blade, cutting off the portion of the leg that projects beyond the edge of the jig. Be sure your taper begins at the foot of the leg. Make one taper cut on

TABLE, PLAN VIEWS

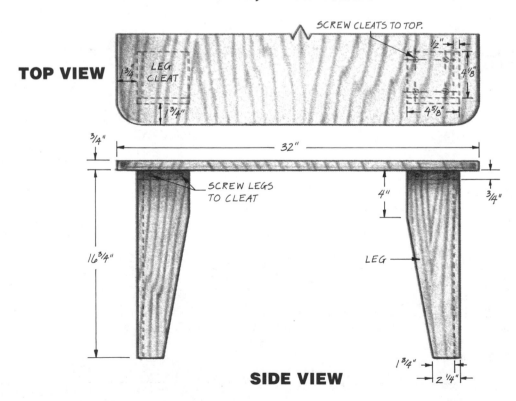

TOP VIEW

SCREW CLEATS TO TOP.

LEG CLEAT

³⁄₄"

1³⁄₄"

½"

4¹⁄₈"

4⁵⁄₈"

³⁄₄"

32"

SCREW LEGS TO CLEAT

4"

³⁄₄"

16³⁄₄"

LEG

1³⁄₄"

2¹⁄₄"

SIDE VIEW

each leg assembly before moving to the second cut.

To make the second cut, you must move the fence to the opposite side of the blade. After moving and setting the fence, turn the jig over, and make the cut on each assembly.

Cut the plywood for the leg cleats to the dimensions specified by the Cutting List. Drill and countersink four $\frac{3}{16}$-inch holes in each cleat as shown in the *Table, Top View*. Align each piece with the top of the leg assembly, its countersunk side down. Using the holes already bored into the legs, drill $\frac{3}{32}$-inch pilot holes into the cleats, then screw the legs to the cleats with $1\frac{3}{4}$-inch drywall screws.

3 **Apply the finish.** Smith finished the top of his table with three coats of polyurethane varnish. He finished the legs with a coat of latex primer and two coats of semigloss latex enamel. You can follow his lead, or you can use some other finishing scheme if you prefer.

4 **Assemble the table.** After the finish has dried, turn the tabletop over and set up one leg at each corner, $1\frac{3}{4}$ inches from the sides. Screw the legs to the top through the holes in the cleats with $1\frac{1}{4}$-inch drywall screws.

SHOP TIP: An L-shaped scrap of plywood can help in placing the legs. Cut each leg of the L $1\frac{3}{4}$ inches wide. Hold this alignment jig flush with the tabletop corner. Then place the leg inside the L for perfect alignment.

TAPERING JIG

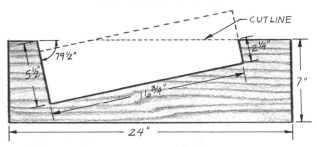

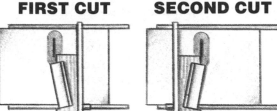

FIRST CUT   **SECOND CUT**

CHAIR

1 **Make the sides.** From $\frac{1}{2}$-inch cabinet-grade birch plywood, cut the sides to the size specified by the Cutting List. On the outside surfaces of the sides, lay out the angles and curves as shown in the *Chair, Front View* and *Chair, Section View*. On the inside surfaces, lay out the elevations for the stretchers, seat, and back while there are still square edges from which to measure.

Saw the final shape on the band saw or with a saber saw. Clean up the edges with scrapers and sandpaper. After finalizing the overall shape, finish laying out the locations for the crosspieces (stretchers, seat, and back) on the inside surfaces.

CHAIR, PLAN VIEWS

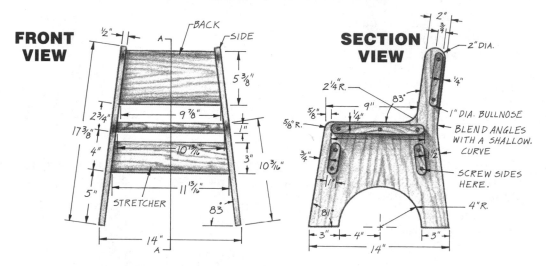

Drill ³⁄₁₆-inch holes as indicated in the *Section View* for the screws that attach the sides to the crosspieces.

2 **Cut the crosspieces.** Cut the stretchers, seat, and back to the sizes specified by the Cutting List. Set the table saw's miter gauge to an 83-degree angle, and cut the angles on both ends of the stretchers and the back. Set the miter gauge back to 90 degrees and tilt the blade to 83 degrees (7 degrees off vertical), then cut the bevels on the ends of the seat. After cutting all the angles, shape the exposed edges of the crosspieces with a 1-inch bullnose cutter (part #765 from MLCS Ltd., P.O. Box 4053 C4, Rydal, PA 19046). Alternatively, a ³⁄₈-inch rounding-over bit could be used.

3 **Assemble the chair.** One by one, hold the crosspieces in position against the sides. Through the holes already in the sides, bore ³⁄₃₂-inch pilot holes into the crosspiece ends.

Assemble the chair with the truss-head screws. Check the fit of the crosspieces, and recut any joint that does not fit well. When everything joins perfectly, take the chair apart, marking the joints for reassembly.

4 **Apply a finish.** Sand all the parts. Finish the crosspieces with a clear wood finish. Coat the sides with latex primer, then apply two coats of semi-gloss latex enamel.

After the finish dries, realign the parts according to their markings and screw the chairs together.

PART THREE

KITCHEN PROJECTS

CHOPPING TRAY

Did you ever grate a large piece of mozzarella cheese for homemade pizza, and have cheese spill out over the top and squeeze out from under the grater? Or dice three or four onions on the counter, and then have to scoop them up to put them in a pan? Nothing to get upset about, certainly. But a chopping tray will alleviate problems of this nature and will keep your counters clear.

As you grate or cut, simply push the grated cheese or diced onions onto the tray. When you are ready to use the ingredient, just slide it into the bowl or pan. If a larger cutting area is needed for slicing bread or carving meats, the reverse side of the tray may also be used.

This chopping tray is a good project for the beginning woodworker. Although cutting and gluing 35 1-inch squares may seem tedious, there are no complicated angles or curves to cut, and the experience of gluing up the tray is good practice for more complicated projects later on. This is not to say that the tray is no more than practice material. A little care will render a beautiful tool from just a little wood.

EXPLODED VIEW

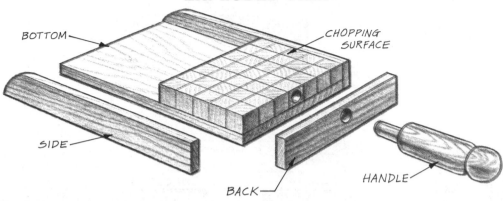

CUTTING LIST

Part	Quantity	Dimensions	Material
Bottom	1	$\frac{1}{2}'' \times 7'' \times 12''$	Cherry
Sides	2	$\frac{1}{2}'' \times 1\frac{1}{2}'' \times 12''$	Cherry
Back	1	$\frac{1}{2}'' \times 1\frac{1}{2}'' \times 8''$	Cherry
Chopping surface	1	$1'' \times 5'' \times 7''$ *	Cherry
Handle	1	$1'' \times 1'' \times 6\frac{1}{2}''$	Cherry

Hardware

Resorcinol glue

* Glued up from 1″ cubes.

1 Select the stock and cut the parts. You can build this chopping tray from almost any hardwood, but cherry, maple, and birch seem to be particularly good choices. The example in the photo was made from cherry. Choose straight, flat stock, free of defects.

From 1/2-inch-thick stock, cut the bottom, sides, and back. From 1-inch-thick stock, cut seven strips, each 1 inch wide × 6 inches long, for the chopping surface and one strip 6½ inches long for the handle.

2 Make the chopping surface. The easiest way to do this is to glue the 1 × 1 × 6-inch strips together, forming a piece measuring 6 × 7 inches. Use resorcinol glue, which is waterproof. After the glue has dried, cut this built-up piece to form five pieces measuring 1 × 1 × 7 inches, as shown in *Gluing Up the Chopping Surface.* Turn the pieces so that their end grain faces up, and glue them together. The pieces are weak, so use scrap strips to spread the clamp pressure. After the glue has dried, plane and sand the piece to a smooth finish.

PLAN VIEWS

TOP VIEW

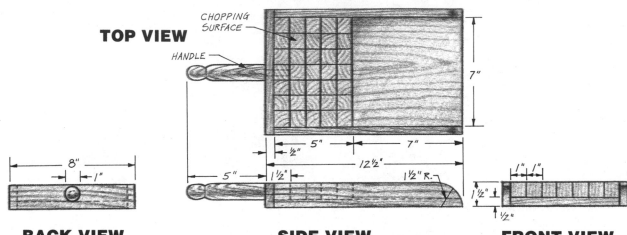

CHOPPING SURFACE

HANDLE

7"

½" 5" 7"

12½"

5" 1½"

1½" R.

BACK VIEW

8"

1"

SIDE VIEW

FRONT VIEW

1" 1"

1½"

½"

GLUING UP THE CHOPPING SURFACE

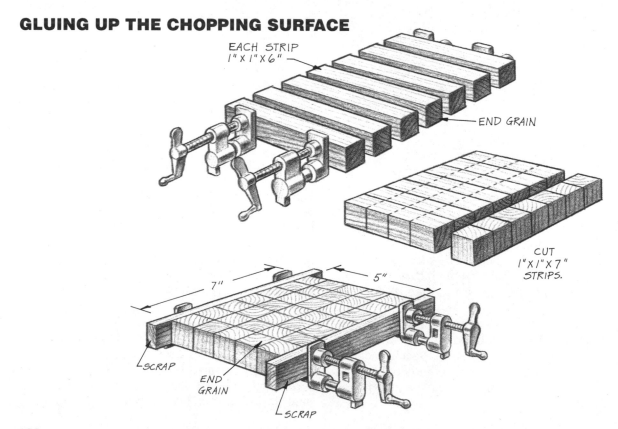

EACH STRIP
1" X 1" X 6"

END GRAIN

CUT
1" X 1" X 7"
STRIPS.

7" 5"

SCRAP

END GRAIN

SCRAP

HANDLE DETAIL

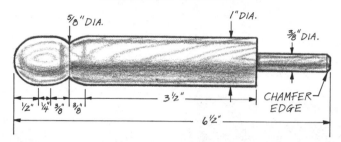

5/8" DIA. 1" DIA. 3/8" DIA.

1/2" 1/4" 3/8" 3/8" 3½" CHAMFER EDGE

6½"

SHOP TIP: Planing the chopping surface after glue-up will give you a crisper surface than if you sand it. Planing end grain is the forte of the low-angle block plane. With its iron fixed at just 12 degrees off horizontal, it cleanly severs the vertical wood fibers. To avoid splitting the edges away, plane only from the edge to the middle of the wood (not from edge to edge).

3 Round off the sides. Each side has a rounded corner. With a compass set to a 1½-inch radius, mark one corner of each, then cut along the line with a saber saw. Sand the sawed edges smooth.

4 Turn the handle. The handle is a simple spindle turning. As shown in the *Handle Detail*, form a decorative knob on one end, a ⅜-inch-diameter × 1½-inch-long tenon on the other.

5 Assemble the tray. The entire tray is glued together using resorcinol glue. Glue the chopping surface to the bottom piece. After the glue has dried, trim the edges of the bottom, if necessary, so that they are flush with the edges of the chopping surface.

Glue the side and back pieces in place next. After the glue has dried, trim the edges, if necessary, so that they are flush.

Using a ⅜-inch bit, drill a 1%16-inch-deep hole into the back of the tray to accommodate the handle's tenon. Apply glue inside the hole with a cotton swab, as well as to the tenon, then force the tenon into place.

6 Finish the project. After the glue has dried, a hole may be drilled into the end of the handle to accommodate a thong for hanging the tray. Remove any excess glue, sand the tray to a smooth finish, and apply several coats of vegetable oil.

KNIFE BLOCK

Here's a sharp way to store your kitchen knives. The portable block allows the knives to be moved easily from one

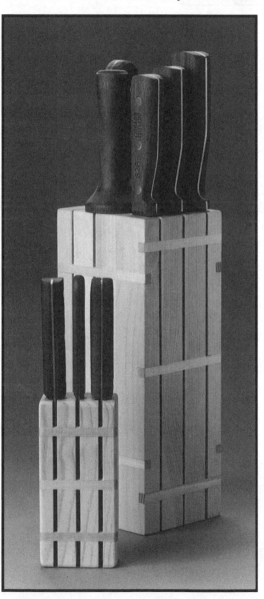

kitchen counter to another. At the same time, it protects the edges of the blades.

The solid wood construction makes the knife block heavy enough to prevent tipping, and the open slots make it easy to clean.

Of course, kitchen knives come in all sizes and shapes, so you should customize the slots in your block to fit the knives in your collection. This is easy enough to do. Just measure how wide each blade is, and cut the slots a little bit deeper or a little bit shallower to accommodate them. Moreover, you can customize the height and width of the knife block, as the photo demonstrates, to hold different sets of knives. Make a small one for steak knives, a larger one for the cook's assortment. After you make the block as directed, it will be clear how to resize the project.

1 Select the stock and cut the parts. The prototype of this knife block is made from pine, and frankly, it is a rather plain-Jane affair. Durability is no problem; the knife block has been in regular use in one of the Rodale Press cafeterias for about ten years.

Since a relatively small amount of stock is at stake here, I'd suggest using contrasting hardwoods to make this knife block—a blond variety like maple or white oak for the blocks, a darker accent like walnut or even redwood for the tie strips. (Or make the blocks dark, the accent strips light.)

After selecting your materials, cut the parts to the sizes specified by the Cutting List.

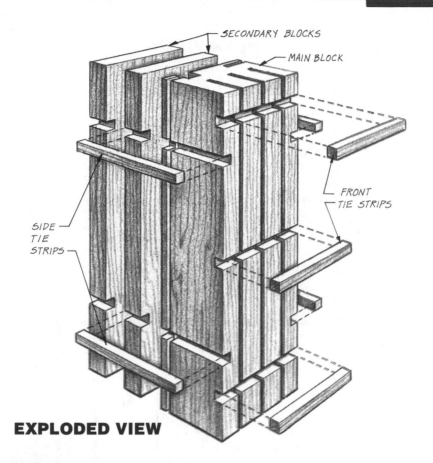

SECONDARY BLOCKS

MAIN BLOCK

FRONT TIE STRIPS

SIDE TIE STRIPS

EXPLODED VIEW

CUTTING LIST

Part	Quantity	Dimensions	Material
Main blocks	5	$\frac{3}{4}''$ × $2\frac{5}{8}''$ × $11''$	Pine
Secondary blocks	2	$\frac{3}{4}''$ × $3\frac{3}{4}''$ × $11''$	Pine
Side tie strips	4	$\frac{5}{16}''$ × $\frac{5}{16}''$ × $4\frac{1}{4}''$	Pine
Front tie strips	3	$\frac{5}{16}''$ × $\frac{5}{16}''$ × $3\frac{3}{4}''$	Pine

2 **Glue up the main block.** Coat the blocks with glue and clamp them together to form a single block $3\frac{3}{4}$ inches thick.

After the glue has dried, remove any excess. Plane the edges, if neces-sary, so that they are flush. Measure $\frac{5}{8}$ inch from the edge of one of the $2\frac{5}{8}$-inch faces, and cut a $\frac{1}{2}$ × $\frac{1}{2}$-inch groove to hold your steel. This groove can be cut with a router and straight bit or on the table saw.

PLAN VIEWS

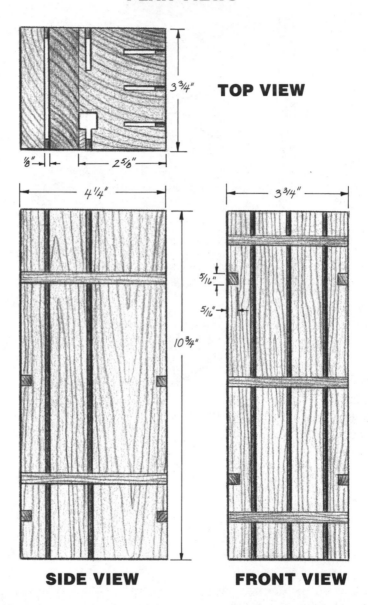

TOP VIEW

3 3/4"

1/8"   2 5/8"

4 1/4"

3 3/4"

5/16"

5/16"

10 3/4"

SIDE VIEW

FRONT VIEW

3 Glue one secondary block to the main block. Apply glue to the face of one secondary block and to the main block. Clamp the two pieces to-gether to form a single block. After the glue dries, remove any excess. Plane the edges, if necessary, so that they are flush.

4 **Cut the knife slots.** Measure the width of the blades of your kitchen knives, and cut slots in the block to accommodate them. Each slot should be a bit larger than the blade it is to hold, so cut the slots about $\frac{5}{16}$ inch deeper than the blades are wide. The knife rack shown has an ornamental slot cut in the groove that holds the steel. This balances the knife slot on the opposite side and makes both sides of the block look alike.

5 **Assemble the knife block with the tie strips.** The remaining secondary block is attached to the main block by the tie strips. To position it while you cut the dadoes and glue the tie strips into place, make a $\frac{1}{8} \times 3 \times 11$-inch spacer. Clamp the main block and the remaining secondary block together, with the spacer between them. Use a try square to make sure that the pieces are clamped flush and square. The

clamps, of course, must be positioned to allow you to cut the dadoes.

Cut $\frac{5}{16} \times \frac{5}{16}$-inch dadoes on three sides of the block for the tie strips as shown in the *Side View* and *Front View*. Use a dado cutter or a router and straight bit. Glue the tie strips into the dadoes.

When the glue is dry, remove the clamps and force the spacer out of the assembly. The spacer will have created a slot the width of the block for a large, broad knife. Your block is now ready for the finishing touches.

6 **Apply a finish.** Trim $\frac{1}{8}$ inch off each end of the block to square it. This will make the finished block $10\frac{3}{4}$ inches high.

Remove any excess glue around the tie strips; if necessary, sand the edges of the strips so that they are flush. Sand the entire block smooth, and apply several coats of whatever finish is desired.

TRIVETS

When you're holding a hot pot you want to set down, it's handy to have a trivet, so that you won't mar a countertop or scorch a tablecloth. Pots and pans come in different sizes and styles, and so do trivets.

There's no hard-and-fast rule on what size a trivet should be. When we originally made these trivets, we called one the large trivet, by virtue of its being about an inch and a half longer and wider than the other. Obviously, they're quite close in size, but you can change that simply by adding (or removing) slats or by lengthening (or shortening) the slats.

The two trivets shown are easy to make. They are the sort of project that's great for a weekend woodworker: They go together quickly, don't require elaborate shop tools, and don't use a lot of wood. (In fact, these are good projects for using up scraps, because the slats are so small.) They are practical, and they make good surprise gifts.

These particular trivets, in my opin-

EXPLODED VIEWS

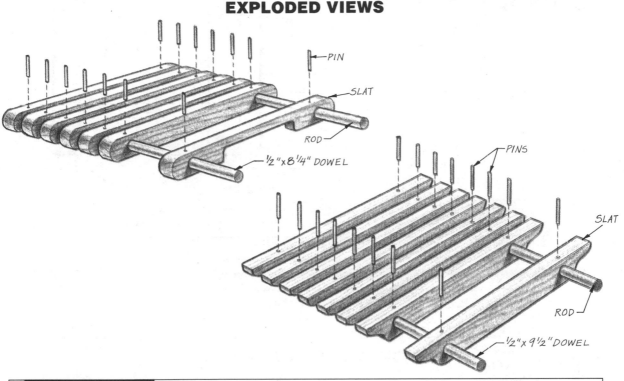

PIN

SLAT

ROD

½" x 8¼" DOWEL

PINS

SLAT

ROD

½" x 9½" DOWEL

CUTTING LIST

Part	Quantity	Dimensions	Material
Small trivet			
Slats	7	¾" × 1¼" × 11"	Pine
Rods	2	½" dia. × 8¼"	Hardwood dowel
Pins	14	⅛" dia. × ¾"	Hardwood dowel
Large trivet			
Slats	8	¾" × 1¼" × 12½"	Pine
Rods	2	½" dia. × 9½"	Hardwood dowel
Pins	16	⅛" dia. × ¾"	Hardwood dowel

ion, go a little further by giving the fledgling woodworker some experience with small-scale production techniques— the use of jigs and fixtures. One of the challenges in woodworking is mastering the craft of producing a lot of identical parts. With the drilling box, a handful of scrap-wood spacers, and a tenoning jig, you can produce dozens of these trivets in short order, and all will be the same.

PLAN VIEWS

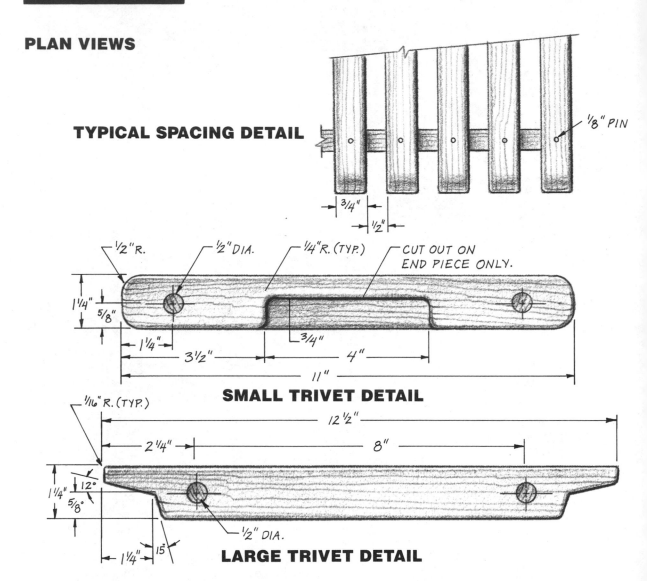

TYPICAL SPACING DETAIL

¹⁄₈" PIN

³⁄₄"

¹⁄₂"

¹⁄₂" R.

¹⁄₂" DIA.

¹⁄₄" R. (TYP.)

CUT OUT ON END PIECE ONLY.

1¹⁄₄"

⁵⁄₈"

1¹⁄₄"

3¹⁄₂"

³⁄₄"

4"

11"

SMALL TRIVET DETAIL

¹⁄₁₆" R. (TYP.)

12¹⁄₂"

2¹⁄₄"

8"

12°

1¹⁄₄"

⁵⁄₈"

¹⁄₂" DIA.

1¹⁄₄"

15°

LARGE TRIVET DETAIL

1 **Select the stock and cut the parts.** Although the prototype trivets are made from commonplace pine, you can dress up the project by using a more showy wood. Redwood, cedar, and even Philippine mahogany are readily available and yield interesting color; they are lightweight, which is good, but soft and easily dented, which could be bad.

American hardwoods are nice, too. One possibility is to use walnut dowels—available from several sources via mail order—for the rods and pins; this dark wood would contrast attractively with a blond wood—maple, oak, even good old pine. And of course, you can always just rummage through the scrap bin to see what's there.

Whatever wood you choose, cut the parts to the sizes specified by the Cutting List. When you cut the slats, cut several extras to make the drilling box, to serve as routing cauls, and to test setups. The dowels can be cut by hand. After you cut the pins, taper, bevel, or round one end of each with sandpaper to ensure that you can get it started in its hole easily during final assembly.

You also need some scraps not listed in the Cutting List. Half-inch stock—plywood, particleboard, even solid wood—is required for the base of the drilling box and for the spacers used in assembling the trivets.

2 Drill holes in the slats for the rods. The construction and use of the drilling box is outlined on page 116. Make a box for whichever size trivet you are making.

On one of the slats, mark the center points of the holes for the rods. Place this slat in the newly constructed drilling box, and use a ½-inch bit to drill holes at the marks. Drill through both the slat and the box's bottom.

Now drill ½-inch-diameter holes into all the other slats by fitting the box over each one and using the holes in the box as guides for the drill bit. Hold the box and slat firmly to a scrap board, so that the slat doesn't split out as the bit breaks through it.

3 Shape the slats. This is the step in which the two trivet designs truly differentiate.

Small trivet: Cut handle notches in the two slats that will be on the outside, as shown in the *Small Trivet Detail.*

These notches should be 4 inches long, ¾ inch deep, and centered 3½ inches from either end. The inside corners of the notches can be rounded in several ways. You can simply round them with a scroll saw or saber saw, or you can first drill ¼-inch-diameter holes in the corners and then cut to the holes. Use a rattail file or a dowel wrapped with sandpaper to finish these inside corners, regardless of how you cut them. The outer edges of the holes also should be filed or sawed round.

Clamp the seven slats tightly together, with the extra slats—the cauls—on the outside of the assemblage. Round the edges of the slats with a router and a ½-inch rounding-over bit. The cauls keep the good slats from splitting out. Round both the top and bottom edges as shown in the *Small Trivet Detail.* Unclamp the slats, and sand the sides and rounded edges.

Large trivet: Bevel the ends of each slat, as shown in the *Large Trivet Detail.* Do this on the table saw, as though you were cutting tenons. Make the "shoulder" cut first. Tilt the saw's arbor to 15 degrees. Adjust the depth of cut to ⅝ inch, and position the rip fence 1¼ inches from the outside of the blade. With the slat cradled in the miter gauge, its nose against the fence, guide it over the blade. After testing the setup on an extra slat (and adjusting it if necessary), make this cut on both ends of each slat.

Break out the tenoning jig next. Position the rip fence so that the saw blade, when tilted, leans away from it. Tilt the blade to 12 degrees. Set the tenoning jig over the fence, stand a test slat in it, and adjust the fence placement and the depth of cut so that the kerf just intersects the shoulder cut. Test the setup. If it's right, complete the cut on all the slats.

Sand all the slats.

4 **Assemble the trivets.** Slide the slats onto the two rods. Place ½-inch-thick spacers between the slats. Clamp the slats and spacers together. With a ⅛-inch bit, drill two ¾-inch-deep holes through the top of each slat into each rod. One by one, apply glue to the pins and insert them into the holes, locking each slat in place on the rod. Remove the spacers, and with a wet rag, wipe up any glue squeeze-out.

When the glue has dried, trim any protruding pins with a chisel. Sand the trivet smooth, then apply whatever finish is desired. Keep in mind that the trivet will be exposed to heat, which could burn off varnish.

USING A DRILLING BOX

One of the challenges in woodworking is contriving ways of making uniform parts. These trivets, and the baker's cooling rack on the opposite page, require you to make several identical parts, each with holes drilled into the same spots. The better you position the holes, the better the completed project will look.

By using a drilling box, you can position the holes uniformly in each trivet slat, regardless of whether you are using a hand drill or a drill press. The box shown will work for the small trivet; alter the dimensions to accommodate a slat of a different size. The guiding principle in building a drilling box is to make the sides the same length as the slat, but thinner. Use plywood or particleboard for the base, and even for the sides and end. When assembling the fixture, see to it that the end piece is square to the sides and that a slat fits snugly.

To lay out the holes in the drilling box, first lay them out on a slat. Drop the slat into the fixture and drill the holes, boring completely through the slat *and* the bottom of the fixture. If the project calls for slats with "through" holes, you have the first piece done.

To use the fixture, fit it over the slat, butting its end tightly against the slat's end. Drill through the holes in the box. Every subsequent slat should be a duplicate of the first.

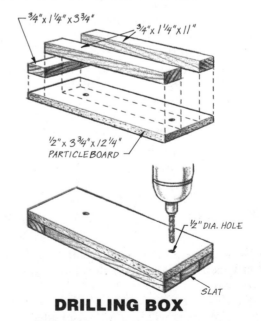

¾" x 1¼" x 3¾"

¾" x 1¼" x 11"

½" x 3¾" x 12¼"
PARTICLEBOARD

½" DIA. HOLE

SLAT

DRILLING BOX

BAKER'S COOLING RACK

You can cool your bread and other baked goods on a wire rack that you buy in a store. But here's a beautiful hand-made wooden rack that you will want to keep out on the counter or hang where it can be admired.

This rack can be made just about any size. The instructions here include a drilling fixture that you assemble from

scrap wood. It's just a three-sided box that allows you to drill into both side pieces at the same time, thus lining up the holes exactly. Of course, you can measure and drill your holes without it. But once you make the drilling fixture, you will be able to make many side pieces in a short time, so it will be easy to turn out racks for gifts.

EXPLODED VIEW

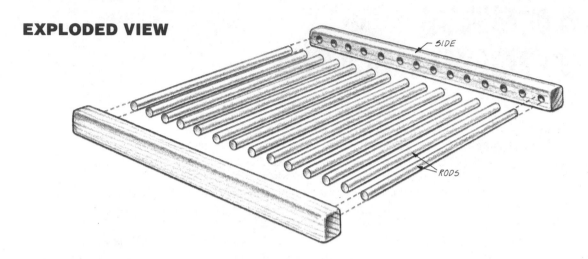

SIDE

RODS

CUTTING LIST

Part	Quantity	Dimensions	Material
Sides	2	¾″ × 1″ × 15″	Maple
Rods	14	⁵⁄₁₆″ dia. × 8¾″	Hardwood dowel

PLAN VIEWS

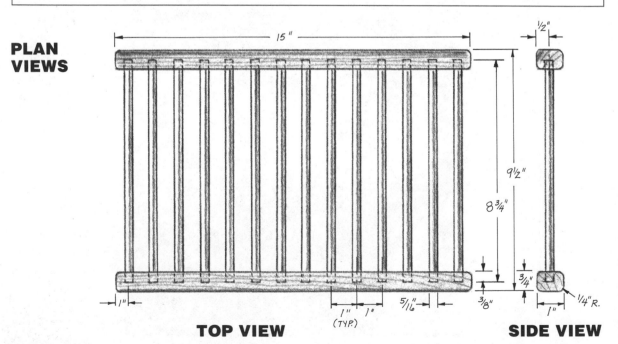

15″

½″

9½″

8¾″

1″

1″ 1″
(TYP.)

⁵⁄₁₆″

3/4″

3/8″

1″

¼″ R.

TOP VIEW

SIDE VIEW

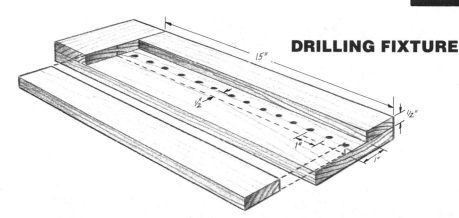

DRILLING FIXTURE

1 **Make a drilling fixture.** The purpose of the drilling fixture is to help you make duplicate sides. The illustration shows one size for this project; you can find more information in "Using a Drilling Box" on page 116.

2 **Make the sides.** Cut two pieces of soft maple for the rack sides. Place the drilling fixture over one piece, with its closed end snug against the side's end. Drill the 14 holes, each 5/16 inch diameter × 3/8 inch deep. Drill the holes in the second side in the same manner.

Rout a 1/4-inch radius on all the edges of your side pieces, or if you prefer, just break the edges with sandpaper.

3 **Cut the rods and assemble the rack.** Cut 14 pieces of 5/16-inch-diameter dowel. You can make them any length you want, but the rack shown has 8¾-inch lengths. We settled on this dimension because the standard 36-inch dowel yields four 8¾-inch rods. You also can cut three 11¾-inch rods from a 36-inch dowel, which would give you a 12½-inch-wide cooling rack.

Sand the dowels and side pieces. Put a drop of glue into each hole and insert the dowels. True up the assembly on a flat surface, and let it dry. Finally, finish your rack with clear Deft or a comparable finish.

SHOP TIP: If you are using a portable drill to bore the holes into the rack sides, making sure that each hole is perpendicular and just the right depth is a little tricky. Control the depth by marking the bit with paint or nail polish; stop drilling when the stripe is flush with the fixture's surface. Align the bit with the little guide shown.

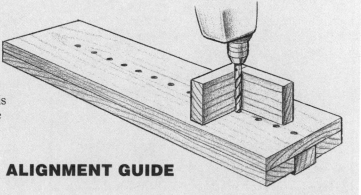

ALIGNMENT GUIDE

VEGETABLE STORAGE BINS

"We keep the food processor in the top bin, the carrots, onions, and potatoes in the second," explains Rodale Press woodworking photographer Mitch Mandel. "The cat food is in the bottom. I don't know what we have in the other one. But there it is—a quick and easy project."

An avid woodworker, Mandel built this vegetable storage bin for his family's kitchen. The project is made from both one-by and 5/4 (five-quarters) pine, with a lauan plywood back: standard lumberyard stock, already cut to thickness and dressed. It's glued together, with the exception of the top, which is attached with screws, and the doors, which are hung with commercial hardware.

How long does it take to build? Not terribly long; you'll spend as much time watching the glue dry as you will actually cutting and machining the boards.

1 **Select the stock and cut the parts.** Mandel built his vegetable bins using standard #2 pine. (Many of the parts were cut from wood he had on hand.) You could substitute other species—poplar for a painted unit, oak, or maple. But the design looks good in pine, and upgrading with wood simply adds to the cost.

Cut the parts to the sizes specified by the Cutting List. Mandel glued up stock to achieve the width necessary for

EXPLODED VIEW

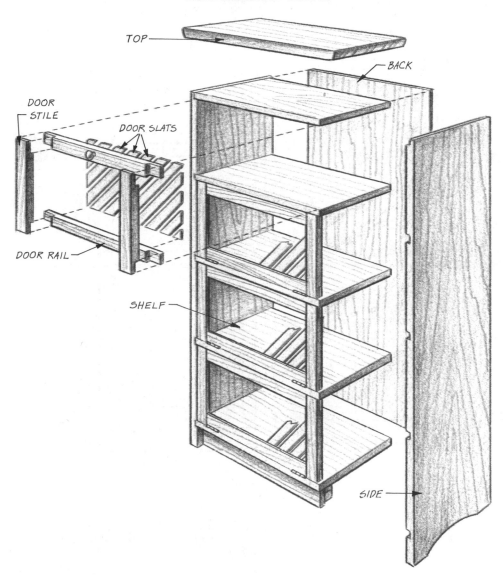

TOP

BACK

DOOR STILE

DOOR SLATS

DOOR RAIL

SHELF

SIDE

the sides and top. By gluing up narrow boards to make the wide components, you can help counter pine's tendency to cup. Hold off cutting any of the slat stock.

2 Dado and rabbet the sides. The sides need to be rabbeted for the top shelf, dadoed for the other shelves, and rabbeted for the back. After removing the clamps and trimming the sides to

121

PLAN VIEWS

SECTION VIEW

FRONT VIEW

BOTTOM VIEW

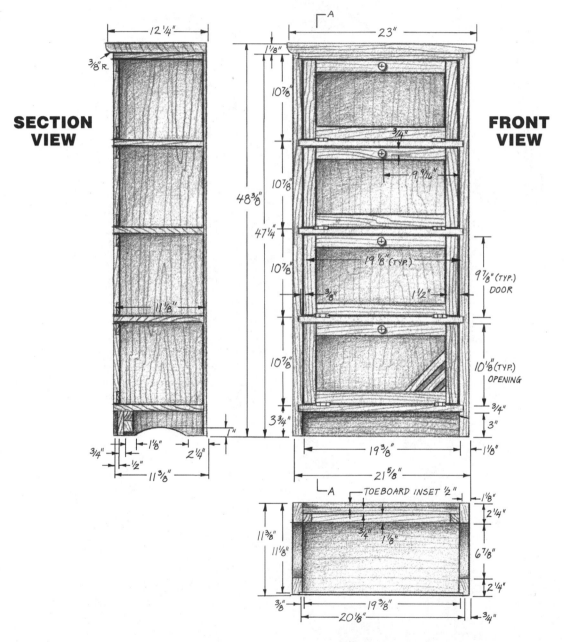

DOOR DETAIL

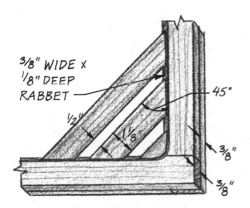

3/8" WIDE x 1/8" DEEP RABBET

45°

1/2"

1/8"

3/8"

3/8"

making each cut straight across both sides, you'll simultaneously save work and achieve perfect alignment. Clamp a straightedge to the sides to guide the router. These are big dadoes, so don't cut more than 1/8 inch of wood per pass; three passes per dado should get you to the required 3/8-inch depth.

The rabbets for the back can be routed with a piloted 1/4-inch rabbeting bit. Rest the router on the broad face of the sides to cut this rabbet.

Before assembling the case, lay out and cut the feet on the sides. The arc can be created using a 1-gallon paint can as a template. Measure and mark points 2¼ inches from the front and rear edges of the side. Align the can with the marks and scribe around it. Cut the arc on the band saw or with a saber saw.

size, lay them on your workbench and clamp them edge-to-edge. Lay out and cut the top rabbet and the dadoes with a router and a ¾-inch straight bit. By

CUTTING LIST

Part	Quantity	Dimensions	Material
Sides	2	1⅛″ × 11⅜″ × 47¼″	5/4 pine
Top	1	1⅛″ × 12¼″ × 23″	5/4 pine
Shelves	5	¾″ × 11⅛″ × 20⅛″	1-by pine
Back	1	¼″ × 20⅛″ × 47¼″	Lauan plywood
Toeboard	1	¾″ × 3″ × 19⅜″	1-by pine
Cleat	1	1⅛″ × 1⅛″ × 19⅜″	5/4 pine
Glue blocks	2	1⅛″ × 1⅛″ × 1⅛″	5/4 pine
Door rails	8	¾″ × 1½″ × 19⅛″	1-by pine
Door stiles	8	¾″ × 1½″ × 9⅞″	1-by pine
Door slats	As needed	⅛″ × 1⅛″ × (variable) *	5/4 pine

Hardware

6 flathead wood screws, #10 × 1½″
8 brass roundhead wood screws, #4 × ¾″
⅜″ staples
4 pairs brass butt hinges, 1″ × 1½″

4 double-roller catches
60″ brass sash chain
4 ceramic knobs, 1″ dia.
4d finishing nails

* Cut individual pieces to fit.

3 **Assemble the case.** Glue the shelves into their dadoes. The shelves should be flush with the front edges of the sides and with the shoulder of the rabbet at the back. Before the glue can set, drop the back panel into place and attach it with 4d finishing nails. Although installing the back should square the case, you should confirm that it is square either with a framing square or by measuring the diagonals.

4 **Install the toeboard and top.** Stand the case on its head and fit the toeboard into place. Glue the toeboard to the shelf bottom and the sides. Reinforce this simple joinery by gluing a cleat to the back of the toeboard and the shelf bottom, and a glue block to the side and each end of the toeboard. The blocks should be oriented with their long grain parallel to the sides.

The top is fastened with 1½-inch screws driven through the top shelf. Before attaching it, round over the bottom edge of the top's front and ends with a router and a ⅜-inch rounding-over bit. Leave its top edges square.

5 **Build the door frames.** Each door consists of a half-lapped frame, with diagonal slats stapled into rabbets cut around its inner perimeter.

Cut the half-laps on the table saw using a tenoning jig. Set the saw with a ruler for the shoulder cut, then test the depth of cut on a scrap of the frame stock and adjust as necessary. Set the rip fence the width of the stock from the outside of the blade—use the scrap to do this—and use the miter gauge in making

one shoulder cut on each end of each frame piece.

After all the shoulders are cut, use the tenoning jig to guide each piece as you cut away the waste. Again, use a workpiece to set the depth of cut and the rip fence position.

Glue up the four door frames. When the glue has set, use a router and a piloted ⅜-inch rabbeting bit to machine a ⅛-inch-deep rabbet around the inner perimeter of each frame. You can use a chisel to square the corners, although this isn't necessary.

Finally, test fit each frame in the openings in the case. You may want to mark each frame for a specific bin. As necessary, trim each frame with a plane to ensure a good fit.

6 **Cut and install the slats.** The slats are produced by ripping ⅛-inch-thick strips from the edge of a 5/4 board. Rip several feet of the slat material, then cut pieces to fit, mitering the ends at 45 degrees. The first piece should be a triangle. Round off a corner of this piece with a file so that it will fit into the corner of the door frame. Staple it. Miter one end of the next slat, posi-

SHOP TIP: Avoid having saw marks on the exposed face of the slats. Between cuts, joint the cut edge of the board from which you are ripping the slats. The slat's face will be smooth; its back—which is only visible when the door is open—will be rough. This will save you the vexation of trying to sand or plane yards of thin strips.

tion it ½ inch from the first piece, and mark the uncut end. Miter that end and staple the slat into place. Continue fitting, cutting, and stapling until all the doors are completed.

7 Finish the bins and hang the doors. After completing any necessary touch-up sanding, apply a finish to the case and the doors. Mandel wiped on a stain, then applied a couple of coats of a satin polyurethane.

When the finish is dried, install the knobs—Mandel used a 1-inch-diameter ceramic knob in the center of the top rail of each door. Mortise the hinges into the bottom rail of each door, one aligned inside the vertical seam of each lap joint. The hinges are surface-mounted on the shelves; this provides the appropriate clearance for the door. As each door is hinged to the case, install a double-roller catch to keep it closed. Align the catch with the knob. To limit the distance the door can be opened, install a length of sash chain between the upper corner of the door and the inner side of the case using ¾-inch screws.

SHAKER-STYLE WALL CABINET

This handsome cabinet is an adaptive reproduction. Although its builder, Kenneth Burton, Sr., can point to a specific cabinet as its antecedent, the piece shown here is not a duplicate of that original. Rather, it copies the style, the proportions, the deceptively simple joinery, and the craftsmanship. The dimensions are different.

Over a period of years, Burton has made dozens of small country accent pieces for a friend who operates a furniture business. Among the pieces are copies of a small wall cabinet the friend owns. It is old, and the friend calls it a Shaker cabinet, though Burton doesn't know if it is authentic.

At any rate, when Marge Burton

EXPLODED VIEW

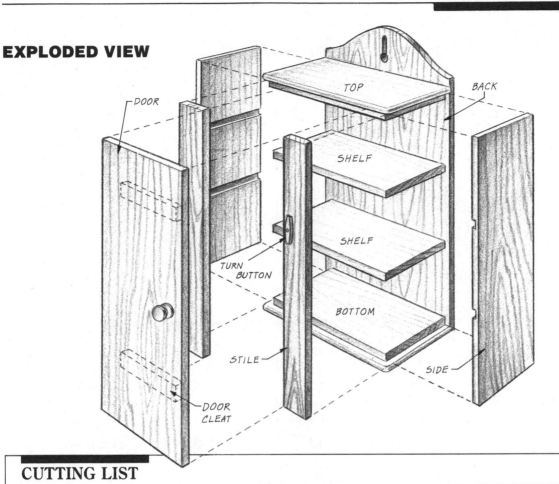

CUTTING LIST

Part	Quantity	Dimensions	Material
Bottom/Top	2	$\frac{3}{4}'' \times 6\frac{7}{16}'' \times 11\frac{1}{2}''$	Pine
Sides	2	$\frac{1}{2}'' \times 5\frac{11}{16}'' \times 16''$	Pine
Back	1	$\frac{5}{16}'' \times 11'' \times 20''$	Pine
Shelves	2	$\frac{1}{2}'' \times 5\frac{11}{16}'' \times 10\frac{1}{4}''$	Pine
Stiles	2	$\frac{1}{2}'' \times 2'' \times 16''$	Pine
Door	1	$\frac{1}{2}'' \times 7'' \times 15\frac{7}{8}''$	Pine
Door cleats	2	$\frac{1}{2}'' \times \frac{3}{4}'' \times 6''$	Pine
Turn button	1	$\frac{1}{2}'' \times \frac{3}{8}'' \times 2''$	Pine

Hardware

4 flathead wood screws, #6 × ¾"
1 black roundhead wood screw, #6 × 1"
1 pair brass butt hinges, 1" × 1½"

1 wooden knob, 1" dia.
Cut finishing nails

PLAN VIEWS

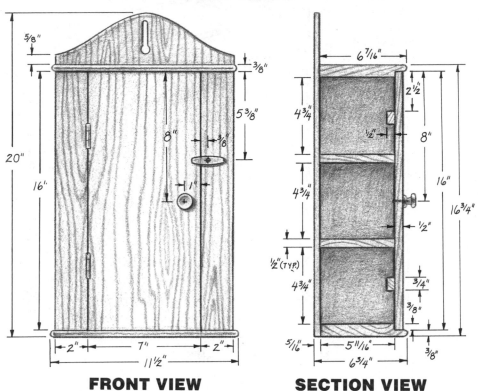

FRONT VIEW

SECTION VIEW

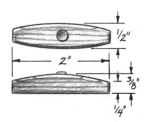

TURN BUTTON DETAIL

asked her husband for a spice cabinet, he turned to his friend's little Shaker cabinet as a model. His version is a bit taller and deeper than the original. A self-described "table saw woodworker," Burton performed a lot of the construction steps with hand tools rather than power tools. After resawing the lumber on his homemade band saw, he hand planed it. The dadoes and rabbets were cut with a dado cutter, but the edges of the top and bottom were shaped with a block plane.

The cabinet is an excellent weekend project. It requires a relatively modest amount of material, and the joints are easy to make. Take your time in making it to achieve tight joints.

1 **Select the stock and cut the parts.** The cabinet shown is made entirely from pine. To me, this seems the appropriate choice, given the character and construction of the piece. Pine is readily available, utilitarian, and easy to work. Poplar would be a reasonable choice for a painted version of this cabinet. But the likes of cherry and walnut seem too dear to be nailed together. Whatever your choice of wood for the cabinet, select straight-grained boards that are free of loose knots and serious defects.

To obtain the 5/16- and 1/2-inch stock required for this project, you probably need to resaw 5/4 (five-quarters) or 6/4 (six-quarters) stock. Resawing is best done on the band saw. More information on the process can be found in "Resawing" on page 174.

After resawing and dressing the required amount of stock, cut the parts to the sizes specified by the Cutting List. To form the back panel and the door, glue up narrow boards. Burton believes this minimizes warping of these key components, especially when they are made from pine.

2 **Cut the joinery.** The cabinet's joinery is pretty simple. The sides and stiles fit into rabbets cut in the top and bottom. The shelves ride in dadoes cut in the sides. The back overlays the bottom, sides, and top.

Cut the 3/4-inch-wide × 3/8-inch-deep rabbets along the front and across both ends of the top and bottom. Use a router or a dado cutter.

Shape what will be the exposed edges of the bottom and top as indicated in the *Section View*. The cabinet shown has what is known as a thumbnail shape to the edge. Burton used a block plane and a file to form it. With some experimentation on scraps, you might be able to duplicate it with a table-mounted router and a large-radius rounding-over bit. The tricky part is addressing the rabbeted edge.

Turn to the sides next, cutting 1/2-inch-wide × 1/8-inch-deep dadoes for the shelves. Position the dadoes as shown in the *Section View*. Again, use a router or a dado cutter for this job.

3 **Cut the back's profile.** Enlarge the pattern for the back's top profile and transfer it to the back panel. Cut the profile either with a saber saw or on a band saw or scroll saw. Sand away any saw marks.

Lay out and cut the keyhole to hang the cabinet. Drill a 1/2-inch-diameter hole at the base of the keyhole and a 1/4-inch-diameter hole at its top. Saw away the waste between the holes, maintaining the familiar keyhole shape as you do so. Sand the cut edges.

PATTERN FOR THE BACK'S TOP PROFILE

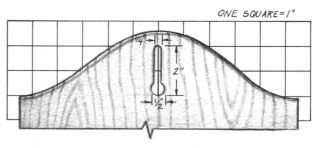

ONE SQUARE=1"

4 **Assemble the cabinet.** Use glue and cut finishing nails. (If you can't locate cut finishing nails, just file the heads from regular cut nails, which is what Burton did.) Glue the shelves to the sides—no nails. Then fit the top and bottom into place, using a bit of glue and driving about three nails through each side into the top and bottom. Add the stiles next, driving nails through them into the edge of the sides as well as into the top and bottom. Finally, position the back and nail it in place, driving nails into the shelves, sides, top, and bottom. Countersink the nails slightly.

5 **Hang the door.** Begin by attaching the cleats to the door as shown in the *Section View*.

The door is hung with two pairs of small butt hinges. Lay out and cut mortises for the hinges in the door edge as well as in the edge of one stile. Install the hinges. Drill a screw hole for the door knob as indicated in the *Front View*, then install the knob. (Burton turned his own knob.)

The door is held closed by a hand-whittled turn button. Form it as shown in the *Turn Button Detail*, then attach it to the cabinet with the roundhead screw.

6 **Apply a finish.** Burton finished the cabinet shown with Minwax Wood Finish, a stain-and-sealer product. The cabinet has a bit of color introduced by the stain, but lacks varnish's film. Apply whatever finish appeals to you, following the manufacturer's instructions.

FOLDING STEPLADDER

Stepladders are designed to be underfoot when they are in use. But some are underfoot when you don't want them to be. You find yourself tripping over them, or moving them to the basement or attic just to get them out of the way. This little folding ladder is light, handy, and strong; yet it folds up in a second to be tucked into a cabinet, placed on a shelf, or hung in a closet.

It has its limitations, of course. It is not designed to hold more than 200 pounds, and it won't get you more than two feet off the ground. But for household use, it will pay for itself in beauty and convenience. It will do fine for getting the good dishes or the canner down from the top shelf in the cupboard.

This is not a difficult project. The lumber will cost you relatively little—even at today's prices. Chances are you have scraps left over from another pro-

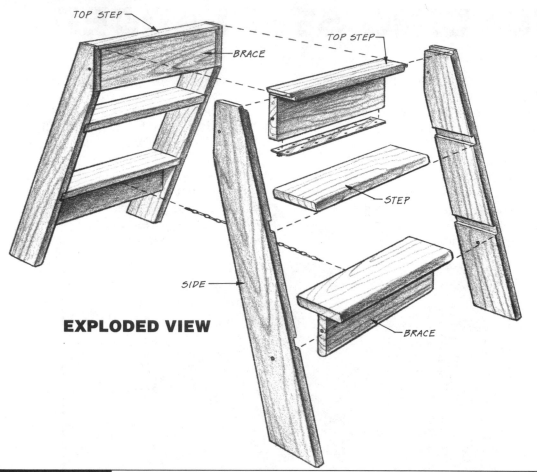

EXPLODED VIEW

CUTTING LIST

Part	Quantity	Dimensions	Material
Sides	4	¾″ × 3½″ × 25¾″	Pine
Braces	4	¾″ × 3½″ × 14½″	Pine
Top steps	2	¾″ × 2½″ × 16″ *	Pine
Steps	4	¾″ × 3⅝″ × 15¼″ *	Pine

Hardware

8 flathead wood screws, #12 × 1½″
2 eyescrews, #6 × ¾″
1 piano hinge, 1½″ × 14½″

12″ steel jack chain
8d finishing nails

* Bevel as specified in Step 2.

ject that you can use. And it takes no special skill to make the necessary cuts, although you will have to be careful and precise as you make the various angles, rabbets, and grooves.

1 Make the sides. Cut the four sides from relatively clear (that is, without large knots) 1 × 4 stock to the length specified by the Cutting List.

The sides are made in mirror-image pairs; there's a left side and a right side in each pair. Study the *Side View*. All four sides are mitered at 70 degrees on both ends, and their tops are tapered at 20 degrees. Make these cuts.

Next cut the rabbets and dadoes for the steps. To mark the locations of these cuts, lay out the pairs of sides in their A-shaped configuration, as shown in the *Side View*. The rabbets are at the top, and they are most easily cut with a router and a ⅜-inch piloted rabbeting bit. Make them ⅜ inch deep.

Cut the ¾-inch-wide × ⅜-inch-deep dadoes next, doing this job on the table saw fitted with a dado cutter. Because you aren't cutting all the way through the wood, you can use the rip fence to position the dadoes. Guide the sides with the miter gauge set to the required 20-degree angle. Set the fence and the miter gauge, and cut the first dado in two sides. Reset the miter gauge to the opposite angle, and dado the remaining two sides. Then reset the fence for the second dado, and repeat the cutting sequence.

Round off the bottom corners of the sides with a belt sander, then radius the exposed edges with a router and a ¼-inch rounding-over bit. Sand the sides.

2 Cut the steps. For the steps, cut four 15¼-inch pieces out of 1 × 6 stock. Tilt the table saw's arbor (or table) to 20 degrees, and bevel-rip the steps to a 3⅝-inch width. The edges must be parallel.

For the top step, cut a 16-inch piece of 1 × 6 stock and rip it in two. Bevel one edge of each piece at 20 degrees, an action that should leave the narrower face 2⅛ inches wide. Complete the top step by cutting a ⅜-inch-wide × ⅜-inch-deep rabbet across the ends of each half to fit into the rabbets already cut in the sides. The rabbets must be in the broader face of the step halves.

3 Cut the braces and glue them to the steps. Cut four braces out of 1 × 4 stock, as specified by the Cutting List. Glue one brace to the bottom of each of the top step halves, flush with the inside edge. Glue the other two braces to the bottom steps; each should be perpendicular to the step, about 1½ inches away from the step's outer edge. Center these braces end-to-end, so that the steps will fit into the dadoes. Round off the bottom edges of the braces, and sand the steps.

4 Assemble the two halves of the ladder. As you clamp the parts together, make sure the subassemblies are square. Finishing nails driven through the side pieces into the steps strengthen the structure. Before the glue dries, drill and countersink holes for two 1½-inch screws into each end of the top step braces. Drive the screws and fill or plug the holes.

PLAN VIEWS

SIDE VIEW

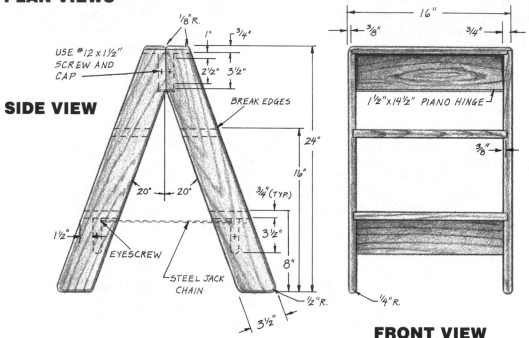

USE #12 x 1½"
SCREW AND
CAP

⅛" R.

1"

¾"

2½" 3½"

BREAK EDGES

24"

16"

20° 20°

¾" (TYP.)

1½"

EYESCREW

3½"

8"

STEEL JACK
CHAIN

½" R.

3½"

16"

⅜" ¾"

1½" x 14½" PIANO HINGE

⅜"

¼" R.

FRONT VIEW

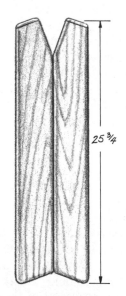

25¾

**LADDER IN
CLOSED POSITION**

5 **Finish the ladder and complete
its assembly.** After the final sanding of both halves of the ladder, apply
whatever finish you like—varnish, lacquer, or polyurethane.

When the finish is dry, join the two
halves. To do this, fasten a 1½ × 14½-
inch piano hinge to the bottom of the top
step braces. Then insert an eyescrew
into each bottom step brace to hold the
safety chain. Attach a piece of steel jack
chain to both eyescrews, adjusting the
length so that the chain is taut just when
the two halves of the top step are tight
together.

PART FOUR

TOY PROJECTS

ROCKING HORSE

The rocking horse has always been a popular toy, and Nintendo notwithstanding, it probably always will be. The general lines for the rocking horse you see here are patterned after Fred Matlack's childhood mount, which dates back to the 1920s. That original Matlack steed had a much lighter undercarriage—thin laminated rockers with slats fastened between them.

"That old horse of mine had two drawbacks," says Matlack, head of the Rodale Press Design Group. "It was so light it tended to buck me off frequently,

EXPLODED VIEW

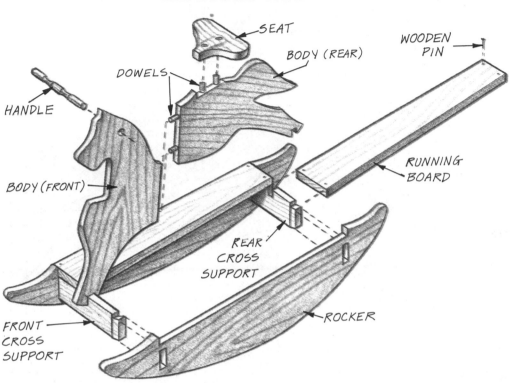

CUTTING LIST

Part	Quantity	Dimensions	Material
Body (front)	1	1¼″ × 12″ × 20″	Pine
Body (rear)	1	1¼″ × 12″ × 18″	Pine
Dowels	4	½″ dia. × 3″	Pine
Front cross support	1	⅞″ × 2¼″ × 10½″	Pine
Rear cross support	1	⅞″ × 2¼″ × 8½″	Pine
Rockers	2	⅞″ × 6¼″ × 37″	Pine
Running boards	2	¾″ × 4⅞″ × 24½″	Pine
Wood pins	10	¼″ × ¼″ × 2″	Pine
Seat	1	⅞″ × 4¾″ × 7″	Pine
Handle	1	¾″ dia. × 7″	Pine

Hardware

#8 × 2½″ drywall screws

ROCKING HORSE LAYOUT

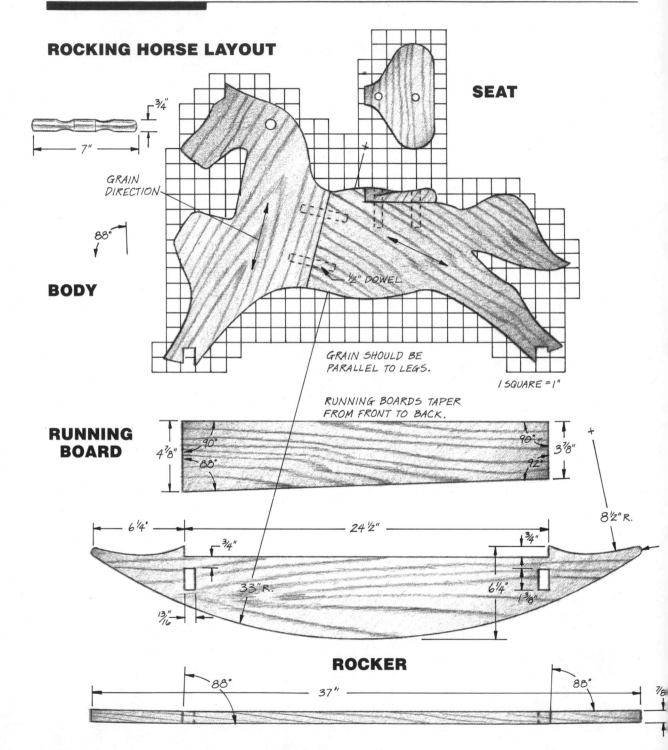

SEAT

BODY

GRAIN DIRECTION

88°

¾"

7"

½" DOWEL

GRAIN SHOULD BE PARALLEL TO LEGS.

1 SQUARE = 1"

RUNNING BOARDS TAPER FROM FRONT TO BACK.

RUNNING BOARD

4⅛"   90°   88°   90°   92°   3⅞"

6¼"   24½"   ¾"   ¾"   8½" R.

33" R.   6¼"   1⅜"

13⁄16"

ROCKER

88°   37"   88°   ⅞"

FRONT CROSS SUPPORT

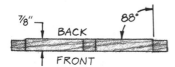

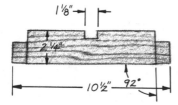

REAR CROSS SUPPORT

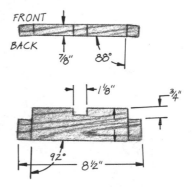

and my toes often got caught between the slats. That made my rides on 'Old Charlie' a bit of a hazard."

Fred's grandfather came to the rescue by screwing a couple of boards across the supports to form running boards. That kept toes out of danger and added much-needed extra weight to the base. Fred borrowed that principle when he built the rocking horse pictured here, making running boards part of the design and cutting the rockers from solid hardwood. The extra weight of the hardwood makes the horse quite stable, and the rockers wear better, too.

The rocking horse is fairly simple to build. You can do most of the cutting on the band saw or with a saber saw. The rockers splay at the bottom, and they're farther apart at the front of the horse than they are at the back. To position the rockers, you must cut the tenons on the cross supports at a compound angle—the tenons point slightly up and to the rear. That way, the corresponding mortises in the rockers can be cut straight through at 90 degrees.

1 Select the stock and cut the parts. Fred assembled the horse from a collection of oak, cherry, chestnut, and maple boards; the body is white pine. Use your imagination (and your scrap pile) to determine which woods to use. You can always alter the dimensions a bit to fit the wood you have on hand.

If necessary, mill your stock to the specified thicknesses, then cut all the parts to the sizes specified by the Cutting List.

2 Make the horse's body. Start by gluing up two pieces of stock for the body. Fred Matlack used two pieces of 1¼ × 12-inch pine (a lumberyard commodity) to form the shape shown. Join the two boards in a butt joint reinforced with ½-inch-diameter dowels. For the greatest strength, it's important to orient the boards so that the grain of each piece runs nearly parallel to the legs, as shown in the *Rocking Horse Layout.*

Enlarge the pattern included in the *Rocking Horse Layout* and transfer it to the workpiece. Cut the shape of the

TENONING SEQUENCE

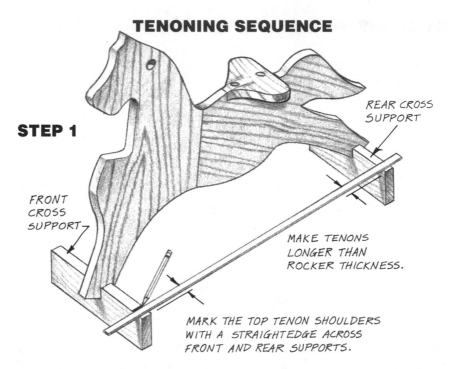

STEP 1

REAR CROSS SUPPORT

FRONT CROSS SUPPORT

MAKE TENONS LONGER THAN ROCKER THICKNESS.

MARK THE TOP TENON SHOULDERS WITH A STRAIGHTEDGE ACROSS FRONT AND REAR SUPPORTS.

horse's body on a band saw or with a saber saw. Sand and radius all the edges that will be exposed, but leave the seat area flat and square-edged.

The cross supports should be joined to the body before you cut the tenons on them. Carefully fit the supports into the horse's legs. When the joints are snug, glue and screw the supports to the body.

3 **Lay out and cut the tenons on the cross supports.** The compound tenons are the trickiest part of the construction. You'll probably find it easier to make these joints with hand tools and a cut-to-fit style of working than to go to all the trouble of setting up power tools to do it.

First make pencil marks on the ends of each cross support to establish the approximate length of the tenons. (Make

them a little long—you'll trim them later.) To mark the top shoulders of the tenons, lay a straightedge on these pencil marks, spanning from the front cross support to the rear cross support, as shown in Step 1 of the *Tenoning Sequence.* Draw a line against the straightedge to mark the top shoulders. These shoulder lines also determine the front-to-back angle of the rockers.

Next, using a try square, mark the cheeks of the tenons at 90 degrees to the top shoulder line, as shown in Step 2. Then mark the vertical shoulders of the tenons with a sliding T-bevel set to 92 degrees, as shown in Step 3. This angle determines the splay of the rockers.

Carefully saw to these lines with a backsaw to form the top shoulders and cheeks of the tenons. After you've made these cuts, place a try square against the

STEP 2

MARK THE CHEEKS OF
THE TENON WITH A TRY
SQUARE.

STEP 3

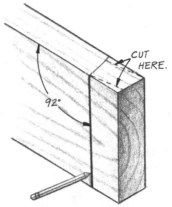

CUT HERE.

92°

MARK THE VERTICAL
SHOULDERS 92° FROM TOP
EDGE OF CROSS SUPPORT AND
CUT OUT WITH BACKSAW.

STEP 4

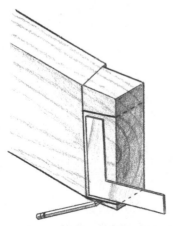

MARK TENON TOP AND BOTTOM
WITH A TRY SQUARE AGAINST
THE SHOULDER. CUT TO THE
LINES.

STEP 5

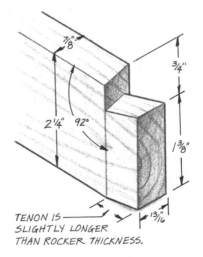

$\frac{7}{8}$"

$\frac{3}{4}$"

$2\frac{1}{4}$"   92°

$1\frac{3}{8}$"

$\frac{13}{16}$"

TENON IS
SLIGHTLY LONGER
THAN ROCKER THICKNESS.

FINISHED COMPOUND-ANGLE
TENON

shoulders to mark the tops and bottoms of the tenons, as shown in Step 4. Cut out the tenons with the backsaw.

4 Make and install the rockers. Lay out the rockers as indicated in the *Rocking Horse Layout*, then cut them out. It may save you some time if you lay out and cut one rocker, then use it as a template to lay out the second. To

mark the mortises, position each rocker against the ends of the tenons on the cross supports. Because you cut the tenons at compound angles, the through mortises can be cut perpendicular—straight through the rockers.

After cutting the mortises, glue the rockers onto the cross supports. Then cut out the slightly tapered running boards and fasten them in place with

SHOP TIP: Whether you use a string compass or a trammel to lay out a curve, locating the arc's center point when it is far off the workpiece can be tricky. Here's a quick and easy approach:

• Place the workpiece (a rocker) on a work surface, and adjust your trammel or string compass to the proper radius.

• Set the pivot on the midpoint of the rocker's edge, and scribe an arc on the work surface. The center point will be somewhere along this arc.

• Set the pivot on an inner corner of the rocker, and scribe an arc on the work surface. Then set the pivot on the opposite corner and scribe a second arc, intersecting the first.

• Sight (or scribe a line) from the midpoint of the rocker to the crossing arcs. The center point is where this line intersects the first arc.

The process takes longer to describe than it does to perform.

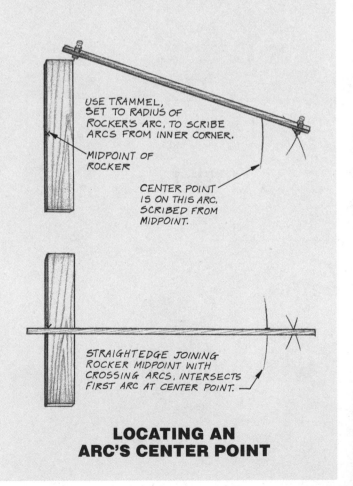

USE TRAMMEL, SET TO RADIUS OF ROCKER'S ARC, TO SCRIBE ARCS FROM INNER CORNER.

MIDPOINT OF ROCKER

CENTER POINT IS ON THIS ARC, SCRIBED FROM MIDPOINT.

STRAIGHTEDGE JOINING ROCKER MIDPOINT WITH CROSSING ARCS, INTERSECTS FIRST ARC AT CENTER POINT.

LOCATING AN ARC'S CENTER POINT

glue and ¼ × ¼ × 2-inch pins, butting the boards tightly against the horse's legs.

5 **Saddle up your horse.** Cut out the seat and carve it to a comfortable saddle shape. Glue it to the back of the horse. Then drill through the seat into the body of the horse, and glue in two ½-inch-diameter dowels to reinforce the joint.

Turn the handle, then glue it into the horse's head. If you don't have a lathe to shape the handle, you could use a spokeshave.

6 **Finish your horse.** Paint the horse to suit your (or your child's) taste, and it's ready to ride. If your "Old Charlie" turns out to be the heirloom that Fred's did, it's worth taking time to add your signature in a place on the bottom where years of hard riding won't wear it away.

WALKING DUCK

Fed up with plastic toys that dance the same routine every time you throw the switch (provided the batteries are fresh)? Here's an old-fashioned alternative.

Homemade, gravity-powered, and unpredictable, this wooden duck will provide a youngster with hours of mirth. Set the duck on a table, hanging the weight over the opposite edge. Give the duck a sideways nudge, and he'll waddle across the table. Driving weights can be changed to suit different table surfaces. You can produce anything from a cautious waddle to a careening quickstep.

This is a great one-evening project—and a short evening at that. You spend more time waiting for the paint to dry than you do cutting out the parts.

1 **Make the body.** Cut the body blank to the size specified by the Cutting List. Enlarge the pattern for the body and sketch it on the blank. Mark the locations of the eye and the pivot. Cut the shape on a scroll saw or band saw or with a saber saw, then drill the ¼-inch-diameter eye and pivot holes. Sand the cut edges with a drum sander chucked in a drill, and round over the

EXPLODED VIEW

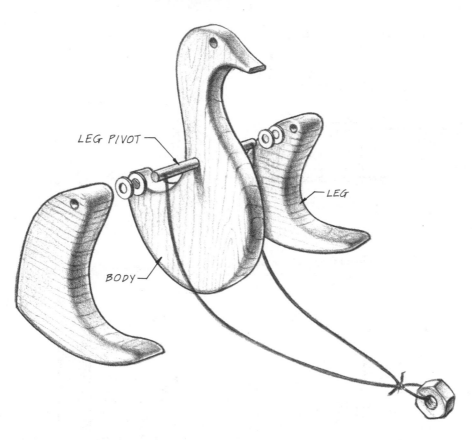

LEG PIVOT

LEG

BODY

Part	Quantity	Dimensions	Material
Duck body	1	$\frac{3}{4}'' \times 5'' \times 8\frac{1}{2}''$	Pine
Leg pivot	1	$\frac{1}{4}''$ dia. $\times 4''$	Hardwood dowel
Legs	2	$1\frac{1}{8}'' \times 5\frac{1}{2}'' \times 6''$	Pine

Hardware

1 steel hex nut, $\frac{5}{8}''$ dia.
4 flat washers, $\frac{1}{4}''$ I.D.
2 pcs. cotton kitchen twine, 36" long

PLAN VIEWS

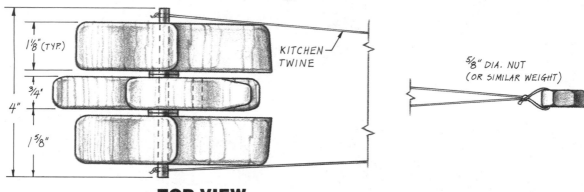

1 1/8" (TYP.)

3/4"

4"

1 5/8"

KITCHEN TWINE

5/8" DIA. NUT
(OR SIMILAR WEIGHT)

TOP VIEW

ONE SQUARE = 1"

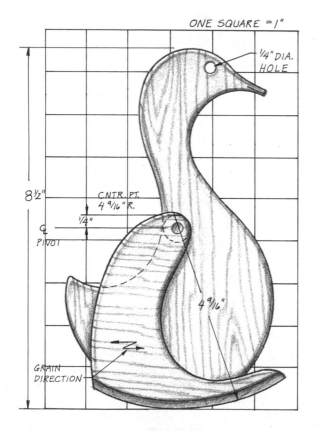

1/4" DIA. HOLE

8 1/2"

CNTR. PT.
4 9/16" R.

1/4"

℄ PIVOT

4 9/16"

GRAIN DIRECTION

SIDE VIEW

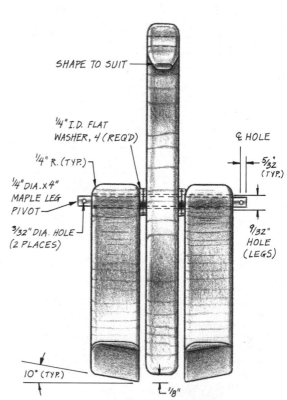

SHAPE TO SUIT

1/4" I.D. FLAT WASHER, 4 (REQ'D)

1/4" R. (TYP.)

1/4" DIA. x 4" MAPLE LEG PIVOT

3/32" DIA. HOLE (2 PLACES)

℄ HOLE

5/32" (TYP.)

9/32" HOLE (LEGS)

10" (TYP.)

1/8"

FRONT VIEW

edges with a ¼-inch rounding-over bit in a table-mounted router. Finally, finish sand the body.

2 **Install the pivot.** The pivot is a short piece of ¼-inch dowel. Cut the pivot to the length specified by the Cutting List. Drill two ³⁄₃₂-inch-diameter holes through the pivot, ³⁄₁₆ inch from the ends. These are for the twine. Glue the pivot into the body, as indicated in the *Front View.*

SHOP TIP: To prevent the pivot from turning when you try to drill the twine holes, cradle it in a small V-block. Make the block by grooving a short scrap of wood with a router and ⅜-inch V-groove bit.

3 **Make the legs.** Cut the blanks for the two legs to the size specified by the Cutting List. Enlarge the pattern overlaid in the *Leg Layout* and sketch it on each blank. Mark the location of the pivot hole. Be sure that the legs are laid out with the feet parallel to the wood's grain (the toes will break off if you fail to do this). Drill the pivot hole, making it ⁹⁄₃₂ inch in diameter—slightly larger than the pivot dowel. As you did with the body, sand the cut edges with a drum sander, round over the edges on a table-mounted router, then finish sand the legs. With a belt sander, bevel the feet as indicated in the *Front View.* Be sure to make a left and right leg as you do this.

LEG LAYOUT

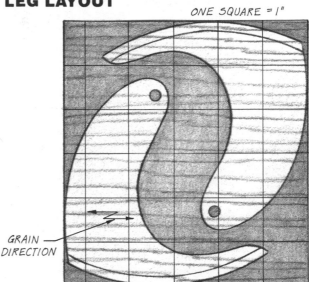

ONE SQUARE = 1"

GRAIN DIRECTION

4 **Apply a finish.** The duck shown was given a couple of coats of polyurethane to finish it. If you have a knack for painting, try a more ducklike approach.

5 **Assemble the duck.** When the finish is dry, assemble the duck. Slide two flat washers onto each end of the pivot. Install the legs next. Tie a piece of twine to each end of the pivot by threading it through the hole, looping it around the pivot a couple of times, then tying it. The twine keeps the legs from dropping off the pivot. Bring the two pieces together, looping them through a hex nut—the drive weight—and knotting them.

Now take him for a walk. Too slow? Increase the drive weight. Too fast? Try a lighter nut.

XYLOPHONE

If you think that those tinny, high-pitched, glockenspiel-like toys are really xylophones, you'll be surprised to learn that a xylophone *should* be made of wood. *Xylophone* is a term derived from *xylon* 'wood' and *phonos* 'sounding'.

So this little project, which uses scraps of pine and walnut left over from more prestigious pieces, will yield a real xylophone. And it does produce a pleasant sound. If your youngster is at the rhythm band stage—driving everyone crazy by beating on a pot with a spoon—surprise him or her with a "look-what-I-made-for-you" gift.

1 Select the stock and cut the parts. The scrap bin is a good place to find most of the pieces you need for this little project. Though the base rails of our model are pine, you could use that strip of oak or the fir 2 × 4. The dowels are dowels; either you have what you need or you spend a buck and buy it.

Substituting another wood for walnut in making the tone bars could be problematic, however. We chose walnut for its visual, as well as its vocal, beauty. With a little tuning as explained later, the sizes listed produce a close approximation of a major scale. Any hard, dense

EXPLODED VIEW

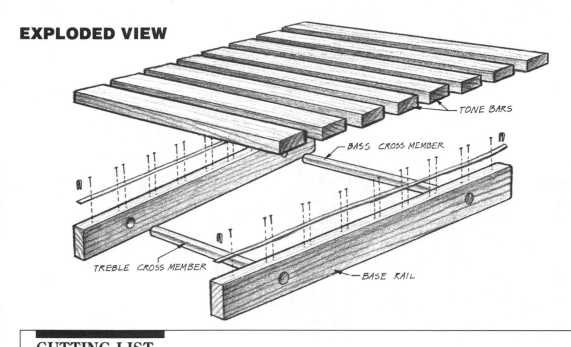

TONE BARS

BASS CROSS MEMBER

TREBLE CROSS MEMBER

BASE RAIL

CUTTING LIST

Part	Quantity	Dimensions	Material
Base rails	2	¾″ × 1½″ × 14″	#2 pine
Bass cross member	1	½″ dia. × 6¾″	Hardwood dowel
Treble cross member	1	½″ dia. × 5⅜″	Hardwood dowel
Tone bar	1	½″ × 1″ × 12″	Clear walnut
Tone bar	1	½″ × 1″ × 11½″	Clear walnut
Tone bar	1	½″ × 1″ × 11″	Clear walnut
Tone bar	1	½″ × 1″ × 10¾″	Clear walnut
Tone bar	1	½″ × 1″ × 10¼″	Clear walnut
Tone bar	1	½″ × 1″ × 9¾″	Clear walnut
Tone bar	1	½″ × 1″ × 9¼″	Clear walnut
Tone bar	1	½″ × 1″ × 9″	Clear walnut
Mallet handles	2	¼″ dia. × 10″	Hardwood dowel

Hardware

4 wire staples, ½″
32 finishing nails, 3d

Miscellaneous

Cotton butcher's cord
1 pair leather shoelaces, 36″

PLAN VIEWS

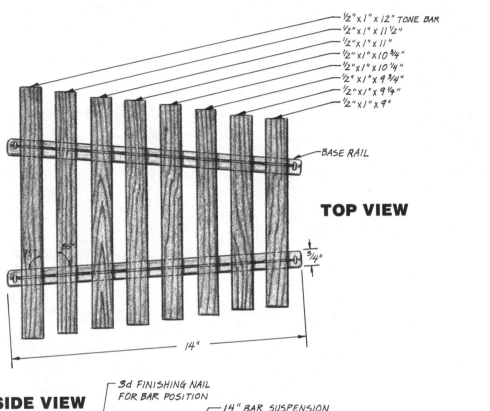

½" x 1" x 12" TONE BAR
½" x 1" x 11½"
½" x 1" x 11"
½" x 1" x 10¾"
½" x 1" x 10¼"
½" x 1" x 9¾"
½" x 1" x 9¼"
½" x 1" x 9"

BASE RAIL

TOP VIEW

¾"

14"

95°   85°

SIDE VIEW

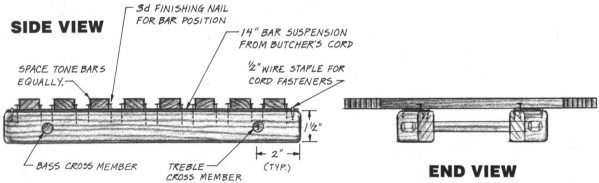

3d FINISHING NAIL
FOR BAR POSITION

14" BAR SUSPENSION
FROM BUTCHER'S CORD

½" WIRE STAPLE FOR
CORD FASTENERS

SPACE TONE BARS
EQUALLY.

BASS CROSS MEMBER

TREBLE
CROSS MEMBER

1½"

2"
(TYP.)

END VIEW

MALLET HANDLE

MALLET HEAD FROM
36" LEATHER SHOELACE
GLUED TO END

MALLET DETAIL

wood sings well. Rosewood generally is accepted as having "the best voice in the business," but few of us have rosewood in the scrap bin. Maple or oak will work. But if you substitute, you may have to do more tuning.

Cut the wood you select to the sizes specified by the Cutting List.

2 Make the base frame. The base frame is made by joining the two rails with the bass and treble cross members, which are dowels.

Drill two ½-inch-diameter holes through each rail for the cross members. The holes should penetrate at an 85-degree angle, as depicted in the *Top View*. Set a sliding T-bevel to that angle to visually align the drill bit as you bore these holes.

Break the edges of the rails using a block plane or a ¼-inch rounding-over bit in a table-mounted router.

Glue the cross members into their holes. After the glue sets, trim the dowel ends flush and sand the base. Apply a finish.

3 Install the tone bar suspension. The tone bars rest on cotton butcher's cord and are held in alignment by finishing nails. Cut two 14-inch lengths of the string. Stretch one piece along the top of each base rail. Staple it in place with a single staple at each end. You might want to knot the string ends to prevent fraying.

The nails are positioned as shown in the *Side View* and *Top View*, one on each side of each tone bar. Drive them through the string, leaving about ⅜ inch projecting above the rail. Use a tone bar to help you position the nails. The tone bars should be spaced evenly, about ⅝ inches apart.

4 Make the mallets. Each mallet is made from a dowel and a leather shoelace. Glue an end of the shoelace to the dowel, then wind it around the end of the dowel, forming a ball. As you use up the shoelace, glue the free end to the dowel.

5 Tune the tone bars. Lay the tone bars in place, take up the mallets, and try your xylophone. Though you'll probably recognize the scale (do-re-mi), you'll undoubtedly need to do a little tuning. To raise the pitch of a bar, shave away some wood at the end. To lower the pitch, shave away some thickness at the middle of the bar. Don't be too enthusiastic with your shaving—a very little trimming can affect the pitch dramatically. If you are concerned about pitch perfection, borrow a pitch pipe or use a piano to compare corresponding notes.

BENCH/DOLL CRADLE

Whoever said "Less is more" probably didn't have this project in mind. But that aphorism nevertheless applies.

This quick and easy doll's cradle uses very little material. Yet it first engages the purposeful woodworker, and later charms the child who plays with dolls. The make-believe "parent" can tuck a doll into the cradle and gently rock it to sleep.

It's a small toy, and it brings such pleasure. But wait! There's more. Flip the cradle over, and it's a bench—just the right height to give a child a step up to see in the dresser mirror or to get a toy from the closet shelf. It's only little, but it's a lot.

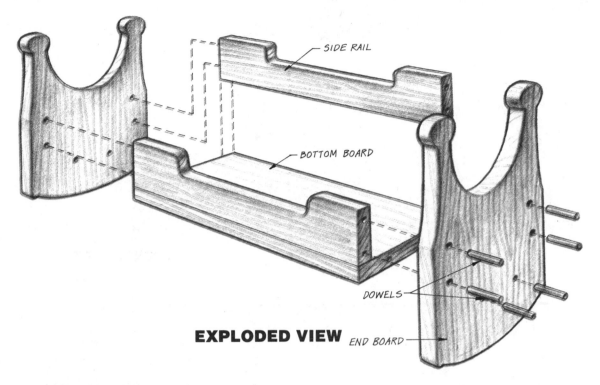

— SIDE RAIL

— BOTTOM BOARD

DOWELS —

EXPLODED VIEW END BOARD —

CUTTING LIST

Part	Quantity	Dimensions	Material
End boards	2	$\frac{3}{4}''$ × 8″ × $10\frac{1}{2}''$	Mahogany
Side rails	2	$\frac{3}{4}''$ × $2\frac{1}{2}''$ × $14\frac{1}{2}''$	Mahogany
Bottom board	1	$\frac{3}{4}''$ × 7″ × $14\frac{1}{2}''$	Mahogany
Dowels	12	$\frac{1}{4}''$ dia. × $1\frac{1}{2}''$	Maple dowel

1 **Select the stock and cut the parts.** For this project, you may have to look no further than your scrap bin. The model shown is made from mahogany, and it was given a natural finish to show off its attractive color. But use what you have on hand. You even can use a piece of this and a piece of that, if you paint it. The child probably won't mind.

Having picked your material, cut the individual pieces to the sizes specified by the Cutting List.

2 **Lay out and cut the ends and rails.** The ends and rails are cut to shape either with a saber saw or on the band saw.

Study the *End View*; the ends can be laid out by either enlarging the pat-

PLAN VIEWS

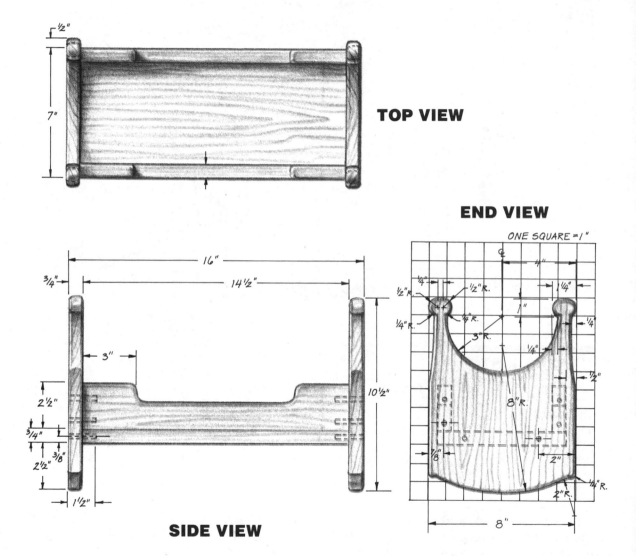

TOP VIEW

END VIEW

ONE SQUARE = 1"

SIDE VIEW

tern or using a compass to scribe the various arcs and curves. Lay out one end, then stack the two end blanks and cut both at the same time. Lay out one rail as shown in the *Side View*, then stack the two rail blanks and cut them out as well.

Smooth the sawed edges with a drum sander chucked in a drill. Then with a router and a ¼-inch rounding-over bit, machine all the edges of the ends and the top edges of the rails. At the same time, you can machine the two exposed edges of the bottom board.

3 **Glue up the cradle.** Begin by gluing the rails and the bottom board together. Clean up any squeeze-out with a wet rag. After the glue dries, sand the assembly as well as the end pieces. Glue the end pieces in place.

4 **Reinforce the assembly with dowels.** To reinforce the cradle so that it can also be used as a stool, drill holes through the ends into the rails and bottom, then glue dowels into the holes. The *End View* shows where to position the dowel holes. Drill ¼-inch-diameter holes, making them 1½ inches deep. After the glue dries, sand the dowels flush with the surface.

5 **Apply a finish.** Do any touch-up sanding necessary, then apply two coats of your preferred finish. It's advisable to use a nontoxic finish.

SNAKE-IN-THE-BOX

I just love this little project—it's a "gotcha!" When Phil Gehret, one of our ace woodworkers, lent it to me, I walked around harassing people with it. Not just kids, but everyone. It's a great folk toy, and we big kids probably will like it better than the small ones.

Dubbed the Box Ness Monster by a colleague, it's a snake-in-the-box, kin to the familiar jack-in-the-box. It's pocket-sized, though, and has no springs or other metal parts. The small size is what catches people. Slide open the lid, and a little wooden snake suddenly pops out.

The toy shown was made by Phil's son Rod back when he was a teenager.

It is a good project for the beginning woodworker: The amount of material needed is small; it can be completed using hand tools; and it won't take long to finish.

1 **Make the snake.** The snake is a whittling project. Start with a piece of hardwood of the size specified by the Cutting List. Rod Gehret made his snake from a scrap of oak. Use whatever is available in your scrap bin.

Following the pattern incorporated into the *Side View*, cut the basic shape of the snake with a coping saw. With a carving knife—actually, even a sharp

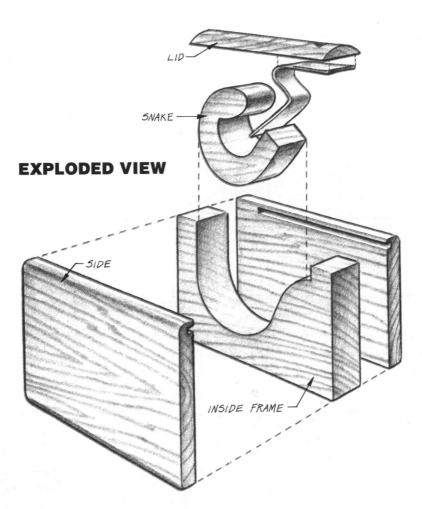

EXPLODED VIEW

LID

SNAKE

SIDE

INSIDE FRAME

CUTTING LIST

Part	Quantity	Dimensions	Material
Snake	1	$^{11}/_{16}'' \times 2^{1}/_{8}'' \times 2^{1}/_{4}''$	Oak
Inside frame	1	$^{3}/_{4}'' \times 2^{7}/_{8}'' \times 4^{1}/_{8}''$	Clear pine
Sides	2	$^{5}/_{16}'' \times 2^{7}/_{8}'' \times 4^{1}/_{8}''$	Clear pine
Lid	1	$^{1}/_{4}'' \times {}^{15}/_{16}'' \times 3^{3}/_{4}''$	Clear pine

Miscellaneous

1 leather snake pull, $^{5}/_{8}'' \times 3^{3}/_{4}''$

PLAN VIEWS

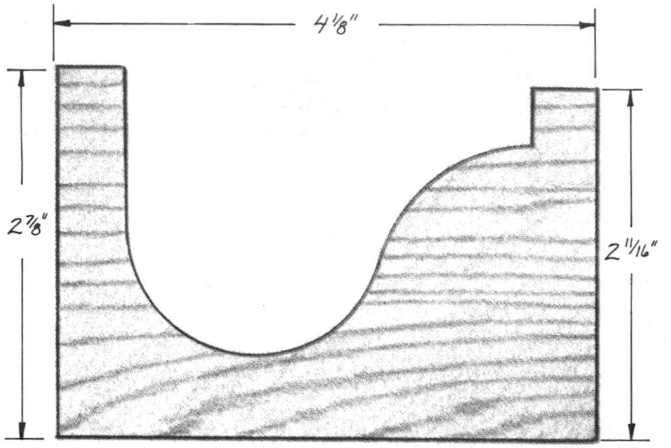
4 1/8"
2 7/8"
2 11/16"

INSIDE FRAME PROFILE

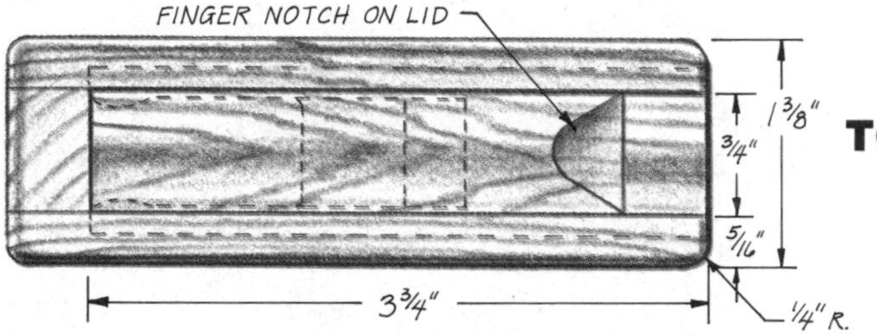
FINGER NOTCH ON LID
1 3/8"
3/4"
5/16"
3 3/4"
1/4" R.

TOP VIEW

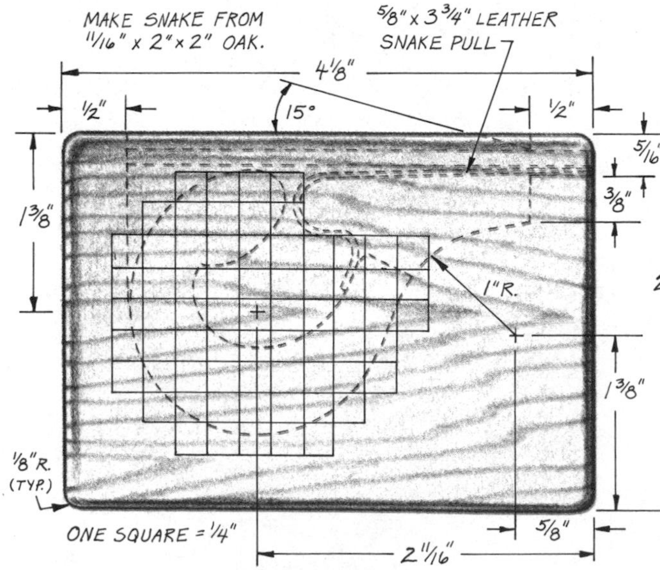
MAKE SNAKE FROM
11/16" x 2" x 2" OAK.
5/8" x 3 3/4" LEATHER
SNAKE PULL
4 1/8"
1/2"
15°
1/2"
5/16"
3/8"
1 3/8"
1" R.
2 7/8"
1 3/8"
1/8" R.
(TYP.)
ONE SQUARE = 1/4"
5/8"
2 11/16"

SIDE VIEW

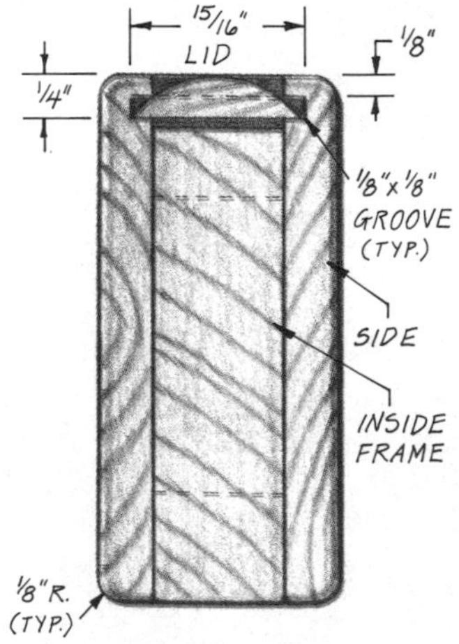
15/16"
LID
1/8"
1/4"
1/8" x 1/8"
GROOVE
(TYP.)
SIDE
INSIDE
FRAME
1/8" R.
(TYP.)

END VIEW

jackknife will do—whittle away at the edges, giving it some snakelike character. Be creative. Make the head somewhat wedge-shaped . . . just like a poisonous copperhead.

2 **Make the box.** The box is made from clear pine. It is small enough that you can cut usable pieces from a #2-grade board. Cut the wood to the sizes specified by the Cutting List.

Mark the inside frame profile on the stock for it, and cut it out with a saber saw or a coping saw. Test fit the snake in its den; if it doesn't fit, either the snake or the den has to be revised, perhaps even redone.

Next cut kerfs in the sides, creating grooves for the lid. The grooves should be ⅛ inch wide × ⅛ inch deep and positioned ⅛ inch from the top edge, as shown in the *End View*. Cut these kerfs on the table saw. This being done, glue the sides to the inside frame. Use wood putty to fill the holes created by the lid grooves on the box's back end.

Make the lid next. Trim its edges with a block plane, file, or spokeshave so that they'll fit the grooves in the box. As you do this, shape the lid's top surface into an arch, as indicated in the *End View*. At one end of the lid, make a finger notch by filing across the grain.

3 **Paint the snake and the box.** Sand the snake, the box, and the lid. Cut a strip of leather for the snake pull, and glue one end of it to the snake. Paint the snake a good snaky color, and when it dries, add eyes and decorative markings with a felt-tip pen. Paint the inside of the box black. Paint or varnish the outside of the box, including the lid.

4 **Put the snake in the box.** Drop the snake into its den, with the leather pull hanging out. Slide the lid into its grooves. For the toy to work properly, there must be some slack in the pull; roughly speaking, the pull should be taut and beginning to move the snake when the lid is open about 1¼ inches. Glue the end of the pull to the bottom of the lid; apply glue to ½ inch of the pull, and attach it to the very end of the lid.

STILTS

Want a raise? Here's the old-fashioned way to get one. These stilts will lift you above the crowd more quickly than any amount of positive thinking. As a matter of fact, we've included room for growth. As you master each level, you can easily move up to the next, simply by adjusting the foot blocks.

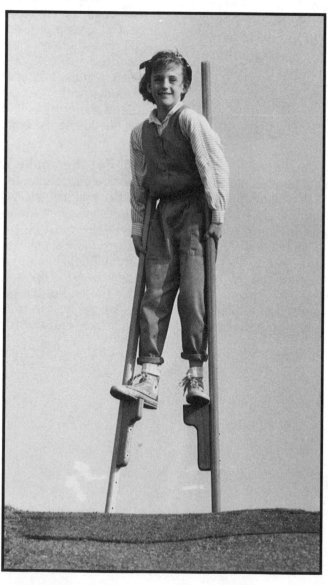

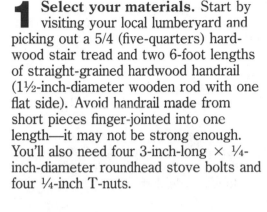

EXPLODED VIEW

1 **Select your materials.** Start by visiting your local lumberyard and picking out a 5/4 (five-quarters) hardwood stair tread and two 6-foot lengths of straight-grained hardwood handrail (1½-inch-diameter wooden rod with one flat side). Avoid handrail made from short pieces finger-jointed into one length—it may not be strong enough. You'll also need four 3-inch-long × ¼-inch-diameter roundhead stove bolts and four ¼-inch T-nuts.

2 **Make the foot blocks.** Cut two foot blocks from the stair tread, following the dimensions shown in the illustration. For strength, the grain should run parallel to that of the handrail. Rout a ⅜-inch radius on the outside edges of each foot block. Counterbore each foot block at 4 inches on center to accept two T-nuts, then drill ¼-inch-diameter holes the rest of the way through.

3 **Make the poles.** Drill a series of ¼-inch-diameter holes through the lower portion of each pole, as shown. Starting the holes on the handrail's flat side makes drilling easier. Make sure the

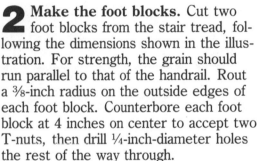

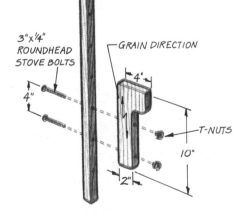

3"x¼" ROUNDHEAD STOVE BOLTS

4"

GRAIN DIRECTION

4"

T-NUTS

10"

2"

CUTTING LIST

Part	Quantity	Dimensions	Material
Poles	2	1½" dia. × 72"	Oak
Foot blocks	2	1⅛" × 4" × 10"	Oak
Hardware			

4 roundhead stove bolts, 3" × ¼" dia.
4 T-nuts, ¼"

holes match the ones in the foot blocks. Rout a ⅜-inch radius on each end of the poles.

4 **Finish and assemble the stilts.** Sand the parts and apply two coats of your favorite finish. Put the T-nuts into the foot blocks, and bolt the foot blocks to the stilts. Let your conscience be your guide, but we'd suggest setting the blocks as low as possible until the pilot logs a little flight time.

5 **Walk tall.** Learning to operate these marvels of engineering is no great challenge. It's easiest if you don't hold the tops of the stilts in front of your body. Stand with the stilts behind your shoulders, your arms passing down in front of the stilts. Grab the stilts at thigh level and pull them up, to keep them tight against your feet, and forward, to keep them snug against your shoulders. How's the view up there?

TOY DUMP TRUCK

Let's face it: This is a sizable project. As it should be, this truck is *big*—a good two feet long, a foot wide, more than a foot tall. It will haul sand or dirt from pile to pile all day long. Its *operator* will wear out before this truck will.

Patterned after the massive trucks manufactured in the 1920s, it has a boxy, open cab, fenders that *are* fenders (and not shrouds), and some major ground clearance. Since this is toy-making, not model-making, the truck has the primitive character of traditional wooden toys—plain wooden disks for wheels, for example.

Besides yielding a physically large toy, the project itself is a fairly substantial undertaking. Look at that Cutting List; the truck requires more parts than any other piece in this book. And not only are there a lot of parts, but they are labor intensive, with many requiring resawing and planing. But don't let this aspect of "big" deter you. The truck shown was designed and constructed by Rod Gehret when he was a teenager. (You know: If a kid can deal with it, why can't you?)

This is a perfect project for the weekend woodworker, because the truck lends itself to construction in sporadic, short sessions. Build the chassis in one session, the cab in another, and so forth.

Just bear in mind that this is a job for a band saw. I wouldn't tackle the project without one.

EXPLODED VIEW

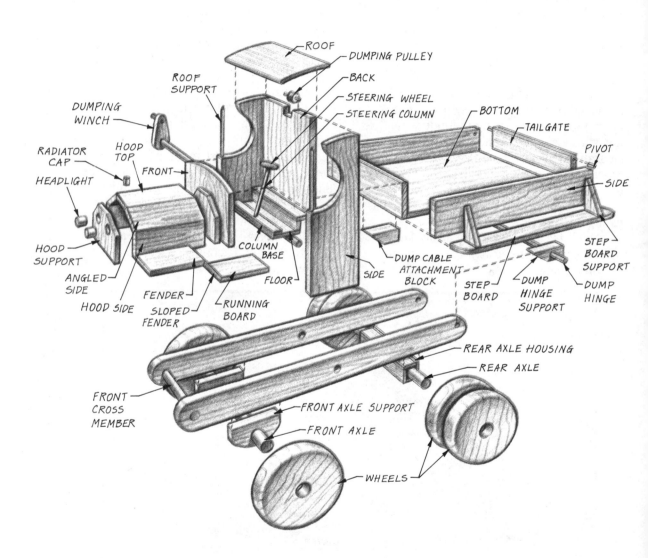

ROOF

DUMPING PULLEY

BACK

ROOF SUPPORT

STEERING WHEEL

STEERING COLUMN

DUMPING WINCH

BOTTOM

TAILGATE

RADIATOR CAP

HOOD TOP

PIVOT

FRONT

HEADLIGHT

SIDE

HOOD SUPPORT

STEP BOARD SUPPORT

COLUMN BASE

ANGLED SIDE

DUMP CABLE ATTACHMENT BLOCK

SIDE

FLOOR

DUMP HINGE

FENDER

HOOD SIDE

SLOPED FENDER

RUNNING BOARD

STEP BOARD

DUMP HINGE SUPPORT

REAR AXLE HOUSING

REAR AXLE

FRONT CROSS MEMBER

FRONT AXLE SUPPORT

FRONT AXLE

WHEELS

1 Select the stock. Wooden toys generally are made from pine. It's light, easily worked, and widely available. Although pine is expensive, this project needs clear stock. Many of the parts *are* small, so you may be able to work around knots and defects. But by all means, keep them out of the truck.

The Cutting List calls for five different thicknesses of stock, only two of which are standard. I'd suggest using 5/4 (five-quarters) pine as your basic stock, resawing it to produce three of the other thicknesses required. The basics of this

CUTTING LIST

Part	Quantity	Dimensions	Material
Chassis			
Wheels	6	5″ dia. × 1⅛″	Clear pine
Rear axle housing	4	¼″ × 1⅜″ × 6½″	Clear pine
Front axle supports	2	1⅛″ × 4″ × 1¾″	Clear pine
Chassis rails	2	1⅛″ × 1⅞″ × 25½″	Clear pine
Front cross member	1	1″ dia. × 6½″	Hardwood dowel
Front axle	1	1″ dia. × 8⅞″	Hardwood dowel
Rear axle	1	1″ dia. × 11¾″	Hardwood dowel
Cab			
Dumping pulley	1	½″ dia. × ¼″	Hardwood dowel
Back	1	½″ × 6½″ × 9⅛″	Clear pine
Front	1	½″ × 6½″ × 4⅜″	Clear pine
Sides	2	½″ × 4¼″ × 11″	Clear pine
Seat	1	5⁄16″ × 1¼″ × 6½″	Clear pine
Seat front	1	5⁄16″ × 1⅛″ × 6½″	Clear pine
Floor	1	5⁄16″ × 2 5⁄16″ × 6½″	Clear pine
Column base	1	5⁄16″ × ¾″ × 1¾″	Clear pine
Steering column	1	3⁄16″ dia. × 4⅜″	Hardwood dowel
Steering wheel	1	1¼″ dia. × ¼″	Clear pine
Roof	1	5⁄16″ × 5″ × 8½″	Clear pine
Roof supports	2	3⁄16″ dia. × 5¼″	Hardwood dowel
Hood			
Hood supports	2	¾″ × 4¼″ × 3½″	Clear pine
Hood sides and top	3	½″ × 2″ × 6″	Clear pine
Angled sides	2	½″ × 2 5⁄16″ × 6″	Clear pine
Headlights	2	1″ dia. × ⅝″	Hardwood dowel
Radiator cap	1	5⁄16″ dia. × ½″	Hardwood dowel
Fenders			
Running boards	2	5⁄16″ × 1⅜″ × 4¼″	Clear pine
Fenders	2	5⁄16″ × 2″ × 4⅝″	Clear pine
Sloped fenders	2	5⁄16″ × 1⅜″ × 2⅞″	Clear pine

(continued)

CUTTING LIST—*Continued*

Part	Quantity	Dimensions	Material
Dumping winch			
Crank handle offset	1	$\frac{1}{4}'' \times 1'' \times 1\frac{3}{4}''$	Clear pine
Crank	1	$\frac{7}{16}''$ dia. $\times 8''$	Hardwood dowel
Crank handle	1	$\frac{5}{16}''$ dia. $\times 1\frac{1}{4}''$	Hardwood dowel
Retaining pin	1	$\frac{1}{8}''$ dia. $\times 1''$	Hardwood dowel
Dump bed			
Bottom	1	$\frac{1}{2}'' \times 8\frac{1}{2}'' \times 12\frac{1}{2}''$	Clear pine
Step board supports	4	$\frac{1}{2}'' \times 1\frac{1}{8}'' \times 2\frac{1}{2}''$	Clear pine
Dump hinge supports	2	$1\frac{1}{8}'' \times 1\frac{1}{8}'' \times 2\frac{3}{4}''$	Clear pine
Dump cable attachment block	1	$1\frac{1}{8}'' \times 1\frac{1}{8}'' \times 3\frac{1}{4}''$	Clear pine
Sides	2	$\frac{1}{2}'' \times 3\frac{1}{4}'' \times 13''$	Clear pine
Tailgate pivots	2	$\frac{3}{16}''$ dia. $\times 1''$	Hardwood dowel
Tailgate	1	$\frac{1}{2}'' \times 2\frac{5}{8}'' \times 8\frac{7}{16}''$	Clear pine
Dump hinge	1	$\frac{3}{8}''$ dia. $\times 8\frac{3}{4}''$	Hardwood dowel
Front	1	$\frac{1}{2}'' \times 3\frac{1}{4}'' \times 8\frac{1}{2}''$	Clear pine
Step boards	2	$\frac{1}{4}'' \times 1\frac{1}{4}'' \times 13''$	Clear pine

Hardware

1 sheet-metal screw, #4 $\times \frac{1}{2}''$
28" mason's cord
1 finishing nail, 3d

procedure are explained in "Resawing" on page 174.

There are many parts, so you'll probably want to avoid trying to cut all of them at one time. The hope is that as your truck takes shape, everything will fit as initially cut. It's better to work subassembly by subassembly.

2 Cut the chassis parts. Begin the truck's construction with the chassis. Cut the parts for the chassis to the dimensions specified by the Cutting List. When making the front axle supports, be sure to cut 1¾-inch lengths of 4-inch-wide stock; note the grain direction indicated in the *Chassis, Side View.*

The wheels can be roughed out with a fly cutter, then finished by drilling their center holes to a full 1-inch diameter and radiusing their outside edges with a piloted ¼-inch rounding-over bit in a table-mounted router.

SHOP TIP: When cutting thin parts like the rear axle housing, you'll probably save time if you cut a full-thickness board to the width and length specified, then resaw it to the desired thickness. In more than a few cases, you need two or more pieces of the same size anyway. You'll be able to slice them from the same blank.

3 Make the chassis. Glue together the four pieces for the rear axle housing, butting them edge-to-face as indicated in the *Chassis, Side View*.

While the glue dries, lay out and cut the curve on the bottom edge of the front axle supports. Drill 1-inch-diameter holes in these supports for the axle; slightly enlarge the holes with a round file so that the axle can turn freely.

Round off the ends of the chassis rails; cut the curves on the band saw, then gingerly sand the cuts smooth with a belt sander. Lay out and drill the holes in the rails for the dump hinge, the crank, and the front cross member. You can lay out the holes on one chassis rail, then stack the two together and bore through both at the same time. When boring for the crank, make sure the hole is stopped ½ inch deep in the left rail, as shown in the *Chassis, Top View*. Enlarge the dumping pivot holes with a round file so that the pivot can turn freely.

Before beginning to assemble the chassis, sand the various parts, softening the edges of the rails, the housing, and the supports. Glue the front cross member into the appropriate holes in the chassis rails. Glue and clamp the rear axle housing and the front axle supports to the chassis rails, as shown in the *Chassis, Side View*.

4 Install the axles and wheels. To install the axles and wheels, first glue wheels to one end of each axle. As shown in the *Chassis, Top View*, the ends of the front axle are flush with the outside of the wheels, while the rear axle protrudes about ¼ inch beyond the outside of its wheels.

The dual wheels on the back are spaced about 1/16 inch apart. Use temporary spacers of that thickness—scraps of plastic laminate, for example—to position the two wheels while the glue dries. After the glue has set, install the axles on the chassis and glue the remaining wheels in place. Again, use scrap spacers between the two rear wheels as well as between the wheels and rails on both sides, front and back.

5 Cut the parts for the cab. The next component to be constructed is the cab. Cut the parts for it to the dimensions specified by the Cutting List.

Before cutting the bit of dowel that's to be the dumping pulley, file a groove around its circumference. To do this, chuck a several-inch length of the dowel in the drill press. As the dowel rotates, hold the edge of a file to it, cutting the groove. Cut the pulley from the dowel, and drill a hole through it for the nail-axle. Hold the pulley with needle-nose pliers while you drill.

6 Prepare the cab parts for assembly. Begin this process with the back. Cut a ½-inch-wide × ⅝-inch-deep notch in the center of the top edge, as shown in the *Body, Front View*. The dumping pulley fits into this notch.

For the nail-axle that supports the pulley, you need to machine a ⅛-inch-wide × ⅜-inch-deep slot extending ¼ inch on either side of the notch. To do this, use a ⅛-inch straight bit in a table-mounted router. Adjust the fence to position the slot in the center of the wood. Set the wood over the bit (with the bit in the notch), turn on the router, and make a very short cut to either side of the notch.

CHASSIS, PLAN VIEWS

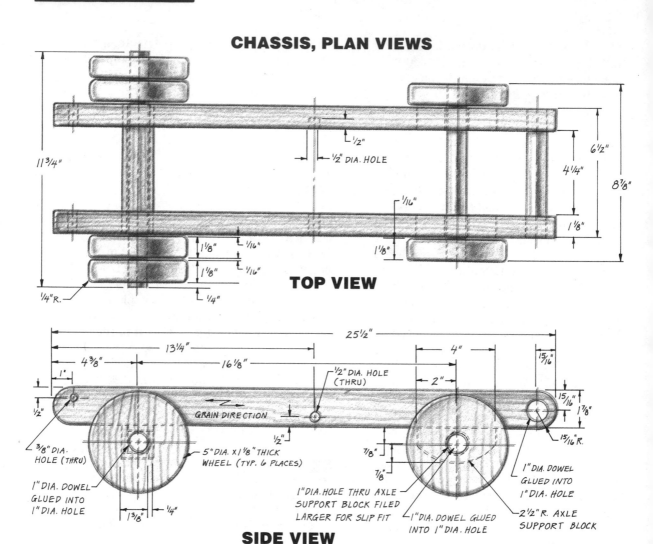

11³/₄"

¹/₂"

¹/₂" DIA. HOLE

6¹/₂"

4¹/₄"

8⁷/₈"

¹/₁₆"

1¹/₈"

1¹/₈"   ¹/₁₆"

1¹/₈"

1¹/₈"   ¹/₁₆"

¹/₄"R.   ¹/₄"

TOP VIEW

25¹/₂"

13¹/₄"

4"

4³/₈"

16¹/₈"

¹⁵/₁₆"

1"

¹/₂" DIA. HOLE
(THRU)

2"

¹⁵/₁₆"

1¹/₈"

¹/₂"

GRAIN DIRECTION

¹/₂"

¹⁵/₁₆"R.

³/₈" DIA.
HOLE (THRU)

5" DIA. X 1¹/₈" THICK
WHEEL (TYP. 6 PLACES)

⁷/₈"

⁷/₈"

1" DIA. DOWEL
GLUED INTO
1" DIA. HOLE

1" DIA. DOWEL
GLUED INTO
1" DIA. HOLE

1"DIA. HOLE THRU AXLE
SUPPORT BLOCK FILED
LARGER FOR SLIP FIT

1"DIA. DOWEL GLUED
INTO 1" DIA. HOLE

2¹/₂"R. AXLE
SUPPORT BLOCK

1³/₈"   ¹/₄"

SIDE VIEW

FRONT VIEW

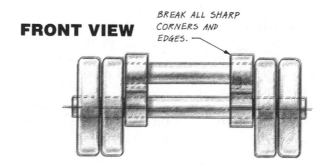

BREAK ALL SHARP
CORNERS AND
EDGES.

BODY, PLAN VIEWS

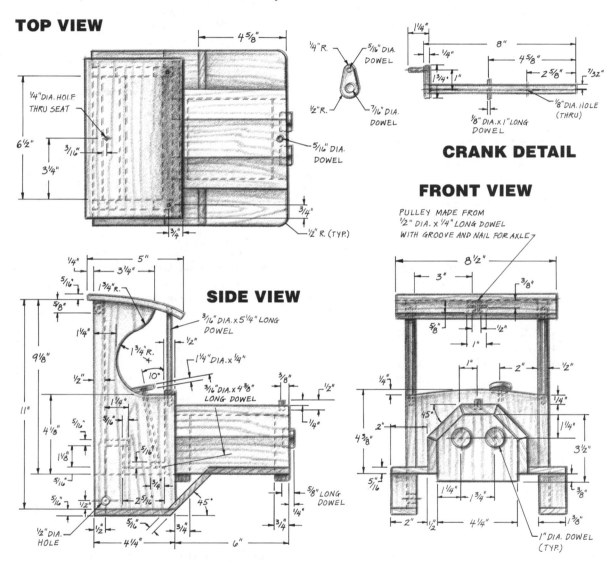

TOP VIEW

CRANK DETAIL

FRONT VIEW

SIDE VIEW

Lay out the arch on the top edge of the front. The arch drops ¼ inch from the center point to the edges; you can duplicate the arch freehand or with a french curve. Cut the arch on the band saw.

Lay out the shape of, and the holes in, the sides. The sinuous window cutout is laid out with a compass. Cut it on the band saw. Only the right side has a ½-inch-diameter hole drilled into it for the dumping crank, as shown in the *Body*,

Side View. This hole must align with the crank hole already drilled into the right chassis rail. Bore this hole into the side. Finally, mark and drill the roof-support holes for each side, as shown in the *Body, Front View* and *Body, Side View.* These holes are ³/₁₆ inch diameter × ¼ inch deep.

Lay out and drill a ¼-inch-diameter hole in the seat for the dumping cable; see the *Body, Top View.*

7 Assemble the cab and fit it to the chassis. Sand all the cab parts. Apply a drop of glue to the dumping pulley, and slip its nail-axle into place. Drop the pulley and axle into their notch in the back.

Preassemble the seat unit, gluing the seat to the seat front. Glue the back, front, and floor to each other and to the chassis, as well as to one side. After these components are in place, add the seat unit and the second side.

Drill a ¼-inch hole in the steering column base. Glue the column into the base and the steering wheel onto the column. Glue this unit into the cab.

Form the roof to the tops of the sides, dampening it if necessary to make it more limber. Mark the location and angle of the holes needed for the roof supports. Drill these holes. Glue the supports into the holes in the sides, then glue the roof onto the supports and the sides.

8 Cut, shape, and assemble the parts for the hood. Set the developing project aside, and cut the parts for the hood. Cut the front and back supports, nipping off the top corners as indicated in the *Body, Front View.* As you rip the hood panels, bevel both edges of the top and angled sides at 22½ degrees. Bevel only one edge of the side panels. Sand the parts.

Drill two stopped holes—1 inch diameter × ³/₈ inch deep—into the front support for the headlights. Into these holes, glue ⁵/₈-inch-long segments of 1-inch-diameter dowel.

Now glue the hood supports and the several hood panels in place.

After the glue sets, drill a ⁵/₁₆-inch-diameter × ¼-inch-deep hole into the hood for the radiator cap. Glue a bit of dowel into the hole.

9 Cut, shape, and assemble the parts for the fenders. Cut the three separate parts that make up the fenders. The running boards must be beveled at 45 degrees across the front end. The fenders are similarly beveled across their back ends. The sloped fender elements are beveled across both ends; see the *Body, Side View.* Round off the outside front corners of the fenders as shown in the *Body, Top View.* Sand these parts.

Glue the fenders and running boards to the truck. Fit the sloped fenders onto the truck, marking where they must be notched to accommodate the cab side. Cut the notches, then glue the fenders in place.

10 Fit the dumping winch to the truck. Cut the parts for the dumping winch to the dimensions specified. Lay out the crank handle offset as indicated in the *Crank Detail.* Drill holes for the crank and the crank handle, then cut the shape on the band saw. Drill two ⅛-inch-diameter holes through the crank—one for the retaining pin, the other for the winch cable.

Slide the crank into its holes in the cab and chassis. Glue the retaining pin into its hole, capturing the crank. Glue the handle into the handle offset, and glue the offset onto the crank.

11 **Cut the parts for the bed.** Cut the dump bed parts to the dimensions specified by the Cutting List. The bottom is wide enough that you may

SHOP TIP: When drilling holes in dowel, cradle it in a V-block so that it won't roll away from the drill bit. To make a V-block, rout a groove in a scrap of wood with a V-groove bit. Mark the hole locations with an awl or a punch, making an indentation to capture the drill bit and to help start the holes.

need to edge-glue two or more narrow boards to make it. Cut the step board

DUMP BED, PLAN VIEWS

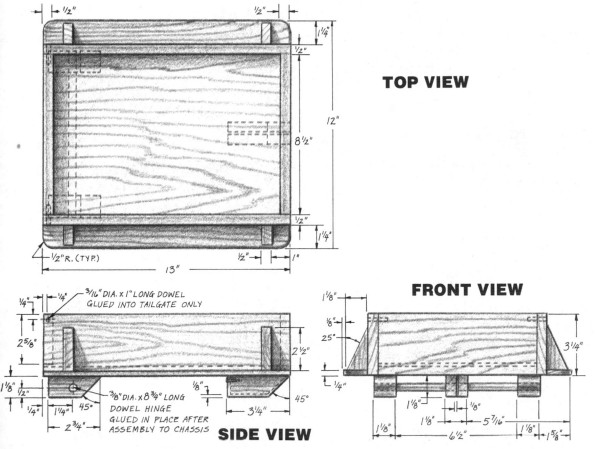

TOP VIEW

FRONT VIEW

SIDE VIEW

supports to the triangular shape indicated in the *Dump Bed, Front View.* As you cut the dump hinge supports and the dump cable attachment block, miter one end of each piece at 45 degrees, as indicated in the *Dump Bed, Side View.* The outer corners of the two step boards should be rounded off as indicated in the *Dump Bed, Top View.*

12 **Assemble the bed and install it.** Before beginning to glue up the dump bed, you must drill a few holes. In each side, lay out and drill a

hole for a tailgate pivot; slightly enlarge this hole so that the pivot is a slip fit. Drill matching holes in the ends of the tailgate, making them ½ inch deep. Lay out and drill a ⅜-inch-diameter hole through each hinge support for the dump hinge; to ensure that the holes line up, clamp the two supports together and drill both at the same time.

The dump cable attachment block must be grooved for the cable. Do this with a table-mounted router and a ⅛-inch straight bit. As you can see in the *Dump Bed, Front View* and *Dump Bed,*

TRUCK ASSEMBLY, PLAN VIEWS

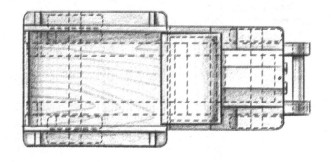

TOP VIEW

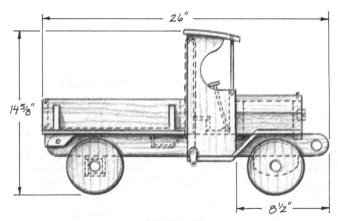

SIDE VIEW

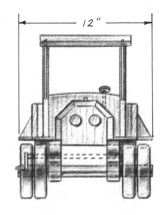

FRONT VIEW

Side View, the groove is centered on the block and extends down the front, across the bottom, and up the back. Drive a ½-inch sheet-metal screw into the groove on the block's back end, near the top edge.

Sand all the parts to ready them for assembly.

Begin assembly by gluing and clamping together the sides, front, and bottom. After the glue dries, install the tailgate, gluing the tailgate pivots into the tailgate only (not into the sides). Add the step boards and supports, gluing and clamping them to the dump bed.

Turn the bed over, and glue and clamp the hinge supports to the bottom. As an aid in aligning these supports, slip the dump hinge into place temporarily; remember that you must be able to remove it to attach the bed to the chassis. Glue and clamp the dump cable attachment block to the bed's bottom.

13 **Apply a finish.** Now the truck is virtually done. Before you complete the assembly, you have to apply a finish. Rod Gehret kept the traditional look of a wooden toy by giving his truck two coats of brushing lacquer. But I can see this with a multicolor paint job—black chassis and wheels and a red or green body. Brushing lacquer certainly is faster.

14 **Mount the dump bed on the truck.** After the finish has dried, complete the truck's assembly. Pull the dump hinge from the bed, fit the bed over the chassis, and replace the hinge. This time, apply a couple of dots of glue to the hinge dowel when it passes through the hinge supports; do not glue it to the chassis.

Thread the cable next. Tie one end to the crank; thread it through the hole in the crank and tightly knot the free end. Thread the cable through the hole in the seat, up and over the pulley, then down the outside of the cab and under the bed. Tie it to the screw in the dump cable attachment block. Leave yourself a little slack when the bed is down, but not a lot. Test the dumping action.

Resawing

Resawing saves an enormous amount of time and wood. Working 4/4 (four-quarters) lumber down to ¼-inch thickness on a small planer takes a long time, and it wastes a lot of wood to boot. From that same 4/4 lumber, you can resaw two or three ¼-inch boards.

The band saw is the best tool for resawing. Its kerf is relatively narrow, and the blade's downward action keeps the wood pressed against the table. It is possible to resaw on the table saw, but the danger of kickback, combined with the limited depth of cut and the relatively wide kerf, makes the table saw a weak second choice.

Choose an appropriate blade for resawing; it's the widest one your saw will accommodate, with as few teeth per inch as possible. For most home-shop band saws, this means a ½- to ¾-inch blade with 3 or 4 teeth per inch. Adjust the upper blade guide to prevent blade distortion in the cut, setting it within ⅛ to ¼ inch of the wood.

While it's possible to resaw stock freehand, you can be more accurate if you guide the board with a fence or pivot. A resawing pivot is easy to make and use. Clamped to the saw table, the pivot braces the workpiece and keeps the cut from wandering, thus helping you to achieve a uniform thickness. Following the plan shown here, you can quickly make the pivot from scraps. Attach it to the table with a C-clamp, lining it up with the blade's teeth.

Prepare the stock by squaring one face and one edge on a jointer; the board must rest squarely on the saw table and against the pivot. Using a marking gauge, or just a pencil and rule, mark a cutting line on the unjointed edge

for each piece to be resawed. Cut with the jointed face of the stock held firmly against the pivot, turning the board as necessary—adjusting the feed angle, in other words—to hold to the line.

Take all appropriate safety precautions, of course. Use a push stick or push shoe. Since resawing generates a lot of fine sawdust, it's a good idea to wear a dust mask and goggle-type safety glasses.

RESAWING PIVOT

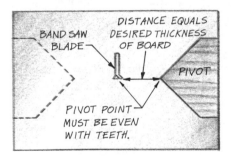

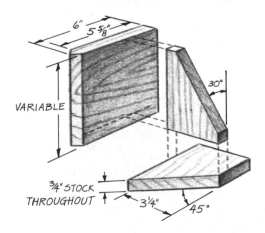

PART FIVE

SHELVING AND STORAGE PROJECTS

WALL SHELF

Walter Morrison wanted a place to display his mantel clock, so the engineer and hobby woodworker designed this wall shelf to look like a fireplace mantel. It's a very simple project to build, and it looks great on the wall. As you can see, the shelf can be used for displaying plates and collectibles, too.

What appears to be a thick, solid base under the shelf is actually hollow. The wide molding is standard 3½-inch pine crown molding, which you can buy at any lumberyard. Morrison made the rest of the shelf from pine to match the molding. The dimensions are the ones Morrison used, but don't be afraid to modify them to suit your needs.

1 Select the stock and cut the parts. The pivotal material in this shelf is the crown molding. Most lumber-

yards will stock it in pine, but some will have it in oak and other common hardwoods. Choose your molding first, then select matching stock for the top and brackets. The spacers probably can be obtained from your scrap bin. The top is taken from 5/4 (five-quarters) stock, and the brackets are glued up from the same stock.

Get started by cutting the top and bottom to the sizes specified by the Cutting List.

2 Make the brackets. Glue up 5/4 stock to make the brackets. Enlarge the pattern shown in the *Bracket Detail*, and transfer it to the bracket blanks. Cut them on a band saw or with a saber saw. With a drum sander chucked in a drill, carefully sand any saw marks from the curved edge—you want those curves to

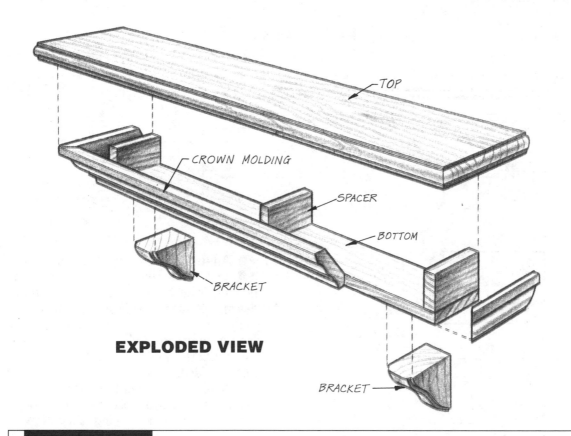

EXPLODED VIEW

CUTTING LIST

Part	Quantity	Dimensions	Material
Top	1	$1\frac{1}{16}'' \times 7\frac{3}{8}'' \times 39''$	Clear pine
Bottom	1	$\frac{3}{4}'' \times 3\frac{3}{4}'' \times 31\frac{1}{4}''$	Clear pine
Brackets	2	$2\frac{1}{8}'' \times 3\frac{9}{16}'' \times 3\frac{7}{16}''$	Clear pine
Spacers	3	$\frac{3}{4}'' \times 2\frac{5}{16}'' \times 3\frac{3}{4}''$	#2 pine
Crown molding	1	$\frac{11}{16}'' \times 3\frac{1}{2}'' \times 39''$ *	Clear pine
Crown molding	2	$\frac{11}{16}'' \times 3\frac{1}{2}'' \times 8''$ *	Clear pine

Hardware

12 flathead wood screws, #6 $\times$ $1\frac{1}{4}''$
6d finishing nails
3 pairs concealed shelf hangers. Available from Constantines, 2050 Eastchester Rd.,
   Bronx, NY 10861.

* Cut to fit.

PLAN VIEWS

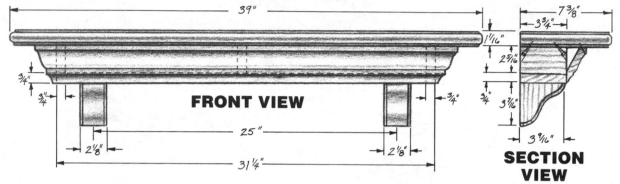

FRONT VIEW

SECTION VIEW

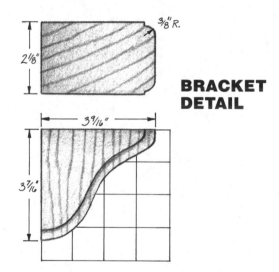

BRACKET DETAIL

be smooth, because you'll be routing the corners of the bracket. The bit's pilot bearing will dip into any bumps and valleys left by the saw, telegraphing the irregularities onto the finished edge.

After you've removed the saw marks, rout the edges of the brackets with a ⅜-inch rounding-over bit. Cut deep enough to create a slight fillet, as indicated in the *Bracket Detail*. This profile creates a shadow line that visually softens the shelf edge and adds interest.

3 **Assemble the shelf.** Prepare the shelf for assembly by routing a bead into the front edge and ends of the top. Use the ⅜-inch rounding-over bit, and as you did with the brackets, cut deeply enough to create a fillet. Rout both the top and bottom edges. Sand the top and bottom pieces.

Begin assembling the shelf by attaching the vertical spacers to the bottom with glue and finishing nails. Now screw the brackets to the bottom, using two #6 × 1¼-inch flathead wood screws per bracket; drive the screws through the bottom into the brackets.

Attach this entire assembly to the top with glue and #6 × 1¼-inch flathead screws, angling the screws upward through the spacers as shown in the *Section View*. Drill pilot holes for these screws to avoid splitting the spacers.

4 **Cut and install the crown molding.** It's easiest to sand the molding before cutting and installing it. Take extra care to sand off chatter marks left by the molding cutter. Faint ridges running perpendicular to the grain, these marks may not be obvious at first, but they'll

SHOP TIP: If you want to display plates on the shelf, you'll need to rout a groove to keep the plates upright on their edges. A groove about ⅜ inch wide × ⅜ inch deep will accommodate most plates. Rout the groove with either a cove bit or a V-groove bit in your router. To keep the groove straight, use a router fence, or guide the router base against a straightedge clamped to the shelf.

show up once you apply stain. You can see them by holding the piece at various angles to the light.

Now you're ready to cut the molding. Crown molding miter joints can be tricky; try a few practice joints before you cut the finished molding. "Crown Molding Miters" on page 180 shows how to do it.

Once you've cut the molding, assemble the pieces without glue to check the alignment; small gaps at the corners can be closed by twisting the molding a little. When everything fits, attach the molding to the top and bottom with glue and 6d finishing nails, as shown in the *Section View*.

5 **Apply the finish and hang the shelf.** Set all the nails with a small nail set, and fill the holes with wood putty. Apply whatever finish you like. Morrison finished his shelf with stain followed by two coats of polyurethane. He rubbed out the second coat with 000 steel wool.

Mount the shelf with the concealed shelf hangers. One part of the hanger mounts on the back of the shelf, a second part mounts on the wall, and the two pieces interlock.

CROWN MOLDING MITERS

You may have seen crown molding gracing the edges of stately parlor ceilings and assumed it was one solid piece. In fact, it is a board nailed at an angle between the ceiling and wall, seldom more than ¾ inch thick. Because of this angle, crown molding miter joints present some special problems. You have to cut the molding upside down. Try it the other way around, and you'll end up with a huge gap at the top of the joint. Here's how to cut the molding for the wall shelf:

First cut the molding for the left-hand side of the shelf. Place the molding upside down in the miter box as shown in the illustration, with the saw handle 45 degrees to the left and the finished molding to the right of the blade. Cut it a little long—you'll trim the back ends of both side moldings later.

Cut the front molding next. Set the saw handle 45 degrees to the right and the finished molding to the left of the blade. This cut produces the left-hand corner. Test fit the molding

against the bottom of the shelf, and mark the right-hand corner with a knife.

Put the molding back in the box (upside down as before), with the saw handle 45 degrees to the left and the finished molding to the right of the blade. Cut to the waste side of the knife mark.

Cut the right-hand side molding with the saw handle 45 degrees to the right and the finished molding to the left of the blade.

You also can cut crown molding miters on a table saw or radial arm saw. Just remember to cut the molding upside down. On a table saw, set the miter gauge to 45 degrees; leave the blade at 90 degrees. Rest the top of the molding on the table, and clamp the bottom of the molding to an auxiliary fence screwed to the miter gauge. On a radial arm saw, set the blade at 90 degrees and the arm at 45 degrees. Clamp the bottom of the molding to an auxiliary fence clamped to the regular fence, and rest the top of the molding on the table.

MITERING CROWN MOLDING

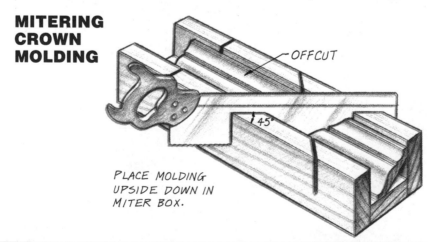

OFFCUT

45°

PLACE MOLDING UPSIDE DOWN IN MITER BOX.

MISSION PLATE RACK

Mission furniture, also known as Craftsman or Arts and Crafts furniture, was a popular American style between 1900 and 1916. Sturdy and simple, with exposed mortise-and-tenon joinery and solid wood construction, Mission furniture heralded a full retreat from the ornate excesses of the fancy Victorian styles popular at the time.

This plate rack is similar to one designed by Gustav Stickley, the best-known furniture designer and manufacturer of the American Arts and Crafts period. Stickley's monthly magazine, *The Craftsman* (published from 1901 to 1916), featured plans for a similar plate

rack, but there's no evidence that Stickley actually manufactured this particular design.

1 Select the stock and cut the parts. Like most of Stickley's original Craftsman furniture, the plate rack shown is made from white oak. Red oak would work just as well.

You need ⅞-inch-thick stock for the posts and upper brackets, ¾-inch stock for the shelves and lower brackets, and ½-inch stock for the back panels and retaining rail. The 15¼-inch-wide lower back panel must be glued up from several narrow boards.

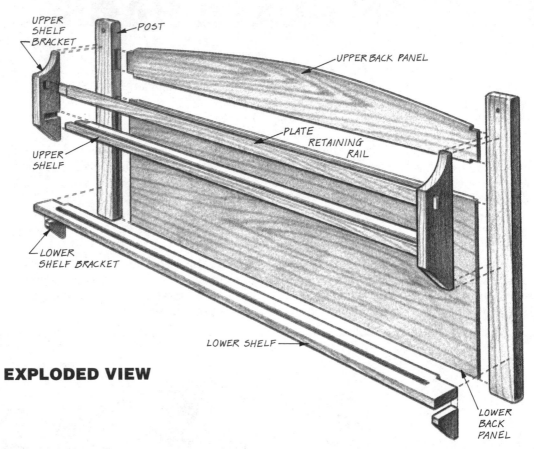

UPPER
SHELF
BRACKET

POST

UPPER BACK PANEL

PLATE RETAINING RAIL

UPPER SHELF

LOWER SHELF BRACKET

LOWER SHELF

LOWER BACK PANEL

EXPLODED VIEW

CUTTING LIST

Part	Quantity	Dimensions	Material
Posts	2	$\frac{7}{8}'' \times 2\frac{1}{2}'' \times 25''$	Oak
Lower back panel	1	$\frac{1}{2}'' \times 15\frac{1}{4}'' \times 44''$	Oak
Upper back panel	1	$\frac{1}{2}'' \times 5'' \times 44\frac{1}{2}''$	Oak
Plate retaining rail	1	$\frac{1}{2}'' \times 1\frac{1}{2}'' \times 47''$	Oak
Lower shelf brackets	2	$\frac{3}{4}'' \times 2\frac{1}{4}'' \times 2\frac{1}{4}''$	Oak
Upper shelf brackets	2	$\frac{7}{8}'' \times 2\frac{3}{4}'' \times 10\frac{1}{2}''$	Oak
Upper shelf	1	$\frac{3}{4}'' \times 2\frac{5}{8}'' \times 45\frac{1}{4}''$	Oak
Lower shelf	1	$\frac{3}{4}'' \times 3\frac{1}{8}'' \times 47''$	Oak

Hardware

12 flathead wood screws, #8 $\times$ $\frac{3}{4}''$

Select your stock and dress it. Then rip and cut the various parts to the dimensions specified by the Cutting List. Glue up the lower back panel.

2 **Make the posts.** The two back panels have ¼-inch-thick offset tenons that fit into mortises in the vertical posts. Cut the mortises in the posts as indicated in the *Side View*. Note that the top mortise should be ¾ inch deep, while the lower one is only ½ inch deep.

Be sure to produce a left post and a right post; they are mirror images, not duplicates, of one another.

3 **Make the back panels.** Remove the clamps from the lower back panel, which you glued up in Step 1. With a cabinet scraper, clean off any glue squeeze-out.

Cut the ¼-inch-thick offset tenons first. Probably the quickest way to do this is on the table saw. Set the rip fence

PLAN VIEWS

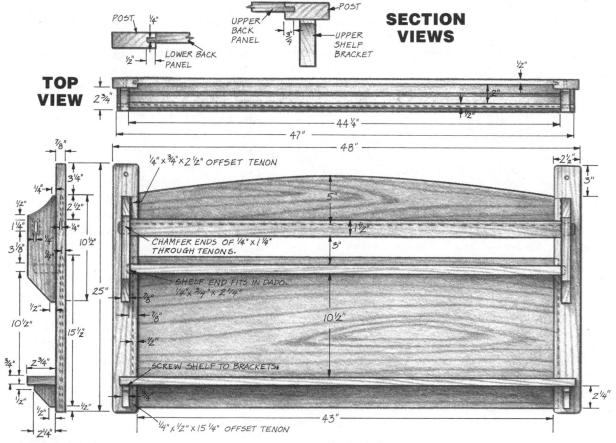

SECTION VIEWS

TOP VIEW

SIDE VIEW

FRONT VIEW

as a stop to control the length of the tenons. Using the miter gauge to guide the stock, make multiple cuts to remove the waste. Note that the upper panel is ½ inch longer than the lower panel. Therefore, the tenons on the upper panel are ¾ inch long, while those on the lower panel are only ½ inch long.

Lay out and cut the arc on the top of the upper panel. The panel is 5 inches wide at the middle and 3 inches wide at the ends. Mark these spots, then draw a fair curve connecting them. Cut the piece with a saber saw or on a band saw.

Finally, use a backsaw to trim ¼ inch from each end of the top panel's tenons, creating a shoulder and reducing the overall length of the tenon to 2½ inches.

SHOP TIP:
You can easily produce a fair curve, such as the one for the top back panel, using a strip of flexible material as a guide. Plastic laminate is good, as is a springy steel ruler or yardstick. Holding each of its ends between the thumb and index finger, position the strip on edge against the workpiece and flex it. When you form a curve you like that connects the appropriate high and low points, have a helper scribe the curve onto the workpiece.

4 **Tenon the plate retaining rail.** The plate retaining rail has ¼ × 1¼ × 1⅛-inch tenons on each end. Forming these tenons involves removing ⅛ inch of stock all around the rail.

Set up your table saw as you did to tenon the back panels, adjusting the fence and the depth of cut to produce a properly sized tenon. Finish the tenons by chamfering the ends with a sharp chisel, block plane, or smooth file.

SHOP TIP:
Because the very ends of the tenons are exposed, you probably will want to pare the saw marks off the tenon cheeks. To avoid having the tenons end up too small as a consequence, rough-cut them a tad over size. After you cut the mortises, pare the tenons for both appearance and fit.

5 **Make the shelf brackets.** The rack uses two different sets of shelf brackets. The lower ones are formed by mitering a corner from a ¾ × 2¼ × 2¼-inch block; see the *Side View*. For safety's sake, if you must use a power saw to make the miter, work with a strip of stock rather than with a block precut to the finished size.

The upper brackets, made of ⅞-inch stock, take more work. On the bracket blanks rough-cut in Step 1, lay out the blind dado for the shelf, the through mortise for the retaining rail, and the profile cuts at the top and bottom. The lower profile is a simple 45-degree miter. The upper profile is a freehand curve; you may want to lay out and cut one bracket, then use it as a template to lay out the second. Make sure you lay out the two brackets as mirror images, not as duplicates; you need a left and a right side.

Cut the blind dado using a dado cutter or a table-mounted router. Drill out the mortise. Square the corners of both with a chisel. Make the profile cuts with a saber saw or on a band saw.

6 **Make the shelves.** Both the upper and lower shelves are notched to fit around the posts. To get the best fit, you should assemble the back and posts without glue. To capture the length of the notch, set the shelves in position and mark their back edge where they intersect the posts. To capture the depth, rest the shelf against the back panel and butt its end against the post, then scribe along the post on the end of the shelf. Cut the notches with a backsaw or saber saw.

Cut the plate grooves next. Use a 3/8-inch core box bit (or a 3/8-inch straight bit) in a router. Position each groove about 1 1/8 inches from the front edge of the shelf. The groove in the upper shelf can be routed through, since the ends of the shelf are housed. The ends of the lower shelf are exposed, however, so you should terminate the groove about 1 to 1 1/2 inches short of the ends.

7 **Assemble the rack.** The four shelf brackets are fastened to the vertical posts with flathead screws. The back panels are not glued into their mortises, so that they're free to expand and contract across the grain without risk of splitting. What holds the assembly together are the shelves, which are attached to the posts with screws, and the plate rail, which is glued into the two upper brackets.

Before assembling the plate rack, test fit all the parts. Disassemble the rack and finish sand the parts.

Reassemble the rack, applying glue only to the tenons of the retaining rail. Clamp the assembly. Drill pilot holes for the screws through the backs of the posts into the brackets and shelves. Drive the screws.

8 **Finish the rack.** Stickley's original Craftsman oak furniture was finished by exposing the wood to concentrated ammonia vapors—a process known as fuming. The ammonia fumes react with the tannin in the oak to darken the wood.

Instead of fuming this plate rack, the wood was darkened with a brown aniline dye. You could also use a brown stain. After staining, dying, or fuming, an oil finish such as Minwax Antique Oil Finish or Watco comes close to duplicating the look of Stickley's original.

MUDROOM BOOT BENCH

Designed for storing wet boots and shoes out of sight but not out of reach, this sturdy boot bench is just the sort of thing you probably need to give your mudroom at least a semblance of neatness and order. It's an unusual and very practical item that makes a good intermediate woodworking project.

The cabinet is made from ¾-inch plywood—strong enough to sit on while putting on or removing footwear. The latticed doors and floorboards, designed especially to allow plenty of air circulation inside, are made from pine. The boot bench shown is painted with two coats of tough interior semigloss latex enamel over a coat of latex primer; the doors and floorboards are finished with polyurethane, for appearance as well as

for durability. The floorboards are raised not only to allow ventilation underneath but also to accommodate a shallow pan or an absorbent material like newspaper to catch water dripping from the articles inside. Both the floorboards and the doors are easy to remove when spring-cleaning time arrives.

Although this project looks complex, it really is not. The plywood cabinet's rabbeted and dadoed pieces are held together with glue and nails. The technique for cutting the doors' gridwork is very similar to that for cutting finger joints, an operation quickly and easily accomplished on the table saw.

Give yourself a couple of weekends to complete the bench—one to build it, one to paint it.

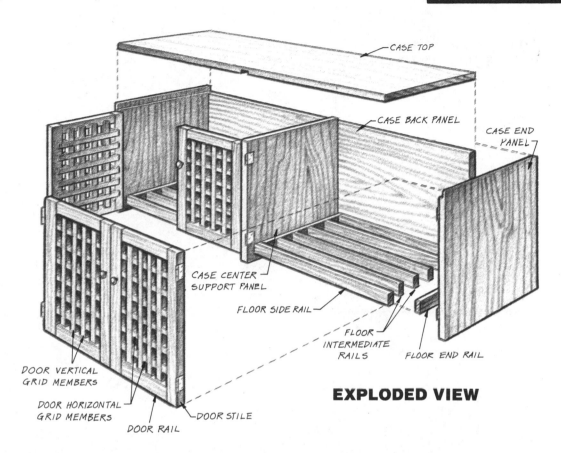

CASE TOP

CASE BACK PANEL

CASE END
PANEL

CASE CENTER
SUPPORT PANEL

FLOOR SIDE RAIL

FLOOR
INTERMEDIATE
RAILS

FLOOR END RAIL

DOOR VERTICAL
GRID MEMBERS

DOOR HORIZONTAL
GRID MEMBERS

DOOR RAIL

DOOR STILE

EXPLODED VIEW

1 Select the stock and cut the parts. The case of the boot bench is built from standard plywood. Buy a sheet with one good side. After cutting the case parts to the sizes specified by the Cutting List, you will have a good-sized piece left for your next plywood project. Although you may be tempted to cut *across* the sheet to make the parts, the case will be stronger if you take them from the length of the sheet—so that the grain of the face veneer parallels the longest dimension of each part.

The remaining parts of the boot bench are cut from #2 pine. This grade does have knots, but generally it costs half of what clear pine costs. In doing

your layout and cutting, try to work around knots that could weaken a part. Cut all the pine parts to the sizes specified by the Cutting List.

2 Build and paint the case. Along the top inside edge of each end panel, cut a ¾-inch-wide × ⅜-inch-deep rabbet for the top panel. Use a router or a table saw for this.

Rout or saw a ¾-inch-wide × ⅜-inch-deep dado along the underside of the top panel for the center support. Cut the dado across the width of the panel, down the centerline.

Glue and nail the ends and the center support panel to the top, making

187

SHOP TIP:

When cutting up full-sized sheets of plywood, it's easiest (and safest) to use a circular saw and this shop-built jig. You actually can make the jig using a strip of the plywood you've bought for this project. Then use the jig to cut the case parts.

To make the jig, rip the factory edge from a sheet of plywood; the strip you cut should be about 6 inches wide. Roll the just-cut strip onto the plywood as shown, align the cut edges, and glue and screw the strip to the sheet. Guiding the saw with the factory edge, cut the jig from the plywood sheet.

To use the jig, lay the plywood on a couple of expendable two-bys that are supported on sawhorses. Lay out the cut, align the edge of the jig with the cutting line, and cut as shown.

PLYWOOD-CUTTING JIG

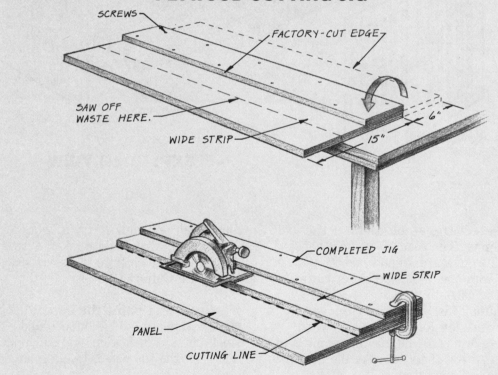

SCREWS

FACTORY-CUT EDGE

SAW OFF WASTE HERE.

WIDE STRIP

6"

15"

COMPLETED JIG

WIDE STRIP

PANEL

CUTTING LINE

sure that the front edges of each panel are flush with the front edge of the top. Then glue and nail the back panel into place. Use white or yellow glue and 6d finishing nails. Clamps are not required when using nails as well as glue.

To make finishing easier, sand, fill, and paint the plywood assembly now, then set it aside while you complete the remaining steps. The bench shown is finished with one coat of primer and two coats of interior semigloss latex enamel.

CUTTING LIST

Part	Quantity	Dimensions	Material
Case			
End panels	2	¾" × 16" × 18"	AC plywood
Top	1	¾" × 16" × 47¼"	AC plywood
Center support panel	1	¾" × 15¼" × 17⅝"	AC plywood
Back panel	1	¾" × 16¼" × 46½"	AC plywood
Floor			
Side rails	4	¾" × 1½" × 22⅞"	#2 pine
Intermediate rails	8	¾" × 1½" × 21⅜"	#2 pine
End rails	4	¾" × 1½" × 12⅝"	#2 pine
Doors			
Rails	8	¾" × 1½" × 11⅜"	#2 pine
Stiles	8	¾" × 1½" × 16¼"	#2 pine
Horizontal grid	24	¾" × ¾" × 9⅞"	#2 pine
Vertical grid	16	¾" × ¾" × 14¾"	#2 pine

Hardware

8 flathead wood screws, #6 × 1¼"   4 magnetic cabinet catches
4 pairs loose-pin hinges, 1½" × 1½"   6d finishing nails
4 wooden knobs, 1" dia.   4d finishing nails

3 Build and install the floor. Glue and nail together the floor section pieces, using white or yellow glue and 4d finishing nails. Clamps are not needed. Sand the floor sections, and finish them with two coats of polyurethane before installing them.

Drill pilot holes through each completed floor section into the ends and center panel of the plywood case. Using four 1¼-inch screws per section, attach the floor to the case.

4 Make the door frames. The rails and stiles that form the door frames are joined with half-laps. Cut half-lap joints on the ends of each rail and stile.

Cut the laps using a dado cutter mounted in the table saw. Use the rip fence to control the length of the lap, and guide the frame pieces with the miter gauge as you cut.

Glue and clamp each frame. Make sure the frame is square and flat as you clamp it. Spring clamps are usually adequate for clamping half-lap joints.

5 Build and install the door grids. The most complex elements of the boot bench project are the half-lapped grid members that make up each cabinet door. The notches in these members must be cut quite accurately and uniformly if the parts are to fit together and their appearance is to be neat.

Cut the notches almost as if you were making finger joints. Read the instructions for "Cutting Finger Joints" on

PLAN VIEWS

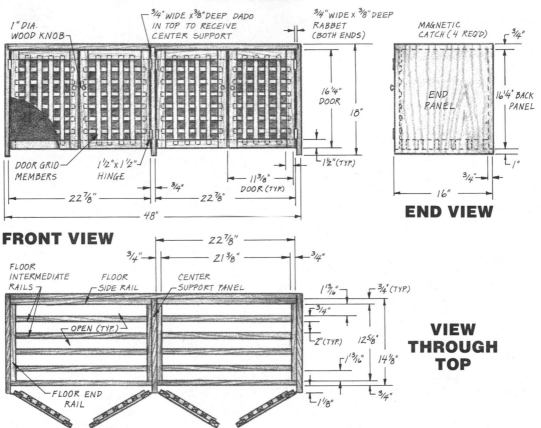

1" DIA. WOOD KNOB

3/4" WIDE x 3/8" DEEP DADO IN TOP TO RECEIVE CENTER SUPPORT

3/4" WIDE x 3/8" DEEP RABBET (BOTH ENDS)

MAGNETIC CATCH (4 REQ'D)

3/4"

16 1/4" DOOR

18"

END PANEL

16 1/4" BACK PANEL

DOOR GRID MEMBERS

1 1/2" x 1 1/2" HINGE

3/4"

1 1/2" (TYP.)

11 3/8" DOOR (TYP.)

22 7/8"

22 7/8"

48"

3/4"

16"

1"

END VIEW

FRONT VIEW

22 7/8"

3/4"

21 3/8"

3/4"

FLOOR INTERMEDIATE RAILS

FLOOR SIDE RAIL

CENTER SUPPORT PANEL

OPEN (TYP.)

1 13/16"

3/4" (TYP.)

3/4"

2" (TYP.)

12 5/8"

1 13/16"

14 1/8"

1 1/8"

3/4"

VIEW THROUGH TOP

FLOOR END RAIL

page 40, then study the *Door Grid Detail* to determine the size and spacing of the notches. The difference between finger joints and the door grids is the disparity in size between the notches and the dentils. In a finger joint, the notches and the dentils are the same width; in the door grids, the dentils are wider than the notches. Therefore, when making the jigs, measure and lay out their second notches to get the proper spacing. Because the notch spacing on the vertical pieces is different from that on the horizontals, you have to make separate jigs.

The horizontals can be notched as shown on the opposite page.

The verticals are a little different. Begin by cutting a ¾-inch-wide × ⅜-inch-deep rabbet on the ends of each piece. Then cut the first notch in each piece before fitting the jig in place. Set up the rip fence to locate this notch, and guide the workpiece over the cutter with the miter gauge. After so notching each vertical, screw the jig to the miter gauge and cut the rest of the notches.

Assemble each of the four grid sections by joining four verticals and six

SHOP TIP:

In cutting laps, the trick is getting the table saw's depth of cut just right, so that the joint fits precisely when assembled.

Try this: Roughly set the depth of cut, using a rule. Nip a corner of a scrap piece taken from the working stock. Roll the piece over, and nip the opposite corner so that the two cuts intersect. By looking at the end of the piece where the cuts intersect, you can tell how you need to adjust the depth of cut. Adjust the setting, then try again on a new scrap.

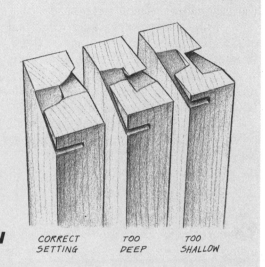

SETTING THE SAW FOR LAPPING

CORRECT SETTING   TOO DEEP   TOO SHALLOW

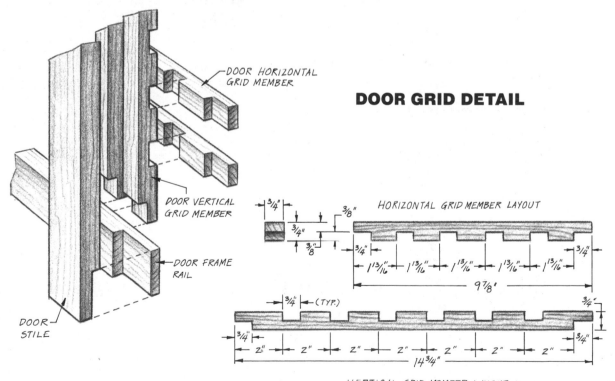

DOOR HORIZONTAL GRID MEMBER

DOOR VERTICAL GRID MEMBER

DOOR FRAME RAIL

DOOR STILE

DOOR GRID DETAIL

HORIZONTAL GRID MEMBER LAYOUT

VERTICAL GRID MEMBER LAYOUT

horizontals. Glue the pieces, clamping the assembly between scrap blocks of lumber and a plywood backing. Glue and clamp the finished grid sections to the finished frames next. The rabbeted ends of the grid pieces should be glued to the undersides of the frames (the underside is where the rails overlap the stiles).

Sand the four completed doors and finish them with polyurethane, as you did the floors. Apply polyurethane to each of the four wooden knobs, too.

6 Hang the doors. The doors are flush-mounted, meaning that they fit inside the case, their faces flush with the edges of the case. First make sure the doors fit. Plane them down a bit, if necessary.

Using a hinge leaf as a pattern, lay out the hinge mortises on the edges of the doors. Line up the hinges with the seams of the half-lap joints, as indicated in the *Front View*. Cut the mortises with a chisel, then screw the hinge leaves in

place. With the case upside down on its top, set the doors in place, and mark the hinge locations in the case. Lay out and cut mortises in the case sides, then install the hinges. Right the case and install the doors.

After the doors are hung, drill a single hole in each of the door frames and attach the knobs. Line up the knobs with each other, parallel to the boot bench's top edge.

To complete the bench, install magnetic cabinet catches on the underside of the bench top. First attach the small metal plates to the doors, then loosely install the magnets on the bench top, adjusting them for a perfect fit.

SHOP TIP: Here's a
nickel's worth of free advice. When fitting flush doors into a cabinet, use nickels (or for a closer fit, dimes) as shims. They're uniform in thickness, and you usually have a couple in your pocket.

PINE BOOKCASE

Styled in the popular country pine vein, this practical bookcase is sturdy and versatile. The four shelves rest on

plastic pins, allowing you to move them to accommodate books, collectibles, or, as the photo demonstrates, a variety of items that you want to display in an orderly fashion.

The bookcase can be anchored to a wall by driving screws through the top cleat into wall studs, but it can also be left freestanding.

Here is the quintessential weekend project. It's made from #2 pine, available at any home center or lumberyard. The joinery is standard, yet runs well beyond mere butt joints. Construction requires only basic tools—router, circular saw, saber saw, drill, and hand tools.

1 **Select the stock and cut the parts.** This is the prototypical bookcase, and the character you envision for the finished piece must influence your choice of stock. If you have a refined bookcase in mind, choose a hardwood with limited defects and attractive figure. If you picture a "comfortable" bookcase, then select pine. A painted bookcase can be built from pine or poplar.

Having selected your stock, cut the parts to the sizes specified by the Cutting List.

2 **Make the sides.** The sides must be rabbeted for the top, dadoed for the bottom, and bored for the shelf support pins.

Across the top of each side, cut a ¾-inch-wide × ⅜-inch-deep rabbet using a router and a straight bit. Cut both sides at the same time by clamping the two pieces together, edge-to-edge. Then

193

EXPLODED VIEW

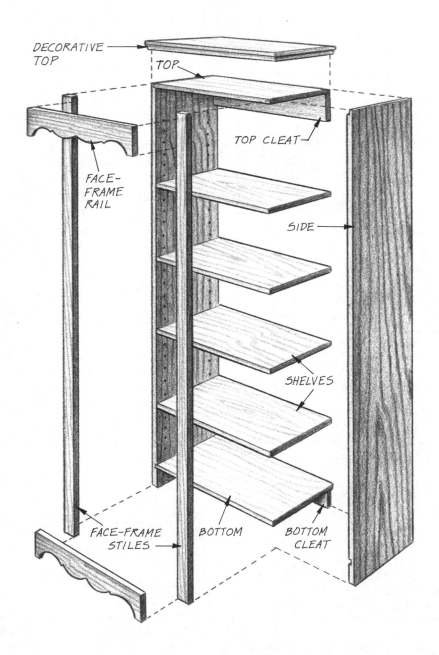

DECORATIVE
TOP

TOP

TOP CLEAT

FACE-
FRAME
RAIL

SIDE

SHELVES

FACE-FRAME
STILES

BOTTOM

BOTTOM
CLEAT

CUTTING LIST

Part	Quantity	Dimensions	Material
Sides	2	$\frac{3}{4}'' \times 11\frac{1}{8}'' \times 71''$	#2 pine
Top and bottom	2	$\frac{3}{4}'' \times 11\frac{1}{8}'' \times 25\frac{3}{8}''$	#2 pine
Top cleat	1	$\frac{3}{4}'' \times 4\frac{1}{2}'' \times 24\frac{5}{8}''$	#2 pine
Bottom cleat	1	$\frac{3}{4}'' \times 3\frac{1}{8}'' \times 24\frac{5}{8}''$	#2 pine
Face-frame rails	2	$\frac{3}{4}'' \times 3\frac{7}{8}'' \times 22\frac{1}{8}''$	#2 pine
Face-frame stiles	2	$\frac{3}{4}'' \times 2'' \times 71''$	#2 pine
Decorative top	1	$1\frac{3}{16}'' \times 12\frac{1}{2}'' \times 27\frac{5}{16}''$	#2 pine
Shelves	4	$\frac{3}{4}'' \times 10\frac{15}{16}'' \times 24\frac{7}{16}''$	#2 pine

Hardware

4–6 flathead wood screws, #8 $\times$ 1½"
16 shelf support pins
8d common nails
8d finishing nails

position and clamp a straightedge across them to serve as a router guide. After cutting the rabbets, reposition the router guide and cut the dadoes for the bottom. Make both these cuts in two or three passes, increasing the depth of cut by about ⅛ inch with each pass until the required depth is reached.

The next task is to lay out and bore

SHOP TIP: Pegboard is a great layout guide for ranks of support holes. The holes in pegboard are located on a 1-inch grid. Clamp an 11-inch-wide strip of pegboard atop the bookcase side, and drill through the appropriate holes. Your holes will be in perfect alignment with one another.

SHOP TIP: Experienced woodworkers usually counsel beginners against using construction-grade material in furniture projects, rightly pointing out that it is dried only to 30 percent moisture content; in comparison, cabinet- or furniture-grade stock is dried to 7 or 8 percent moisture content. A project like this bookcase, however, has no glued-up panels, no doors or drawers, no intricate joinery. Standard one-by #2 pine is satisfactory; we used it in building the bookcase shown in the photo.

the holes for the shelf support pins as shown in the *Side Layout*. The horizontal alignment of the holes is more important to shelf stability than their vertical alignment. Snap or scribe lines the length of the sides, 2 inches from each edge. Use dividers or a compass to step off the placement of the holes. If you are using a hand-held drill equipped with a Porta-lign guide (or some variant), clamp a fence across the two sides to help you align the holes. Be careful that you don't drill all the way through the boards.

PLAN VIEWS

27⁵/₁₆" 1³/₁₆" 3⁷/₈" 2" 72³/₁₆" 71" 22¹/₈" 26¹/₈" 4¹/₈" 3/4"

12¹/₂" 11¹/₈"

1³/₁₆" 3/4" 4¹/₂" 3/4" 3¹/₈"

FRONT VIEW   **SIDE VIEW**   **BACK VIEW**

1/2" 1³/₁₆"

TOP EDGE DETAIL

SIDE LAYOUT

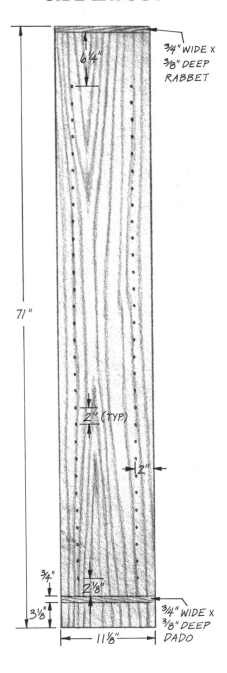

3/4" WIDE X
3/8" DEEP
RABBET

6¼"

71"

2" (TYP.)

2"

3/4"

2⅛"

3⅛"

11⅛"

3/4" WIDE X
3/8" DEEP
DADO

3 **Assemble the case.** The basic case—sides, top and bottom, and cleats—is assembled using glue and nails. You can drive common nails through the top and bottom into the sides; in the bottom, you must angle the nails judiciously—enough to catch the side, but not so much that they break through. Glue and nail the cleats in place, driving common nails through the top and finishing nails through the sides and bottom. Countersink the finishing nails and fill the holes with wood putty. Check the assembly with a framing square or a try square.

4 **Cut the profile of the rails.** Enlarge the pattern for the profile of the face-frame rails, and make a template of cardboard. Bear in the mind that the pattern is for half the overall profile; you must trace the template on one half of a rail, then turn it over and trace it on the other half. Lay out both rails, then cut them out with a saber saw. Use a drum sander chucked in a drill to sand away the saw marks on the edges of the rails.

5 **Install the face frame.** The individual pieces of the face frame are attached to the bookcase, but not to each other. Check the bookcase one last

RAIL PATTERN

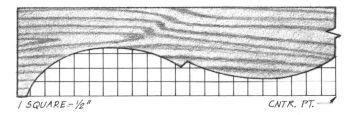

I SQUARE = ½"   CNTR. PT.

197

time to ensure that it is square. Then using glue and finishing nails, join the stiles and rails to the front edges of the bookcase. Countersink the nails and fill the holes with wood putty.

6 **Make and install the decorative top.** The decorative top overlays the structural top and projects beyond the bookcase on the front and sides. It has a Roman ogee profile cut into these edges. Because you must glue up boards to get the necessary width, you should use cabinet-grade stock for this part. Have it milled to the proper thickness, then joint the edges and glue up narrow pieces to achieve the necessary width. After the glue dries, plane and/or sand the top smooth and flat.

With a router and 5/8-inch Roman ogee bit, machine the top's front and side edges.

Install the top with four to six screws, driven from inside the bookcase, penetrating through the structural top into the decorative one.

7 **Apply a finish.** Sand the entire bookcase, including the loose shelves. Apply your choice of finish. We stained our bookcase, then applied two coats of polyurethane varnish.

NEW ENGLAND PINE CUPBOARD

During the last century, cupboards like this one were common in kitchens across the land. Jelly cupboards, as they are called, provided space for canned goods and other foods that would be kept for long periods of time. They didn't need punched tin panels for air circulation, as did pie safes, so their doors were often of frame-and-panel construction.

Jelly cupboards came in all shapes and sizes and were made from whatever wood was available. The cupboard shown here, a reproduction of a New England-style cupboard, was built by Fred Matlack of the Rodale Press Design Group. It's made from pine, with three shelves inside. Placed in your kitchen, dining room, or anywhere around the home, it will fit right in with your country antiques. It would be easy to scale the dimensions of the cupboard larger or smaller to fit a particular space in your home.

The most challenging joinery in the piece is a basic mortise and tenon. The face frame is mortise-and-tenoned together, as are the door frames. But the frame is simply nailed to the sides of the cupboard, as is the top.

The primary embellishment is a bead groove routed into the front edges of the shelves and the outside corners of the face frame. The inside perimeter of each door frame also is decorated with a bead groove to provide a contrast with the simple, flat panel inside it. The bead-

ing work was done using a ⁵⁄₁₆-inch edge beading bit (available from MLCS Ltd., P.O. Box 4053 C2, Rydal, PA 19046) chucked in a table-mounted router. The bit is piloted, so a fence is unneeded.

EXPLODED VIEW

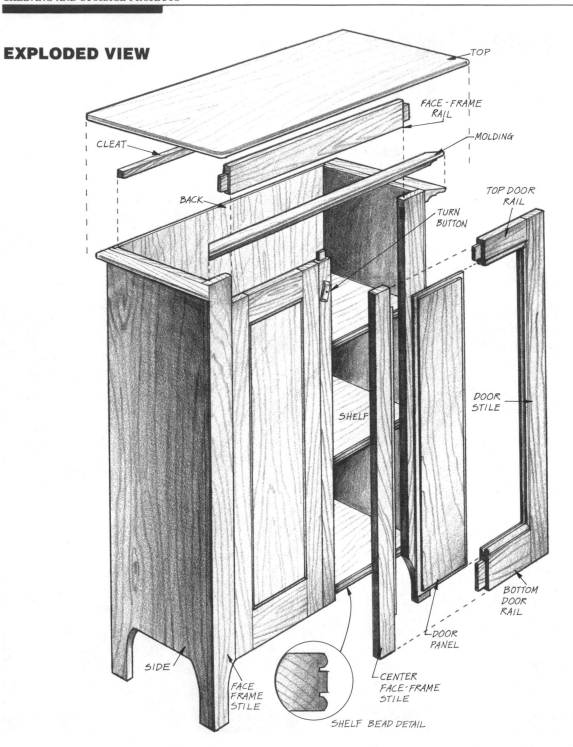

TOP

FACE - FRAME RAIL

MOLDING

CLEAT

BACK

TURN BUTTON

TOP DOOR RAIL

DOOR STILE

SHELF

SIDE

FACE FRAME STILE

CENTER FACE-FRAME STILE

DOOR PANEL

BOTTOM DOOR RAIL

SHELF BEAD DETAIL

CUTTING LIST

Part	Quantity	Dimensions	Material
Sides	2	$3/4'' \times 11'' \times 41\frac{1}{4}''$	Pine
Shelves	3	$3/4'' \times 10\frac{3}{4}'' \times 27\frac{3}{4}''$	Pine
Back	1	$1/4'' \times 27\frac{3}{4}'' \times 35\frac{3}{4}''$	Pine
Face-frame rail	1	$3/4'' \times 2\frac{1}{2}'' \times 24\frac{3}{4}''$	Pine
Center face-frame stile	1	$3/4'' \times 1\frac{1}{2}'' \times 34\frac{3}{16}''$	Pine
Face-frame stiles	2	$3/4'' \times 2\frac{7}{8}'' \times 41\frac{1}{4}''$	Pine
Top	1	$3/4'' \times 13\frac{1}{2}'' \times 32''$	Pine
Cleat	1	$3/4'' \times 3/4'' \times 27''$	Pine
Crown molding	1	$3/4'' \times 1\frac{1}{4}'' \times 65''$	Pine
Door stiles	2	$3/4'' \times 2\frac{1}{4}'' \times 33\frac{1}{8}''$	Pine
Bottom door rails	2	$3/4'' \times 4'' \times 8\frac{5}{8}''$	Pine
Top door rails	2	$3/4'' \times 2\frac{13}{16}'' \times 8\frac{5}{8}''$	Pine
Door panels	2	$3/4'' \times 6\frac{5}{8}'' \times 26\frac{7}{8}''$	Pine
Turn button	1	$1/2'' \times 3/4'' \times 2\frac{1}{2}''$	Pine

Hardware

1 brass roundhead wood screw, #6 $\times$ $1\frac{1}{4}''$
2 pairs brass hinges, $1\frac{1}{2}''$ $\times$ $1\frac{1}{2}''$
2 porcelain knobs. Available from Paxton Hardware, 7818 Bradshaw Rd., Upper Falls, MD 21156.
6d finishing nails

1 Select the stock and cut the parts. The cupboard's construction is simple and straightforward. All the lumber is ¾ inch thick, meaning that it is common lumberyard stock. As you can see in the photo, Fred used common-grade #2 pine, knots and all. The back is a piece of ¼-inch plywood, but you could make the back from ship-lapped or tongue-and-groove boards for a more authentic approach.

After selecting your materials, cut the parts to the sizes specified by the Cutting List. Don't cut the crown molding, however; it should be cut to fit as it is installed. While knots and defects can add to the appearance of the piece, be sure none are large enough or positioned such that they'll weaken the cupboard.

2 Build the carcase. Start construction with the sides. Lay out the feet as shown in the *Side View*, and mark the locations of the dadoes for the shelves. With a router and ¾-inch straight bit, cut ⅜-inch-deep dadoes. If you clamp the sides edge-to-edge on the workbench, you can rout the dadoes in both sides with a single pass, ensuring that they'll line up perfectly. Switch to a ¼-inch rabbeting bit, and rout a ⅜-inch-deep rabbet in the back edge of each side, extending from the bottom dado to the top. Finally, cut the feet with a saber saw or on the band saw.

Bead the shelves next. With a ⁵⁄₁₆-inch edge beading bit in a table-mounted router, cut a bead on the top and bottom front edges of the shelves; see the Shelf

PLAN VIEWS

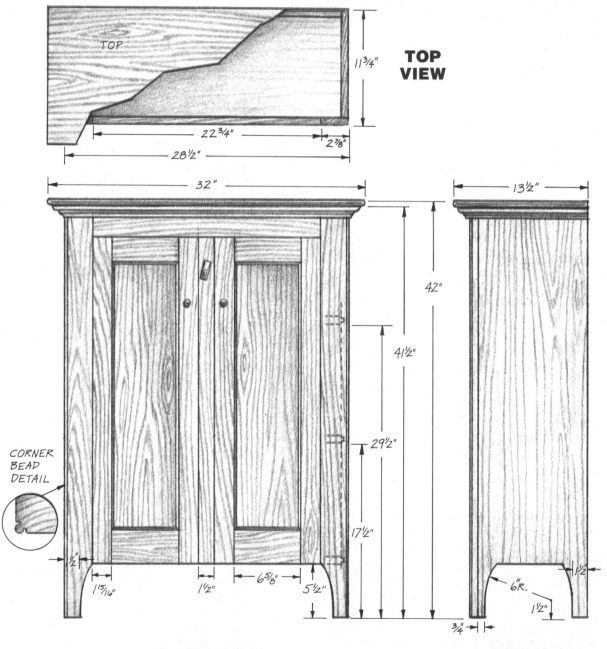

**TOP
VIEW**

TOP

11³/₄"

22³/₄"

2⁷/₈"

28¹/₂"

32"

42"

41¹/₂"

29¹/₂"

17¹/₂"

CORNER
BEAD
DETAIL

¹/₂"

1¹⁵/₁₆"

1¹/₂"

6⁵/₈"

5¹/₂"

FRONT VIEW

13¹/₂"

6"R.

1¹/₂"

1¹/₂"

³/₄"

SIDE VIEW

Bead Detail of the *Exploded View*.

Assemble the carcase. Glue and nail the shelves and sides together; keep the shelves flush with the front edges of the sides. When you add the back, it should square up the assembly for you.

3 **Build and install the face frame.** The face frame of the cupboard consists of two vertical stiles and a center stile, spanned by a rail at the top. The rail is tenoned on both ends, the center stile on one end only. Rough out the tenons on the table saw, forming a ⅜-inch-thick × 1-inch-long tenon ex-

tending the width of the piece. Finish the center stile's tenon by trimming ¼ inch of stock from each end, reducing the tenon to a 1-inch width. Finish the rail tenons by trimming ¾ inch from the top and ¼ inch from the bottom, reducing the width of the tenons to 1½ inches. Use a backsaw to trim the tenons.

Turn your attention to the outer stiles next. With the 5/16-inch edge beading bit, rout a bead along one edge of each stile. This will be the front outside edge when the frame is assembled. To get the three-quarters-round bead (see the Corner Bead Detail of the *Front*

SHOP TIP: Jelly cupboards like this were often built with hand-forged nails. If you like the rustic look of the old fasteners, take a few moments to "customize" the head of each 6d finishing nail to simulate the hand-forged look. Simply lay the side of the nailhead on a vise, and flatten two oppo-

site sides with a ball peen hammer. The steel nails are surprisingly malleable. Then grip the nail's shank in the vise, with the top of the head protruding just over the jaws. Flatten two top faces with the hammer, then the two opposite faces. That's it—centuries-old nails in an instant.

NAIL DETAIL

FLATTEN TWO SIDES OF FINISHING NAIL.

FLATTEN TWO TOP FACES.

FLATTEN TWO OPPOSITE TOP FACES.

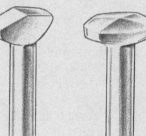

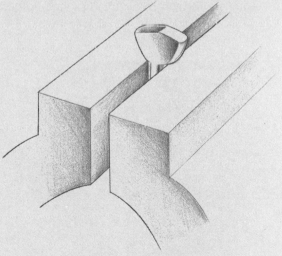

STEP 1   **STEP 2**   **STEP 3**

View), you must rout the edge twice: first with the stile's face on the router table, then with the stile's edge on the router table. Lay out and cut the feet at the bottom of these stiles.

Lay out and cut the mortises to complete the face-frame joinery. Use a ⅜-inch-diameter bit in a drill press (or in a portable drill equipped with a drill guide) to rough out each mortise. Square the corners and sides with a chisel. Pare the mortises and tenons to fit.

Finally, glue up the face frame, then glue and nail it to the carcase.

4 Add the top. Soften the edge of the top with a gentle bullnose. To do this, use a ¾-inch rounding-over bit in a router, but set it for only a ⅜-inch depth of cut. Rout only the front and side edges, not the back edge.

Next nail the cleat to the underside of the top, then nail the top to the carcase. Drive a few nails through the back into the cleat.

Complete the installation by attaching the crown molding. Although you can mill your own molding if you have a

SHOP TIP: The crown molding is a little easier to miter accurately if you set it in your miter box upside down and backwards. In other words, hold the molding in the miter box just as it will fit on the cupboard, except the edge of the molding that contacts the cupboard top should seat on the bottom of the box, and the edge that contacts the cupboard's side (or face frame) should seat against the box's back. Then make the appropriate cut.

shaper, it is easier to use a ready-made profile purchased at a lumberyard.

5 Make the rails and stiles for the doors. First lay out the mortises in the stiles as indicated in the *Door Detail*. Note that the bottom door rail is wider than the top door rail. Cut the mortises.

Next, with the same edge beading bit as before, rout a bead on the inside edges of the stiles and rails.

Plow a ¼-inch-wide groove along the inside of the stiles and rails to accept the door panel. If this groove were centered, it would come too close to the bead groove, weakening the attachment of the bead. So offset the panel groove toward the inside of the door, as shown in the *Door Detail*. You can cut the groove with two passes on a table saw, with a table-mounted router, or on a shaper.

The beads along the inside edge of the stiles and rails are mitered together where they meet. Mark the locations of the miters at the inside corners of the door frames. Make the 45-degree miter across the beads. On each stile, remove part of the bead by cutting straight down the bead groove from the end of each stile to the miter. (It's not necessary to cut part of the bead from the rails, because making the rail tenons will remove that whole area.) Fred Matlack made both the miters and the bead-removal cuts freehand on a band saw.

Finally, cut the tenons on the rails. You can rough them on the table saw and trim the extremities with a backsaw. Then individually fit the tenons into their respective mortises, paring as necessary with a chisel.

DOOR DETAIL

OFFSET GROOVE TOWARD INSIDE.

2 $\frac{13}{16}$"

$\frac{3}{4}$"

$1\frac{9}{16}$"

1"

$\frac{5}{16}$"

$\frac{1}{2}$"

$\frac{3}{16}$"

$\frac{5}{16}$"

2 $\frac{1}{4}$"

$1\frac{5}{16}$"

$\frac{1}{2}$"

MITER BEADS AT INSIDE CORNERS.

4"

1"

2 $\frac{3}{4}$"

$\frac{3}{4}$"

SECTION VIEW

6 **Assemble and install the doors.**
Prepare each door panel for assembly by making a ¼-inch-wide tongue

around its perimeter, either on the table saw or using a router and ¼-inch rabbeting bit. Be sure to offset the tongue so that it matches the offset groove in the door frame.

Assemble the door frames and panels, but don't get any glue into the panel groove.

Mount the doors with the brass hinges, locating the top hinges just below the top rail and the bottom hinges just above the bottom rail. Install the porcelain knobs. To keep the doors closed, make a turn button and fasten it to the center stile with a brass roundhead wood screw.

7 **Apply a finish.** Many of the old jelly cupboards were painted. Fred Matlack finished his cupboard with an oil stain followed by a coat of sanding sealer, which gives a natural, nongloss appearance.

DISPLAY CABINET

It seems a part of human nature to put things on display. This sliding-door wall cabinet makes a perfect showcase for collectibles—fine china, art objects, even well-preserved antique tools. The lines of the cabinet are clean and simple, and the full-width shelves can be adjusted to accommodate your treasures.

The cabinet was designed and built by Pat Warner, a Californian whose specialty is router woodworking. "I prefer to do almost all my joinery with a hand-held router," Warner says, explaining that he likes "the way a router lets me work to fine tolerances, which gives me the accuracy I want in my work."

This cabinet is typical of his woodworking style. In building it, he made use of several shop-made jigs and templates. "I also use a number of different router bit and pilot bearing combinations that you won't find in a router bit catalog," Warner adds. "For example, you won't find a dovetail bit with a pilot bearing in any catalog. There's no great mystery here. I buy the bearings and bits separately, and simply press the bearing on the bit's shaft above the cutters to meet my needs."

The construction is designed for strength. The corners of the case are joined with a half-dovetail rabbet joint

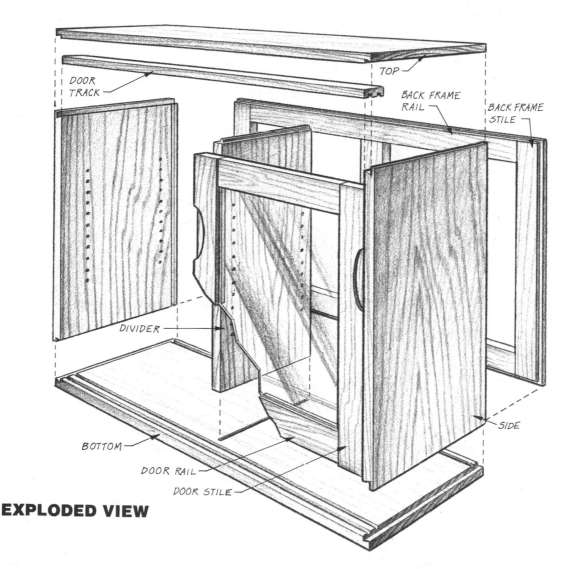

DOOR TRACK

TOP

BACK FRAME RAIL

BACK FRAME STILE

DIVIDER

SIDE

BOTTOM

DOOR RAIL

DOOR STILE

EXPLODED VIEW

that Warner developed especially for casework. Whether screwed or glued together, this joint has proven to be strong. Warner cuts the joint with a router and the help of some shop-built fixtures. (See "Routing a Half-Dovetail Rabbet Joint" on page 214.) The cabinet has a frame but no back panels; "I think the view through the glass doors to a flat, off-white wall lends an air of lightness," Warner explains.

The sliding glass doors are especially intriguing. In most cabinet doors, the glass is held in place by a tacked-on wooden molding, but in these, the glass is captured in grooves routed in the stiles and rails. The top rail is removable, so it's easy to replace the glass.

CUTTING LIST

Part	Quantity	Dimensions	Material
Top	1	$^{11}\!/_{16}'' \times 10^{3}\!/_{4}'' \times 29^{9}\!/_{16}''$	Ash
Bottom	1	$^{11}\!/_{16}'' \times 10^{3}\!/_{4}'' \times 29^{9}\!/_{16}''$	Ash
Sides	2	$^{11}\!/_{16}'' \times 10^{3}\!/_{4}'' \times 20^{5}\!/_{8}''$	Ash
Divider	1	$^{11}\!/_{16}'' \times 8^{5}\!/_{16}'' \times 19^{5}\!/_{8}''$ *	Ash
Back frame stiles	3	$^{3}\!/_{4}'' \times 2^{1}\!/_{4}'' \times 19^{5}\!/_{8}''$ *	Ash
Back frame rails	2	$^{3}\!/_{4}'' \times 2^{1}\!/_{4}'' \times 25^{7}\!/_{16}''$ *	Ash
Shelves	4	$^{5}\!/_{8}'' \times 8^{3}\!/_{16}'' \times 13^{7}\!/_{8}''$ *	Ash
Door stiles	4	$^{3}\!/_{4}'' \times 2^{1}\!/_{16}'' \times 18^{1}\!/_{2}''$	Ash
Door rails	4	$^{11}\!/_{16}'' \times 2^{5}\!/_{16}'' \times 11^{3}\!/_{16}''$	Ash
Door track	1	$^{23}\!/_{32}'' \times 1^{5}\!/_{8}'' \times 28^{9}\!/_{16}''$ *	Ash

Hardware

#8 × 1½" flathead wood screws

Twin-threaded drywall screws, #8 × 3". Available from Cabinet Maker Supplies, 12700 N.E. 124th St., Kirkland, WA 98034; (206) 822-8242.

Twin-threaded drywall screws, #8 × 2". Available from Cabinet Maker Supplies.

16 brass shelf hangers

2 pieces double-strength door glass, 11" × 14⅞"

* Nominal dimensions given; measure inside of case to size parts for your cabinet.

The doors slide in tracks, top and bottom. The bottom track is routed in the cabinet bottom, but the top track is a separate piece. This makes for a tight-fitting door and eliminates the up and down movement common to most sliding-door cabinets.

The cabinet shown here is screwed together, not glued, so that it can easily be knocked down for moving. Just as easily, you can glue the joints permanently.

1 Select the stock and cut the case parts. Warner made the cabinet shown from white ash and left it unfinished. He likes the brilliant "in-the-white" look of this wood. You can make your cabinet from whatever cabinet-quality wood you like (or have on hand). As always, you want straight, flat stock without knots.

Since you'll make the case first, begin by cutting the parts for this element. Glue up stock for the top, bottom, and sides. Leave the center divider a bit long, but rip it to 8⁵⁄₁₆ inches wide. Warner edge-glued the stock with a ³⁄₁₆-inch-square tongue-and-groove joint, though butt joints will work.

2 Cut the case joinery. First cut the half-dovetail rabbet joints for the corners of the case as shown in the Corner Joint Detail of the *Front View*. Warner developed some handy router acces-

PLAN VIEWS

CORNER JOINT DETAIL

11/16"

3/16"   3/16"

1/2"

11/16"

TOP TRACK DETAIL

#8 x 1 1/4" SCREWS

23/32"

11/16"

9/32"   1 3/32"

1 5/8"

ROUT 3/16" SQ. SLOT.

SECTION VIEW

3/4"

8 5/16"

7 3/8"

11/16"

14 3/8"

1"

4 3/8"

10 3/4"

REAR SLOT DETAIL

9/32"

ROUT 3/16" SQ. SLOT.

BOTTOM TRACK DETAIL

1 5/32"

11/32"

ROUT 3/16" SQ. SLOT.

FRONT VIEW

19 1/4"

20 5/8"

11/16"   11/16"

13 15/16"

ROUT 3/8" x 3/16" DADO.

29 9/16"

29 15/16"

sories and a special jig for making the joint, which are explained in "Routing a Half-Dovetail Rabbet Joint" on page 214.

Once you've completed the corner joinery, rout a slot in the rear inside faces of the top, sides, and bottom to receive the tongue of the back frame. Although you can do this with a 3/16-inch straight bit and an edge guide, Warner used a 3/16-inch slotting cutter that cuts a 3/16-inch-deep slot and his right-angle jig.

(The cutter, a Paso Robles Carbide #TA-293K3, is available from The Woodworks, 14007 Midland Road, Poway, CA 92064; 619-748-4363.) At the same time and using the same technique, rout the 3/16-inch-square slots in the inside face of the cabinet bottom for the bottom door tracks (see the Bottom Track Detail of the *Section View*).

Next rout the 3/8-inch-wide × 3/16-inch-deep stopped dadoes in the center of the top and bottom for the divider. Cut the dadoes 8⅛ inches long, measured from the rear slot toward the front. Clamp a fence across the pieces, and rout the dadoes with a ⅜-inch straight bit.

3 **Fit the divider into the case.** Clamp the case together without glue, and measure the length and height of the inside to determine the correct dimensions for the divider and back frame. These measurements are critical for a good fit. When you have them, add ⅜ inch to the length and height to get the overall dimensions for the back frame (including the 3⁄16-inch tongue) and divider. Cut the divider to length, and machine the tongues to fit the dadoes.

4 **Drill the shelf-hanger holes.** Lay out and drill the shelf-hanger holes in the divider and sides so that the holes are 1 inch on center, as shown in the *Section View*. Warner used L-shaped brass hangers with ¼-inch-diameter × ⅜-inch-long studs, but you can use another configuration.

SHOP TIP: It's a good idea to stack the top, bottom, and sides of the cabinet on stickers to prevent these parts from warping while you make the back frame and doors.

5 **Make the back frame.** As mentioned, the back is an open frame (though you could easily use solid panels if you prefer). Size the stiles and rails according to the inside case dimensions.

Be sure to make allowances for the rail tenons and the tongue around the perimeter of the frame. The procedure is to assemble the frame, then cut a 3⁄16-inch-square tongue around the outer edge.

The outer stiles are joined to the rails by mortise-and-tenon joints as shown in the Tenon Detail of the *Back Frame Construction*. Lay out and cut the mortises. Then cut the tenons on both rails at the same time; clamp the rails together, edge-to-edge, and remove the wood with a fence-guided router. Machine one face, turn the rails, reclamp them, rout the next face, and so on until the tenons are formed.

The center stile of the back frame joins the top and bottom rails in half-laps. Rout the laps in the rails, then on both ends of the center stile, following the same basic method you used to cut the tenons.

Glue up the back frame. When it's dry, rout a centered, 3⁄16-inch-square tongue around the perimeter of the frame.

6 **Assemble the case.** Sand all the parts before assembly. The case can be screwed together (as is this one) for knockdown capability, or it can be glued. If you opt for the former method, use #8 × 2-inch twin-threaded drywall screws; the twin threads—one low and one high—offer tremendous gripping power in a ⅛-inch hole, whether it's in face grain or end grain.

Begin assembly by inserting the back frame into its slot in the bottom. Add the sides. Fit the divider into its dadoes, then put on the top. Screw and/or glue the top and bottom to the divider, and the top, bottom, and sides to the

BACK FRAME CONSTRUCTION

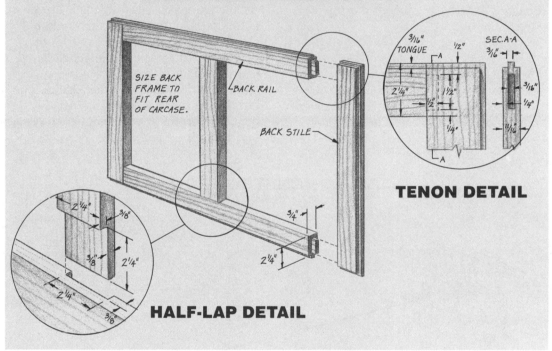

SIZE BACK FRAME TO FIT REAR OF CARCASE.

BACK RAIL

BACK STILE

3/16" TONGUE

2 1/4"

1/2"

1/2"

1/2"

1/4"

SEC. A-A

3/16"

3/16"

1/4"

11/16"

TENON DETAIL

2 1/4"

3/8"

3/8"

2 1/4"

2 1/4"

3/8"

3/4"

2 1/4"

HALF-LAP DETAIL

back frame. The divider can be screwed through the back frame's center stile if you want. Two or three screws per edge is sufficient, unless there's some pesky warp that needs to be pulled flat. In keeping with the knockdown concept, Warner covered the screwheads with colored plastic caps specially designed to fit into the cross-slots of Phillips-head screws.

7 Make the shelves. The four shelves are notched as shown in the *Shelf Construction* to conceal the brass hangers and to prevent the shelves from sliding out. This means the shelves are cut full-length, avoiding the usual unsightly gaps where the shelves meet the cabinet sides. Cut the notches wide enough and deep enough to match your shelf hangers.

Warner shaped the front edge of the shelves in two steps, as shown. First machine a bevel using a 1-inch-diameter, 14-degree dovetail bit that is fitted with a 1½-inch-O.D. (outer diameter) pilot bearing on the shank above the cutter. (This bit, part #69420, is available from the Wisconsin Knife Works, 2710 Prairie Avenue, Beloit, WI 53511; 800-225-5959.) Then use a standard ¼-inch rounding-over bit to smooth the top edge.

8 **Cut the joinery in the door rails and stiles.** As shown in the *Door Construction*, the door frames are joined with ⅜-inch sliding dovetails that allow the top rail to be removed easily for re-placing the glass. The joint makes the doors strong, and it looks nice as well.

Cut the door stiles and rails to the dimensions specified by the Cutting List. The measurements given allow for the dovetails and the sliders on the rails. The doors will overlap about ½ inch when they're closed.

Cut a ⅛-inch-wide slot along the inside edge of each piece to accept the glass. Use a ⅛-inch three flute slotting cutter in a table-mounted router, making the slots ⁵⁄₁₆ inch deep. Since glass thickness varies slightly, adjust the width of the slot accordingly. Note that the stiles and rails are different thicknesses to provide a visual accent, so run the flush face of each piece on the table as you slot it. This will en-

SHELF CONSTRUCTION

SHELF HANGER

13⅞"

7⅜"

¹¹⁄₁₆"

⅝"

¹⁄₁₆"

⅝"

8³⁄₁₆"

1.
ROUT BEVEL ON EDGE OF SHELF WITH 1" DIA. DOVETAIL BIT.

PILOT BEARING
FENCE
SHELF

2.
ROUND-OVER TOP EDGE WITH ⅜" ROUNDING-OVER BIT.

SHELF

DOOR CONSTRUCTION

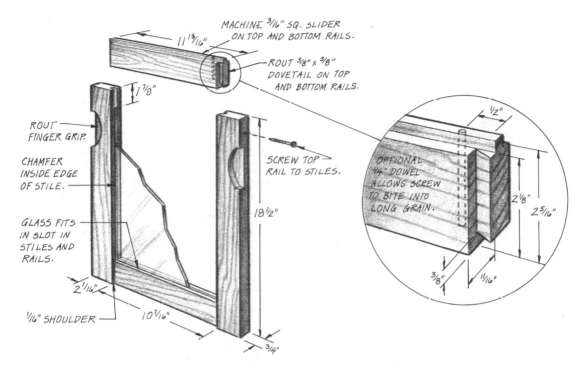

MACHINE 3/16" SQ. SLIDER ON TOP AND BOTTOM RAILS.

ROUT 3/8" X 3/8" DOVETAIL ON TOP AND BOTTOM RAILS.

11 13/16"

1 1/8"

ROUT FINGER GRIP.

CHAMFER INSIDE EDGE OF STILE.

GLASS FITS IN SLOT IN STILES AND RAILS.

SCREW TOP RAIL TO STILES.

18 1/2"

2 1/16"

1/16" SHOULDER

10 1/16"

3/4"

OPTIONAL 1/4" DOWEL ALLOWS SCREW TO BITE INTO LONG GRAIN.

1/2"

2 1/8"

2 5/16"

3/8"

1/16"

sure that the slot is aligned from piece to piece. Cut a slight chamfer on the inside edge of each stile with a block plane. Also cut a 3/16-inch-square tongue, centered on the outside edges of the rails, to act as sliders for the door tracks.

For the dovetail joint, use a 3/8-inch-diameter, 9-degree dovetail bit, and make the cuts on a router table. When the joint is assembled, only the slider tongues should be proud of the stile ends.

9 **Rout the finger grips into the stiles.** Using a 1/2-inch-diameter, 14-degree dovetail bit, press a 5/8-inch-O.D. pilot bearing on the shank. With this setup, use a template shaped like the grip profile, and make the 3/8-inch-

deep cut in one pass. The slight undercut looks nice and provides a better grip for the fingers than a straight-edged recess. The location of the grips is arbitrary, but on Warner's cabinet they're centered 5 7/8 inches from the top of the stiles.

10 **Assemble the doors.** With the top rail in position but not fastened, glue the bottom rail into the stiles. The top rail is held in place with screws; for this, Warner used #8 × 3-inch twin-threaded drywall screws, which hold well in end grain. If you don't have these screws, try driving a 1/4-inch dowel into a hole in the rails, as shown in the *Door Construction*, so that a regular drywall screw can bite into long grain.

ROUTING A HALF-DOVETAIL RABBET JOINT

As an alternative to more familiar case corner joints such as rabbets and lock miters, Pat Warner developed this router-cut corner joint. Fairly simple to make with a router, the joint comes together neatly and squarely. It is more resistant to racking than a conventional rabbet.

As shown in the illustration, the tools you need to cut the joint are: a 1-inch-diameter, 14-degree dovetail bit; a router fence; a router edge guide; and a right-angle jig.

Make the half-dovetail cut on the side pieces first. Warner fits a 1⅛-inch-O.D. pilot bearing on the dovetail bit's shank above the cutter, then clamps a fence to the work for the bearing to ride against. But you can achieve much the same effect by positioning the fence so that the router base rides against it.

Before cutting the actual cabinet pieces, make trial cuts to get the bits and fences set up properly. The idea is to cut the side so that the mating horizontal piece will fit perfectly with a ³⁄₁₆-inch shoulder. When you get the trial cuts to fit right, go ahead and cut the sides.

Next cut the dovetail rabbet on the top and bottom horizontal pieces. This can be done on a router table, but Warner crafted a simple right-angle platform jig that clamps to the work. Clamp the top/bottom as shown in the illustration, and set the router's edge guide to make a cut with a ³⁄₁₆-inch shoulder. The router's depth of cut should be the same as before.

Warner designed—and now sells—a couple of router accessories to make these operations easier and safer. One is an offset subbase made from ½-inch clear acrylic plastic. A large grip knob on the offset allows you to pull the router against the fence while pressing the router down on the inboard side of the work. This eliminates tipping and improves control for most portable routing operations. The other accessory is a custom edge guide to use with the offset subbase. (Both are available from Warner at 1427 Kenora Street, Escondido, CA 92027; 619-747-2623.)

ROUTING A HALF-DOVETAIL RABBET

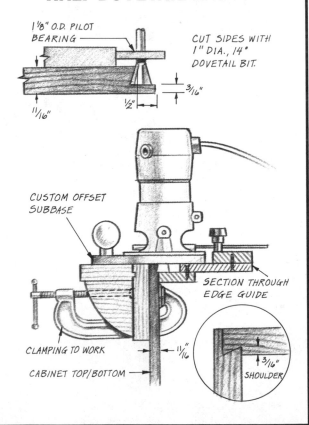

1⅛" O.D. PILOT BEARING

CUT SIDES WITH 1" DIA., 14° DOVETAIL BIT.

³⁄₁₆"

½"

¹¹⁄₁₆"

CUSTOM OFFSET SUBBASE

SECTION THROUGH EDGE GUIDE

CLAMPING TO WORK

CABINET TOP/BOTTOM

¹¹⁄₁₆"

³⁄₁₆" SHOULDER

Cut the pieces of glass to size (the correct dimensions are obtained by adding 9/16 inch to the door's inside measurements). Sand all the members, and polish the sliders with 400-grit sandpaper. Remove the top rail from each door frame, and slide in the glass. Replace each top rail and screw it in place.

11 **Make the door track and install the doors.** A removable track at the top of the cabinet simplifies installation of the sliding doors. And since the tongue slider is centered, the door conceals the slot.

Cut the top door track to size, and machine slots as shown in the Top Track Detail of the *Section View*. Locate the track 1/16 inch inside the top front, and fasten it with countersunk #8 × 1½ inch flathead wood screws centered between the slots. To install the doors, seat them in the bottom slots, tip them out just enough to position the top track, tip them back, and screw the track in place.

CONTEMPORARY QUILT STAND

"This quilt rack was designed to be a quiet, friendly piece for the bedroom," says Ken Burton, Jr. And so it is.

Its gentle curves and graceful lines lend it a contemporary feel, yet its design is not so extreme as to eliminate it from more traditional settings. It provides the perfect place to display and store quilts, coverlets, or other fine linens. The rack also could serve in a guest room, holding towels or extra blankets for your overnight visitors.

Burton, a teacher and maker of fine furniture, built the original as a gift. Although he did that piece in walnut, any hardwood could be used. The joinery is mortise-and-tenon throughout. The curved members were cut on the band saw and shaped with a spokeshave. The details on the feet were created with a simple shop-made jig and a hand-held router; these triangular features offer an excellent opportunity to learn about the marvels of pattern routing.

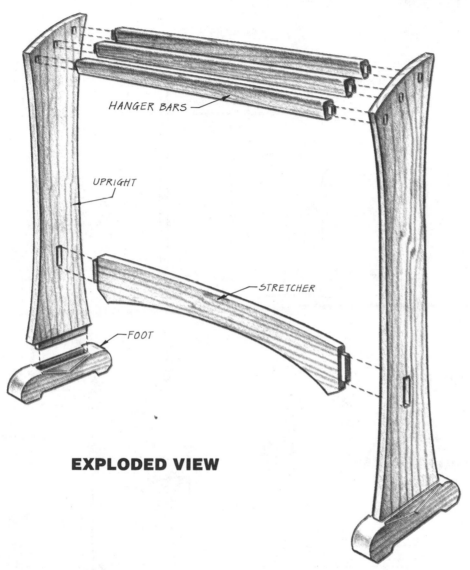

HANGER BARS

UPRIGHT

STRETCHER

FOOT

EXPLODED VIEW

CUTTING LIST

Part	Quantity	Dimension	Material
Feet	2	$1\frac{1}{2}'' \times 2\frac{3}{8}'' \times 10''$	Walnut
Uprights	2	$\frac{3}{4}'' \times 6'' \times 34\frac{3}{8}''$	Walnut
Stretcher	1	$\frac{3}{4}'' \times 4\frac{1}{2}'' \times 30''$	Walnut
Hanger bars	3	$\frac{3}{4}'' \times 1\frac{1}{2}'' \times 30''$	Walnut

PLAN VIEWS

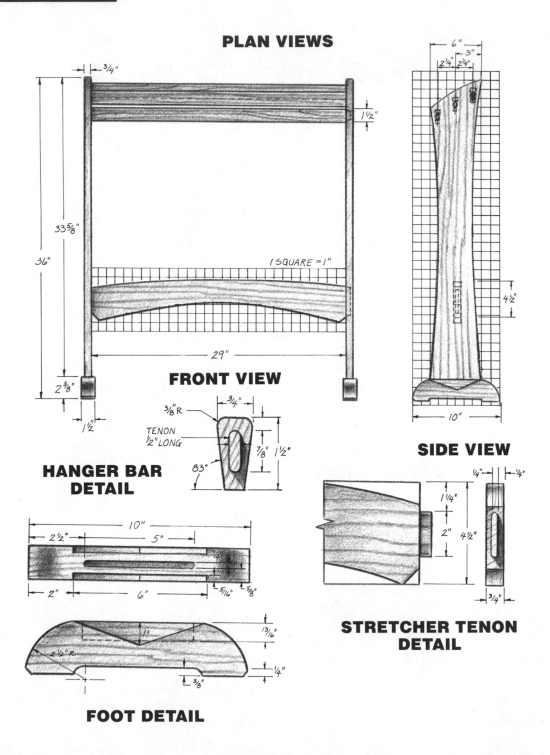

3/4"

1 1/2"

33 5/8"

36"

1 SQUARE = 1"

6"

3"

2 1/4" 2 1/4"

4 1/2"

29"

2 3/8"

1 1/2"

FRONT VIEW

10"

SIDE VIEW

3/8" R.

TENON
1/2" LONG

3/4"

7/8" 1 1/2"

83°

HANGER BAR
DETAIL

10"

2 1/2" 5"

1/4"

2" 6"

5/16" 5/8"

1/4" 1/4"

1 1/4"

2" 4 1/2"

3/4"

STRETCHER TENON
DETAIL

13/16"

1"

2 1/2" R.

3/8"

1/4"

FOOT DETAIL

1 **Select the stock and cut the parts.** This is a display piece, so select some exhibition-quality material for it. The project doesn't require a great deal of wood, so you may be able to absorb the extra outlay required to get some truly magnificent stock—walnut or tiger maple, for example. Burton built the rack shown from walnut. The piece looks especially rich, yet it didn't cost much more to make than if he'd used oak or poplar.

Cut your chosen stock to the sizes specified by the Cutting List. When cutting the feet, mill an extra 24-inch-long piece to the same width and thickness; you'll use it to make the foot-shaping jig.

2 **Cut the mortises in the feet.** When making things with curved and shaped parts, you should do as much machining as possible before cutting the curves. It is much easier to lay out and cut joints while the sides of the wood are still square.

Lay out the mortise on the top of each foot blank as shown in the *Foot Detail*. Clamp one blank to the bench with the bench dogs. Rout the mortise with a ¼-inch-diameter bit in a plunge router. Use an edge guide to position the bit and to guide it through the cut. Make multiple passes, cutting a little deeper each time until the mortise is $13/16$ inch deep. Repeat on the other blank.

3 **Rout the triangular foot detail.** The triangular details on the sides of the feet are cut with the aid of the jig shown.

Make the jig from ¾-inch plywood and the extra length of foot stock. Cut the pieces to the sizes specified in the

illustration. Using glue and screws, assemble the jig around one of the feet you've started to ensure that the jig can hold the stock. Cut the cam lever on the band saw, shaping it to hold the foot blank tightly in the jig.

The templates are cut from ¼-inch plywood. Take your time making them, as any error here will show up on your finished piece. When the templates are completed, line up one on top of the other, clamp them to the jig, and drill through the templates and the jig to place the locating dowels.

With the jig complete, clamp it to your bench. Lock a foot blank in place with the cam lever. *Make sure the mortise faces out.* Set the triangle template on the locating dowels, and check to be sure everything is tight. Set up your router with a ⅜-inch straight bit and a ½-inch-diameter template guide. Set the bit to cut one-half the depth of the finished detail. Rout the detail by running the router along the template. Reset for the full depth and repeat. Rout both sides of the two feet. Clean out the jig between cuts to ensure that chips do not build up in it.

4 **Cut the foot profile.** Lay out the foot cutout on the side of each foot blank as shown in the *Foot Detail*. On the band saw, cut away the waste to within ¹⁄₁₆ inch of the line. Place the blank in the jig with the mortise to the inside, and lock it in with the cam lever. Align the cutout template on the dowels. Set up your router with a ¾-inch straight bit and a ⅞-inch-diameter template guide. Rout the foot cutout, this time making multiple passes until you are halfway through the blank. Then turn the

FOOT-SHAPING JIG

SCREW ON
BLOCKS FROM
UNDERNEATH.

CAM LEVER
TO HOLD IN
WORKPIECE

¼" PLYWOOD

³⁄₈" HOLES FOR
ALIGNMENT

USE WITH
¾" DIA.
ROUTER BIT
AND ³⁄₈" DIA.
TEMPLATE
GUIDE.

4³⁄₄"

5⁷⁄₈"

¹⁄₁₆"

17"

TEMPLATE FOR FOOT CUTOUT

CENTER CUTOUTS OVER
OPENING IN JIG.

USE WITH
³⁄₈" ROUTER
BIT AND ½" DIA.
TEMPLATE
GUIDE.

6¹⁄₈"

1¹⁄₁₆"

TEMPLATE FOR TRIANGLE DETAIL

³⁄₈" TEMPLATE
LOCATING DOWELS

3½"

10"

2³⁄₈"

2³⁄₈"

8"

CAM
LEVER

½" DIA.

TOP VIEW

CUT DOWELS OFF
FLUSH WITH TEMPLATES.

1½"

¾"

FRONT VIEW

PLYWOOD
BASE

HARDWOOD BLOCKS
SCREWED FROM
UNDERNEATH

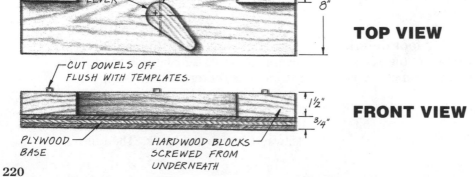

blank over and finish the cut from the opposite side.

Shape the curved ends of the feet next. Draw a 2½-inch-radius circle on a piece of cardboard. Cut out this circle and use it to lay out the curves on the feet. Cut along these lines on the band saw. Use a spokeshave and scraper to refine the sawed curves and to remove saw marks.

Finally, chamfer the "toes" on the table saw. Lay out the chamfers on the bottom of the feet as shown in the *Foot Detail*. Tilt the table saw blade to 45 degrees. Guide each foot past the blade with the miter gauge to cut the chamfers.

5 **Rout the mortises in the uprights.** Lay out the mortises on the uprights as shown in the *Upright Layout*. Note that the right and left sides are mirror images; be sure to make one of each. Rout the mortises with a ¼-inch bit mounted in a plunge router. Use an edge guide to position the bit and to guide the router through the cut. Make multiple passes until the mortises are 9/16 inch deep.

6 **Cut tenons on the uprights, stretcher, and hanging bars.** Set up your table saw with a dado cutter stacked for a ⅜-inch-wide cut.

To tenon the uprights, set the fence ¾ inch from the outside of the blade to act as a stop. Adjust the blade height so that the resulting tenons will fit snugly into their mortises. Cut each tenon by running the upright past the blade with the miter gauge. Make multiple passes until the upright touches the fence. Flip the upright over and repeat. Raise the

UPRIGHT LAYOUT

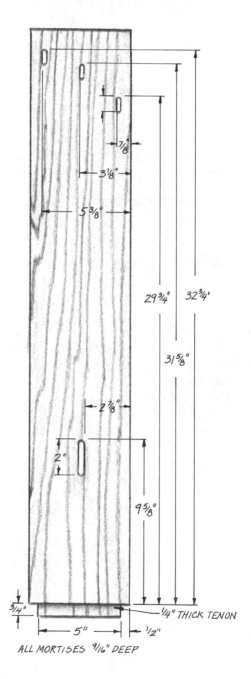

29¾"   32¾'

31⅝"

2⅞"

2"

9⅝"

7⅛"

3⅛"

5⅜"

¾"

5"   ½"

¼" THICK TENON

ALL MORTISES 9/16" DEEP

blade as necessary to cut the edges of the tenons.

Cut the tenons on the stretcher and the hanger bars in the same way. For these tenons, however, set the fence ½-inch from the outside of the blade. Refer to the *Stretcher Tenon Detail* and the *Hanger Bar Detail* for specific dimensions.

To complete all these tenons, shave away the corners with a chisel so that they will fit the router-cut mortises.

SHOP TIP: Use a scrap the same thickness as the piece you are tenoning to make the initial setup. That way, if you happen to make a mistake, you won't waste any good wood.

---

7 **Cut the uprights and stretcher to their final profiles.** Lay out the curves on the uprights using the pattern that is incorporated into the *Side View*. Enlarge the pattern, transfer the curves to the workpieces, then cut to these lines on the band saw. Clean up the curves with a spokeshave and scraper. Finish sand the uprights.

In the same manner, enlarge the stretcher pattern incorporated into the *Front View*, and transfer it to the stretcher. Cut to these lines on the band saw. Clean up the sawed edges with a spokeshave and scraper. Finish sand the stretcher.

8 **Shape the hanger bars.** The hanger bars have a wedgelike cross section that is created next. Begin by rounding the top edge of each bar with a

⅜-inch rounding-over bit chucked in your table-mounted router. Then set the rip fence of your table saw ¾ inch from the inside of the blade. Tilt the blade to cut an 83-degree bevel (7 degrees off vertical). Bevel-rip the hanger bars; be sure to use a push stick when making narrow cuts such as this. Turn the workpiece around to cut the opposite side. Be careful when making this second cut; very little of the bar will actually contact the fence. Finish sand the hanger bars.

9 **Assemble and finish the rack.** Assemble all the pieces without glue, going so far as to clamp the joints. Make any adjustments necessary to ensure that the joints fit and that the whole rack is square. Measure the diagonals; the distance from the top of the left upright to the inside of the right foot should equal the distance between the same points on the right upright and left foot.

Glue the feet onto the uprights. Apply glue to the inside of the foot mortises and to the cheeks of the uprights' tenons, then assemble and clamp the pieces. Clean up any squeeze-out with a moist rag. Set aside the clamped units to dry.

When the clamps are removed, glue the cross members in place. Again, apply glue to the mortises and the tenon cheeks. Fit everything together and clamp. Clean up any squeeze-out, and check the assembly to make sure it is square.

Finish the quilt rack. Go over the whole piece and touch up any blemishes with sandpaper. Apply your favorite wood finish.

PATTERN ROUTING

Pattern routing is a technique that allows you to make multiples of a given cut easily. This is accomplished by making a pattern or template of the shape you want, securing it temporarily to the workpiece, then running a router fitted with a template guide along the template's edge.

The template guide, also called a guide bushing, is attached to the router base plate. The guide has interchangable bushings through which the bit projects. The bushing's inside diameter has to match the diameter of the bit. As shown, the side of the bushing bears on the template, and since the bushing has thickness, the actual line of cut is offset from the template about $1/16$ to $1/8$ inch. (The templates shown for the quilt rack have a $1/16$-inch offset.)

TEMPLATE GUIDES

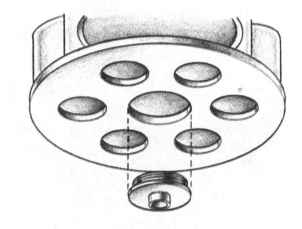

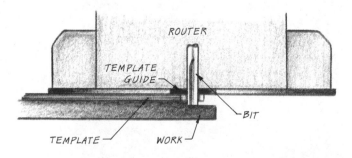

ROUTER

TEMPLATE GUIDE

BIT

TEMPLATE

WORK

PIANO BENCH-CABINET

The piano was a large old upright made of mahogany, still in good condition. A beautifully figured mahogany veneer covered the piano panels. With age or with stain, the finish had darkened to a rich red-brown color. And it needed a bench.

Because the piano's owner was a friend, cabinetmaker David Page accepted the job of building a storage bench—no lift-up lid allowed. "I almost refused the commission," says Page,

"because the client wanted it made in a style that matched the piano. That did not seem to leave much design freedom. The finish, too, had to match the piano finish, and matching finishes is often difficult." But meeting the client's needs within her design strictures was too much of a challenge to pass up.

Page designed and built this bench-cabinet. Since the client wouldn't be putting her feet under the bench, "the space beneath the seat could be anything

EXPLODED VIEW

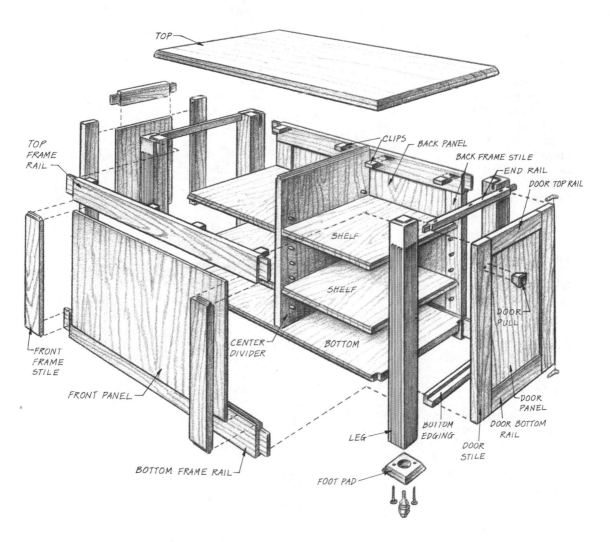

I wanted it to be, as long as it was related by the design to the piano," Page explains. "The simple design reflects fluted columns from the old piano, with figured mahogany panels. The two end doors allow you to reach to each side while sitting on the bench to retrieve sheet music inside. Two adjustable shelves in each compartment provide abundant storage." To keep bugs out of the sheet music, Page made the shelves from aromatic red cedar.

The panel on the front, or piano side, of the bench is higher off the floor than the back panel; this allows the bench to clear the piano pedals when it

CUTTING LIST

Part	Quantity	Dimensions	Material
Legs	4	2″ × 2″ × 18⅛″	Mahogany
Foot pads	4	½″ × 3″ × 3″	Mahogany
Back panel	1	¼″ × 12⅝″ × 23″ *	Plywood
Front panel	1	¼″ × 10⅞″ × 23″ *	Plywood
Door panels	2	¼″ × 11⅛″ × 7½″ *	Plywood
Bottom frame rails	2	¾″ × 2¾″ × 28½″	Mahogany
Top frame rails	2	¾″ × 2″ × 28½″	Mahogany
Back frame stiles	2	¾″ × 1¾″ × 12⅝″	Mahogany
Front frame stiles	2	¾″ × 1¾″ × 10⅞″	Mahogany
Bottom edgings	2	¾″ × 1″ × 10½″	Mahogany
End rails	2	½″ × ¾″ × 13″	Mahogany
Center divider	1	¾″ × 12½″ × 14⅞″	Mahogany plywood
Bottom	1	¾″ × 13″ × 27½″	Mahogany plywood
Top	1	⅞″ × 16½″ × 32″	Mahogany
Clips	8	½″ × 1″ × 1¼″	Mahogany
Door stiles	4	¾″ × 1¾″ × 14″	Mahogany
Door bottom rails	2	¾″ × 2″ × 9⅜″	Mahogany
Door top rails	2	¾″ × 1½″ × 9⅜″	Mahogany
Door pulls	2	1″ × 1″ × 1″	Mahogany
Shelves	4	¾″ × 12⅜″ × 12¼″	Aromatic cedar

Hardware

10 brass flathead wood screws, #8 × 1¼″
14 brass flathead wood screws, #8 × 1″
4 steel casters, 1″ dia. Available from The Woodworkers' Store, 21801 Industrial Blvd.,
  Rogers, MN 55374. Part #24687.
2 pairs brass knife hinges. Available from The Woodworkers' Store. Part #26260.
2 door catches
16 shelf supports with ¼″ posts

Miscellaneous

Approx. 6–8 sq. ft. fiddleback mahogany veneer. Available from Certainly Wood, 11753 Big Tree
  Rd., Rt. 20A, East Aurora, NY 14052.
Approx. 6–8 sq. ft. plain mahogany veneer. Available from Certainly Wood.

* These are final dimensions. For veneering, cut two pieces of plywood ¼″ × 13½″ × 31½″. Cut one frame
panel and one door panel from each piece.

is pushed under the piano, out of the way. "It pushes easily," Page points out, "because of the casters all but hidden within each leg." The overall dimensions were determined by standing in front of the piano with a measuring tape.

Construction of the bench-cabinet is not complicated. Mortises and tenons join the front and back panel frames to the legs and the door rails to the door stiles. A center divider separates the two compartments and strengthens the bench for supporting the weight of one or more people. Page veneered ¼-inch plywood with figured mahogany veneer for the front, back, and door panels. The Cutting List gives a source for the veneer.

1 Select the stock. David Page built this little bench from mahogany and mahogany-veneered plywood panels, a choice dictated by the piano. It easily can be made from any cabinet-grade hardwood, such as walnut, cherry, maple, or oak. Page was able to match the elaborate figure of the piano's wood by using veneer. If you are satisfied with the low-key figure of typical hardwood plywood, then you can circumvent the veneering process (and you may want to). If you choose not to veneer, then order a sheet of the appropriate species of hardwood plywood for the exposed panels.

2 Make the legs. Mill wood for the four legs, and cut them to the dimensions specified by the Cutting List. If necessary, glue together two thinner boards to get the thickness needed.

Cut the mortises for the frame rails first. Since the legs are wide enough to provide safe bearing for a router, cut the mortises with a ¼-inch straight bit in a plunge router. Use an edge guide attachment, which slides against the side of the leg, to guide the router. Lay out the mortises following the *Leg Layout*. Rout them with several passes of the router, lowering the bit ⅛ inch with each pass. Square the ends of the mortises with a chisel. The mortises for the top rails are open, so you can run the router bit out the top of the leg.

If you don't have a plunge router, drill the mortises on the drill press. Sliding the leg along a fence clamped to the drill press table, drill overlapping holes to make the mortise. Clean and square each mortise with a chisel.

Next cut the mortises for the end rails in the same manner that you made the frame rail mortises, using the plunge router and edge guide. These, too, are open mortises, so run the bit out the top of the leg.

After all the mortises are cut, rout the leg flutes. These are cut into the two exposed surfaces of each leg with a ¼-inch fluting bit, as shown in the Flute Detail of the *Leg Layout*. Stop the flutes 2 inches from the top of the leg. Guide a hand-held router with a fence clamped to the leg, or slide the leg against a fence on a table-mounted router.

3 Make and attach the foot pads. For the four foot pads, mill a board to thickness and rip it to the desired width. Then crosscut the foot pads to length. Chamfer the top edges with a chamfer bit in a table-mounted router, sizing the chamfers as indicated in the *Front View*. On the drill press, drill and countersink pilot holes for two #8 × 1¼-inch screws, passing through the

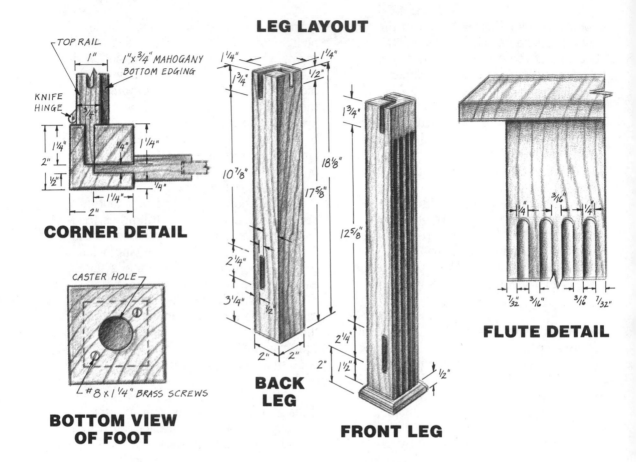

LEG LAYOUT

TOP RAIL

1"

1" x ¾" MAHOGANY BOTTOM EDGING

KNIFE HINGE

¾"

1¼"

2"

½"

¼"

1¼"

¼"

1¼"

2"

CORNER DETAIL

CASTER HOLE

#8 x 1¼" BRASS SCREWS

BOTTOM VIEW OF FOOT

1¼"

1¾"

10⅞"

2¼"

3¼"

½"

2"   2"

BACK LEG

1¼"

½"

1¾"

18⅛"

17⅝"

12⅝"

2¼"

2"   1½"

½"

FRONT LEG

3/16"

¼"   ¼"

7/32"   3/16"   3/16"   7/32"

FLUTE DETAIL

bottom into each leg. Glue and screw the foot pads onto the leg bottoms.

Drill the legs for the casters. Have the casters in hand before doing this, so that you can size the holes properly. (The Cutting List suggests a source for the appropriate casters.) Stand each leg upright on the drill press and bore. Leave ¼ inch of the caster wheel exposed.

4 Cut (and veneer) the front, back, and door panels. The front, back, and door panels of the origi-

nal bench-cabinet were cut from cabinet-grade birch plywood. To match his customer's piano, Page applied veneers of fiddleback mahogany to each panel. The details of applying a veneer are explained in "Veneering" on page 234. Both surfaces of the plywood must be veneered for stability, though the hidden side can be covered with a lesser-quality material.

If instead you plan to use a hardwood plywood that matches the wood chosen for the framework and top, then merely cut the panels to the sizes specified by the Cutting List.

5 Make the rails and stiles. Mill the wood for the framework, and cut the rails and stiles to the dimensions specified by the Cutting List. Mill the bottom edgings to thickness and width, but leave them slightly long. Rout a ¾-inch-wide × ¼-inch-deep rabbet in these edgings.

First cut the grooves in the frame rails and stiles for the front and back panels. Be very careful to match the width of the groove to the thickness of the panels. Hardwood plywood often is slightly undersized. If, like Page, you veneer the panels, they'll *probably* turn out 5/16 inch thick. But if you use the plywood without additional veneer, your grooves *probably* should be 7/32 inch wide. Use a dado cutter to make these grooves, cutting them ¼ inch deep. These are *not* stopped cuts.

Adjust the width of the dado cutter, and use it to groove the bottom frame rails for the bottom. The grooves are ¼ inch wide × ¼ inch deep. Note in the *View through End* that the grooves are in different positions on the two rails. Label the parts clearly, so that you don't mix them up.

Tenon the frame rails next. Cut the tenons to fit the mortises in the legs.

Page used a tenoning jig on the table saw for this procedure. Crosscut the frame rails against a stop block to make the tenon shoulders, then stand the rails upright in the jig to cut the tenon cheeks. Cut the tenons to width in the tenoning jig or on the band saw.

Before setting aside the frame rails, rout slots in the top ones for the wooden clips that attach the top to the framework. Position the slots roughly as shown in the *Top View*; exact placement isn't necessary. Use a ¼-inch slotting cutter to make the 2-inch-long × ⅜-inch-deep slots.

The stiles, which abut the insides of the legs, have a ¼-inch-long tenon on each end that fits into the same rail groove as the panel. Cut these tenons on the table saw with the tenoning jig, as you did the frame rail tenons. Make them the proper thickness to fit into the groove you plowed earlier.

Finally, tenon the end rails, which fit between the legs above the cabinet doors. Size the tenons to match the mortises in the legs. Cut them on the table saw, as you did the tenons in the frame rails and stiles. Complete the rails by drilling and countersinking three pilot holes for #8 × 1-inch screws, which help fasten the top to the bench. Slot the two outside holes, or drill them over size, to allow for seasonal movement of the top.

6 Make the center divider and bottom. Cut ¾-inch mahogany plywood to the sizes specified by the Cutting List for the bottom and the center divider.

These pieces join each other and

PLAN VIEWS

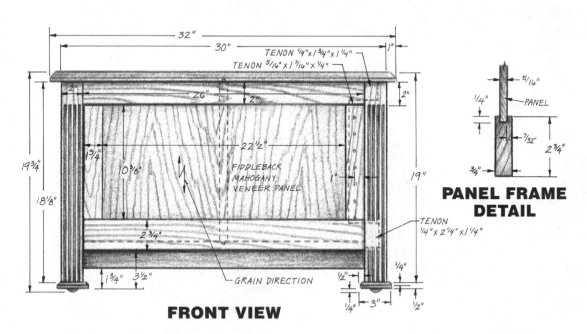

FRONT VIEW

PANEL FRAME DETAIL

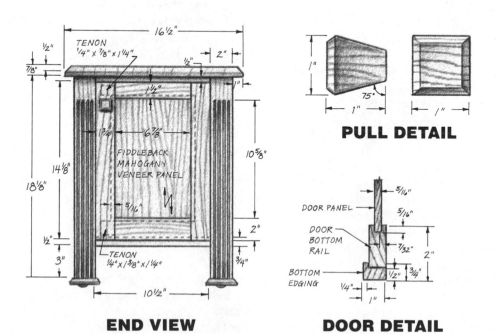

END VIEW

PULL DETAIL

DOOR DETAIL

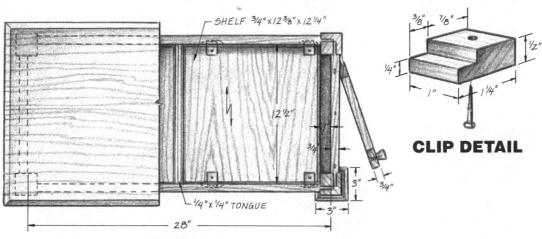

SHELF ¾" x 12⅜" x 12¼"

12½"

¼" x ¼" TONGUE

28"

3" 3"

CLIP DETAIL

⅜" ⅞" ½" ¼" 1" 1¼"

TOP VIEW

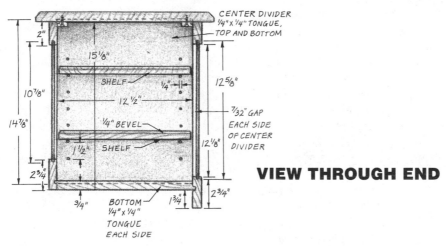

CENTER DIVIDER ¼" x ¼" TONGUE, TOP AND BOTTOM

2" 15⅛" 12⅝"

SHELF ¼"

10⅞" 12½" ⁷⁄₃₂" GAP EACH SIDE OF CENTER DIVIDER

14⅞" ¼" BEVEL

1½" SHELF 12⅛"

2¾" 2¾"

¾" BOTTOM ¼" x ¼" TONGUE EACH SIDE 1¾"

VIEW THROUGH END

the rest of the cabinet in tongue-and-groove joints. Rout ¼ × ¼-inch tongues on the top and bottom edges of the center divider. These tongues fit into grooves that you'll cut in the plywood bottom and the solid mahogany top. Since the tongues on the bottom are off-set (though they are the same dimension), you must adjust the router before cutting them. Be sure to offset the tongue along the front edge to the top,

the tongue along the back edge to the bottom, as shown in the *View through End.*

Rout a ¼-inch-wide × ¼-inch-deep groove, centered across the bottom, for the tongue on the center divider.

The corners of the bottom must be notched to fit around the legs. Lay out and cut the notches either on the band saw or by standing the bottom on edge against the miter gauge on the table saw.

231

7 **Drill holes for the shelf supports.** Lay out and drill ¼-inch-diameter × ⅜-inch-deep holes in the center divider and in the four frame stiles for the shelf supports. Space the holes 1½ inches apart, 1 inch in from the outside edges of the divider and stiles.

8 **Assemble the bench.** This assembly proceeds in two stages. First you glue up the side frames and legs, then you join them with the end rails and bottom. Begin by sanding the legs, rails, stiles, and panels. Test fit both side frames with their adjoining legs. When you are satisfied with the fit of the parts, disassemble the frames.

On a flat surface, glue the frame stiles onto the side panel. Glue the side panel into the grooves in the frame rails, gluing and clamping the stile tenons into the rail grooves. Glue and clamp the rail tenons into their leg mortises, pulling the frame tight. Pull the inside stiles tight against the legs with clamps. Glue each frame separately, measuring across its diagonal corners to make sure it is square.

When the frames are dry, assemble the bench. Glue and clamp the end rail tenons into their leg mortises. At the same time, glue and clamp the bottom into its groove in the bottom frame rails. Crosscut the bottom edgings to fit between the legs on each end of the bench. Glue and clamp the strips to the bottom, hiding the plywood edges. The doors will close into the rabbet machined in the edgings.

9 **Make and attach the top.** Mill the wood for the top. To get the width specified by the Cutting List, you must edge-glue several boards. Calculate the number of boards needed, and crosscut them to the specified length. Joint their edges and glue them up.

Make the clips used to fasten the top to the cabinet. As shown in the *Clip Detail*, rout a ⅜-inch-wide × ¼-inch-deep rabbet in both ends of a ½-inch-thick piece of the working stock. On the table saw, crosscut the ends to length, then rip the clips to width. Drill and countersink holes for #8 × 1-inch screws.

After the clamps are removed and the top has been trimmed to its final size, rout a ¼-inch-wide × ¼-inch-deep stopped groove across its center for the tongue on the center divider. Then rout a ½-inch chamfer around the top edge, as shown in the various plan views. For this procedure, use a bit with a pilot bearing, and chuck it in a table-mounted router.

Lay the top upside down on padding on your workbench. Turn the bench-cabinet upside down onto the top, align them, and clamp the two together. Mark through the pilot holes in the end rails and clips. Remove the bench-cabinet from the top, and drill for the screws.

Before installing the top, sand it. Then glue the center divider's bottom

SHOP TIP: To safely rip the clips on the table saw, use a stop block clamped to the rip fence to set the width of the clip. Then guide the workpiece past the blade with the miter gauge. The stop block allows the rip fence to be offset from the blade, so that the cutoff doesn't get wedged—dangerously—between the fence and blade.

tongue into its groove in the bench-cabinet bottom. Glue the middle 2 to 3 inches of the divider's top tongue into its groove in the top. Do not glue it all the way across, or the top cannot move with seasonal humidity changes.

Position the top on the bench-cabinet and clamp it down. Drive #8 × 1-inch brass flathead wood screws through the end rails and clips into the top.

10 **Make the rails and stiles for the doors.** Mill working stock for the door rails and stiles, then rip and crosscut the parts to the dimensions specified by the Cutting List.

Cut the mortises in the stiles first. Use the plunge router, equipped with an edge guide and a ¼-inch straight bit. Clamp the stiles in a mortising jig, or ride the router on the edge of the stile. To provide a larger bearing surface for the router, clamp together two stiles with a 2 × 2 × 12-inch spacing block between them. Let the guide of the router ride against the side of the stile being mortised. Rout each mortise in a series of passes, lowering the bit ⅛ inch each time. Square the ends of the mortises with a chisel. (If you don't have a plunge router, drill the mortises on the drill press as described earlier.)

Tenon the rails to match the mortises next. Use a tenoning jig on the table saw, cutting these tenons as you did the frame rails' tenons.

Groove the door rails and stiles. As with the frame rails and stiles, the width of the grooves must match the thickness of the panels. Use a dado cutter set to the panel thickness, center the groove on the inside edge of each rail and stile,

and cut ⁵⁄₁₆ inch deep. The rails are grooved from end to end, the stiles from mortise to mortise. On the table saw, complete the stopped cuts by hand. On the router table, slide the stiles and rails against a fence. Drop the pieces over the bit, and cut half the depth of the groove. Raise the bit and complete the groove.

11 **Glue up the doors.** Sand the door parts. On a flat surface, glue and clamp the rail tenons into the stile mortises, setting the door panel in place as you pull the joints tight. Measure diagonally across the corners to make certain the doors are square.

While the glue dries, make the door pulls. Start with an 8-inch length of 1 × 1-inch stock. Rip opposite sides of the stock with the table saw's arbor tilted to 15 degrees. As you crosscut the pulls from the stock, bevel the two remaining sides with the miter gauge set to 15 degrees. Make the small top bevels with a stationary belt sander. Drill a hole into each pull for a #8 × 1¼-inch screw. Once the clamps are removed from the doors, install the pulls.

12 **Finish the piano bench-cabinet.** Do any remaining sanding, then apply the finish of your choice to the bench-cabinet. Apply the same number of coats to the inside of the cabinet as to the outside.

13 **Make the shelves.** Page made the shelves from aromatic red cedar, but this is optional. Mahogany or edged mahogany plywood is fine. Mill, rip, and crosscut wood for the shelves to

(continued on page 236)

VENEERING

Veneering is a frugal way to make use of wildly figured and exotic woods in furniture making. Thin slices—1/64 to 1/16 inch—of showy wood are glued to panels of more utilitarian material, which then is incorporated into a piece of furniture. Here's how to apply veneer:

1 Cut the plywood to size. For the substrate, cut 1/4-inch hardwood plywood (such as birch) to the required dimensions. Cut the plywood so that its grain direction is perpendicular to the direction of the veneer grain.

2 Cut the veneer to size. Trim the veneer sheets to length with a razor knife. The veneer should extend beyond the plywood 1/2 inch on each side. If necessary, edge-join the pieces of veneer to cover the panels. Stack the veneer sheets on your bench, with their edge overhanging the edge of your bench by 1/2 inch. Clamp a 1 × 2 × 36-inch straightedge on top of the veneer and flush with the edge of the bench, as shown in *Edging the Veneer*. Hand plane the rough edges of the veneer flush with the straightedge and bench. Tape together the edges of the veneer with veneer tape or other thin tape.

Prepare enough veneer to cover both sides of the substrate. Both sides must be ve-neered to minimize warping. You can use a plain veneer for the back of the panel.

3 Prepare the veneer sandwich. To bond the veneer to the substrate, you must form a layered sandwich of the substrate panels, glue, veneer, newspaper, and clamping pads. The *Veneer Sandwich* shows the order of the layers. Use yellow wood glue, applying it only to the substrate, not to the veneer; spread it with a 3- or 4-inch paint roller. To clamp the sandwich, you need either a lot of deep-throated clamps (21 for the piano bench-cabinet) or a set of clamping cauls of the sort shown in *Alternative Clamping Cauls*. Cut pieces of inexpensive 3/4-inch fir plywood for the clamping pads. Two such pads, top and bottom, are better than one. They should over-hang the veneer about 1/2 inch on each side. The layers of newspaper prevent sticking and help distribute clamping pressure. You must work fast, so get a helper. Have everything ready before you begin glue-up.

4 Glue the panels. Do the veneering on sawhorses. Here's how:

Rest one or two clamping pads across the sawhorses. Spread several sheets of newspa-

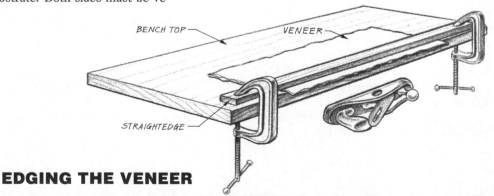

BENCH TOP

VENEER

STRAIGHTEDGE

EDGING THE VENEER

VENEER SANDWICH

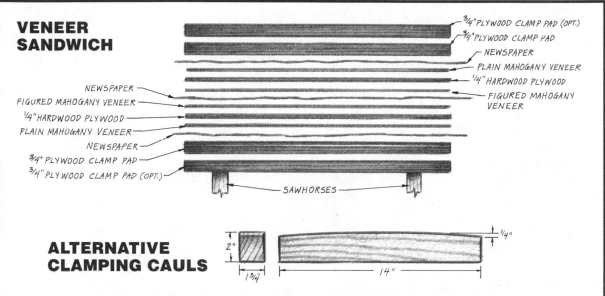

¾" PLYWOOD CLAMP PAD (OPT.)

¾" PLYWOOD CLAMP PAD

NEWSPAPER

PLAIN MAHOGANY VENEER

¼" HARDWOOD PLYWOOD

FIGURED MAHOGANY VENEER

NEWSPAPER

FIGURED MAHOGANY VENEER

¼" HARDWOOD PLYWOOD

PLAIN MAHOGANY VENEER

NEWSPAPER

¾" PLYWOOD CLAMP PAD

¾" PLYWOOD CLAMP PAD (OPT.)

SAWHORSES

ALTERNATIVE CLAMPING CAULS

2"

1¾"

¼"

14"

per on the pads, and lay the backing veneer on the newspaper. Roll glue on one side of the ¼-inch plywood substrate, and lay the substrate on the veneer with its glued side down. Roll glue on the second side of the substrate, and apply the face veneer. Spread newspaper on top of the veneer. The moisture in the glue causes the veneer to curl, so rest the second piece of plywood substrate on the newspaper to keep the veneer flat. Roll glue on this second substrate, apply the face veneer, then quickly flip the panel over so that the face veneer is against the newspaper. Spread more glue, apply the backing veneer, cover the veneer with newspaper, and add the second set of clamping pads.

5 **Clamp the sandwich.** Make certain the clamping pieces and veneers are positioned properly. You can't use too many clamps. Begin clamping in the very center of the sandwich, so that the glue is forced toward the edges. The *Clamping Sequence* shows the relative position of the clamps and the order in which they should be applied.

6 **Cut the panels to size.** Unclamp the sandwich when the glue is dry. Using a chisel, trim excess veneer flush with the plywood. Cut the panels to final dimensions for the frames and doors. Since the ¼-inch plywood usually is undersized, the final thickness of the veneered panel is almost exactly 5/16 inch.

CLAMPING SEQUENCE

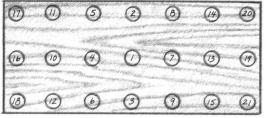

SIZE OF PLYWOOD PADS (APPROX.) 14" x 32"

POSITION OF CLAMPS AND ORDER OF CLAMPING

the dimensions specified by the Cutting List. Edge-glue wood to get sufficient width, if necessary. Chamfer the top edge of the shelves using a piloted chamfer bit in a table-mounted router.

14 **Hang the doors and install the casters.** Page used knife hinges for the doors. Lay out and rout mortises in the doors for whatever hinges you choose. Position the doors, and drill the door rails and their facing pieces for screws. Screw the hinges to the doors and the bench. To latch the doors, Page used small brass double-ball catches, but other hardware is fine. Whatever you choose, latch the doors at the top near the pulls.

Finally, set the casters into the leg holes that you drilled for them earlier. The casters should extend about ¼ inch from the bottom of the leg.

SIX-BOARD BLANKET CHEST

Under this flashy paint job is a very traditional dovetailed blanket chest. Built (and hand painted) by professional woodworker Andy Rae of Princeton, New Jersey, the chest is an amalgam of traditional motifs. Before settling on this particular design, Rae researched the genre fairly methodically. He studied books like Kirk's *American Furniture and the British Tradition to 1830* and

The Antiques Treasury by Alice Winchester, both of which give a broad range of examples, from the simple to the elaborate. He also visited homes and antique stores all over the South (particularly in Mississippi).

"There are literally thousands of heirloom-quality blanket chests to be found," Rae says. "Some undoubtedly found their way here on Spanish and En-

EXPLODED VIEW

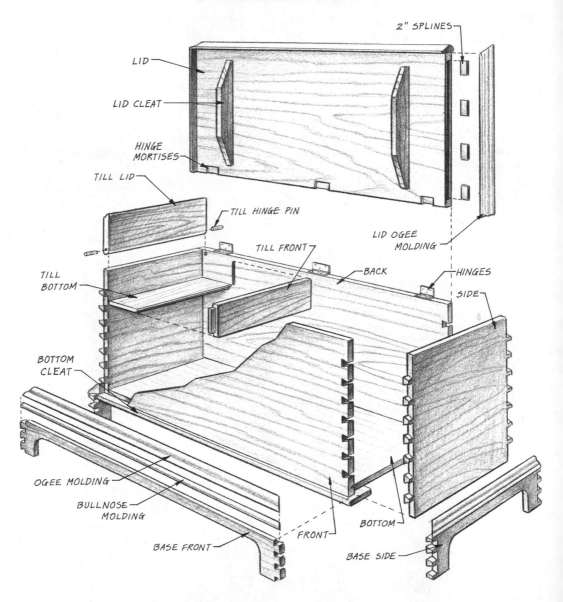

2" SPLINES

LID

LID CLEAT

HINGE
MORTISES

TILL LID

TILL HINGE PIN

LID OGEE
MOLDING

TILL FRONT

BACK

HINGES

TILL
BOTTOM

SIDE

BOTTOM
CLEAT

OGEE MOLDING

BULLNOSE
MOLDING

FRONT

BOTTOM

BASE FRONT

BASE SIDE

CUTTING LIST

Part	Quantity	Dimensions	Material
Sides	2	¾″ × 20″ × 20″	Sugar pine
Front and back	2	¾″ × 20″ × 44″	Sugar pine
Bottom	1	¾″ × 19¼″ × 43¼″	Sugar pine
Lid	1	¾″ × 20⅛″ × 44¼″	Sugar pine
Till lid	1	⅞″ × 6¼″ × 18⁷⁄₁₆″	Walnut
Till bottom	1	½″ × 5¾″ × 19″	Sugar pine
Till front	1	¾″ × 5″ × 19″	Sugar pine
Base front and back	2	1¼″ × 5″ × 46″	Sugar pine
Base sides	2	1¼″ × 5″ × 22″	Sugar pine
Bottom cleats	2	¾″ × 4″ × 44½″	Sugar pine
Bullnose molding	1	¾″ × 1″ × 12′	Sugar pine
Base ogee molding	1	1″ × ¾″ × 12′	Sugar pine
Lid ogee molding	1	1½″ × 1⅛″ × 8′	Sugar pine
Lid cleats	2	1⅛″ × 2″ × 18″	Walnut
Till hinge pins	2	½″ dia. × 1″	Hardwood dowel

Hardware

6 flathead wood screws, #10 × 2½″
8 flathead wood screws, #8 × 1¼″
3 box hinges, ⁵⁄₁₆″ × ¹¹⁄₁₆″ × 2½″. Available from Larry and Faye Brusso, 3812 Cass Elizabeth, Pontiac, MI 48054.
2 coil springs, ½″ dia. × 1″
1″ finishing nails

glish galleons, filled with their owners' belongings and headed for a new world. Many reflect a love for furniture and a passion for organizing ones' household items. The big, wide pine trees of the South also support this proliference; older chests were often made from single boards two feet or more in width."

The chest is fairly easy to build, if your dovetail-cutting skills are up to par. The rest is basic cutting and grooving, most of which can be accomplished on a table saw.

And the paint job? That's up to you. The joinery and detailing almost demand a natural finish, but the genre has a lot of paint in its traditions. The Pennsylvania Dutch, among others, always painted their chests. You may not like Rae's bold creation, but you certainly can't help noticing it.

1 Select the stock and cut the parts. The blanket chest shown is made from clear sugar pine, with two parts—the lid cleats and the till lid—made from contrasting walnut. Pine is the traditional choice for such a chest, and it serves as a good base for the

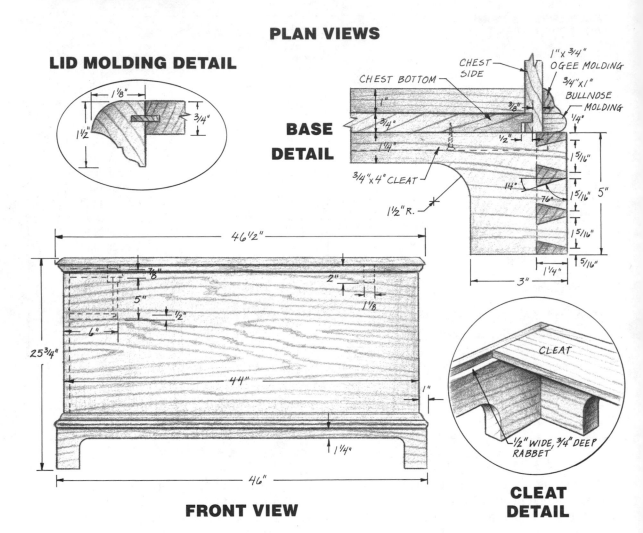

PLAN VIEWS

LID MOLDING DETAIL

1⅛"
¾"
1½"

CHEST SIDE
CHEST BOTTOM
1" x ¾" OGEE MOLDING
¾" x 1" BULLNOSE MOLDING
¼"
3/8"
½"
1"
¾"
1¼"

BASE DETAIL

¾" x 4" CLEAT
1½" R.
14°
76°
1 5/16"
1 5/16"
1 5/16"
1 5/16"
5"
3"
1¼"

FRONT VIEW

46½"
25¾"
⅞"
5"
6"
½"
2"
1⅛
44"
1"
1¼"
46"

CLEAT DETAIL

CLEAT
½" WIDE, ¾" DEEP RABBET

elaborately painted finish. However, any number of hardwoods would be suitable, especially if a natural finish is your preference.

Rae's choice of walnut for the cleats and till lid was based on more than aesthetics. Visual appeal is important, of course, since these parts show. But the cleats are reinforcing the lid, and the till lid serves as a prop to keep the lid open. Both parts need strength.

To make up the width of the sides, front, back, bottom, and lid, you have to edge-glue several boards. Gluing up fairly narrow boards to make these wide panels has the added advantage of minimizing pine's tendency to cup. Choosing flat and straight stock makes assembly easier and more precise. Joint, plane, rip, and cut all of the parts except the molding stock to the dimensions specified by the Cutting List.

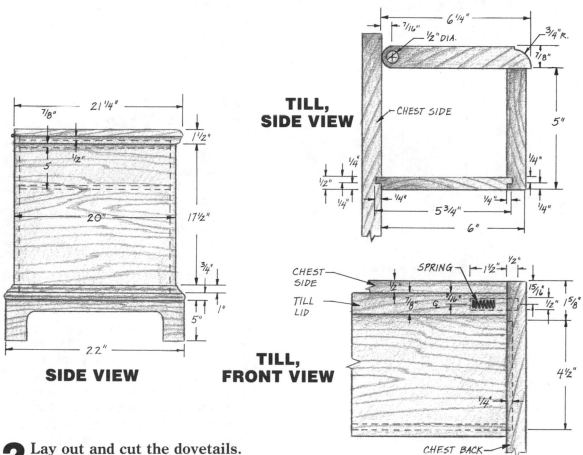

TILL,
SIDE VIEW

CHEST SIDE

SIDE VIEW

TILL,
FRONT VIEW

CHEST
SIDE

TILL
LID

SPRING

CHEST BACK

2 Lay out and cut the dovetails.
Begin by laying out and cutting the tails and pins.

First establish their length. Set a marking gauge to a shade more than the thickness of the stock—the stock is ¾ inch thick, so set the gauge to 13⁄16 inch. Scribe lines around the ends of the front, back, and side pieces.

Lay out the tails next. These are cut on the front and back pieces. The layout sequence is as follows:

• Measure off the tails as indicated in both the *Dovetail Layout* and the *Back Layout Detail*.

• With a sliding T-bevel set to 14 degrees off square, lay out the angle of the tails by extending lines from the layout marks to the line scribed with the marking gauge.

• With a square, extend lines from the layout marks across the end grain.

• Lay out the angle of the tails on the back face of the board, again using the sliding T-bevel.

• Mark the waste clearly.

241

DOVETAIL LAYOUT

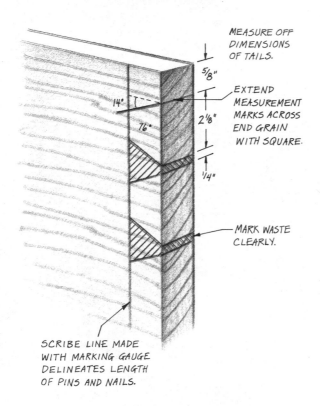

MEASURE OFF DIMENSIONS OF TAILS.

$\frac{5}{8}$"

14°

76°

EXTEND MEASUREMENT MARKS ACROSS END GRAIN WITH SQUARE.

$2\frac{1}{8}$"

$\frac{1}{4}$"

MARK WASTE CLEARLY.

SCRIBE LINE MADE WITH MARKING GAUGE DELINEATES LENGTH OF PINS AND NAILS.

Now cut out the tails. Saw down to the scribe line, cutting on the waste side of the layout lines. A dozuki is easy to control and cuts crisp lines. Watch your layout lines carefully: Follow the angle of the tails, making sure you don't cut through either of the scribe lines. Remove the waste between the tails by chiseling halfway through the board from one side, then turning the board over and chiseling from the other side.

To lay out the pins, hold the tails against the end grain of the sides, and trace around the tails with a marking knife. Carry your layout lines down to the scribe lines, clearly marking the

waste with a pencil. To cut out the pins, saw along the layout lines to the scribe lines, and chisel away the waste as before. Test fit the dovetails. Pare the pins to fit the tails, if necessary.

SHOP TIP: If the dovetail joints are to be a visible element of the chest, Andy Rae recommends spacing the tails more tightly at the ends of each panel than in its middle. Varying the spacing of the dovetails in this way yields a more pleasing proportion when the chest is viewed from a distance. It also brings attention to the fact that these are hand-cut joints—a pleasing detail in this day of mechanized manufacturing.

3 **Groove the front, back, and sides for the bottom.** The bottom of the chest rides in a groove plowed along the inside face of the front, back, and sides. The $\frac{3}{8}$-inch-wide $\times$ $\frac{3}{8}$-inch-deep groove is $\frac{3}{8}$ inch from the bottom edges of these panels. You can plow the groove with a dado cutter or with a straight bit in a router fitted with an edge guide. Because of the molding around the chest's base, you can save yourself the trouble of stopping these grooves; the molding will cover the square holes created where the groove exits the ends of the front and back panels.

4 **Cut the till joinery in the front, back, and side.** The till is the small compartment inside the chest. The chest's front, back, and one side form three of the till's sides. You have to locate and cut stopped grooves and dadoes

BACK LAYOUT DETAIL

in the front, back, and side for the till's bottom and front. In addition, you have to locate and bore pin-hinge holes in the chest's back and front for the till lid.

Lay out the groove and dado on the back as shown in the *Back Layout Detail*. The layout for the front, of course, is a mirror image of the back. The groove in the side connects those in the front and back. All are ¼ inch wide × ¼ inch deep. Cut them with a router, and square their corners and ends with a chisel.

Pin-hinge holes must be drilled into the front and back as well, and their locations are critical for proper hinging of the till lid. First drill 1½-inch-deep holes

in the ends of the lid to accommodate the ½-inch-diameter dowels. Locate these holes by halving the thickness of the lid and using that dimension to measure from the face and the back edge of the lid. Rae's till lid is ⅞ inch thick, so the center of the hole is ⁷⁄₁₆ inch from both the face and the back edge. The top back edge of the till lid must be radiused to allow for clearance when the lid is opened; make this radius half the thickness of your lid—in this case, ⁷⁄₁₆ inch. This is easily done with a block plane and a sanding block.

According to Rae, the best way to position the pin-hinge holes in the chest is to use a mock-up of the front and back (scrap plywood will do) and the actual till lid. Using your mock-up, locate and drill a ½-inch-deep hole into its front and back. The aim is to minimize the clearance between the chest side and the lid's back edge. Once you are happy with the fit, drill the holes into the chest front and back.

5 **Make the bottom and the till parts.** The bottom has already been glued up from several narrower boards. Trim it to the size specified by the Cutting List. Cut a ½-inch-wide × ⅜-inch-deep rabbet around the bottom. The tongue thus formed is ⅛ inch longer than its groove is deep. The result is a ⅛-inch-wide gap between the chest's sides and bottom, which allows these parts to expand and contract without damaging the chest.

Work on the till parts next. Using a router and a piloted ¼-inch rabbeting bit, cut a ¼-inch-deep rabbet around the four sides of the till bottom. Without changing the router setup, form ¼-inch-thick tongues on both ends of the till front. To do this, cut a rabbet across each end of the piece, then turn the piece over and repeat the rabbeting. With a backsaw, shorten the tongues by removing ¼ inch from each end. Complete the front by plowing a ¼-inch-wide × ¼-inch-deep groove along the inside, ¼ inch from the bottom edge. This can be done with a couple of passes on the table saw.

Test fit the tongues in the appropriate grooves or dadoes.

Complete the till lid by routing the front edge with a ¾-inch rounding-over bit, cutting deeply enough to create a slight fillet, as indicated in the *Till, Side View* and the *Back Layout Detail.*

6 **Glue up the chest.** You now can glue up the chest; remember to let in the bottom panel and the till front and bottom. *Do not* glue these parts into the chest—they should float in their grooves, allowing the chest boards to expand and contract without cracking. The two till pieces can be glued up before or, if you feel confident that everything will fit and go smoothly, during the chest assembly. *Do not* install the till lid during glue-up.

Be sure to check that the chest is square. If your dovetails fit tightly, there should be no need to clamp the case as you put it together; but have a few clamps at hand to close up a gap here and there.

7 **Cut the base dovetails and assemble the base.** The dovetails for the base are made in the same manner as those for the chest itself. See the *Base Detail* for the dimensions of the dovetails.

Cut a stopped rabbet in the top edge of all four baseboards to let in the cleats that support the case. The ½-inch-wide × ¾-inch-deep rabbet can be cut with a dado cutter on the table saw, and the rounded corners can be squared up with a chisel.

Lay out and cut the notches that form the feet of each base piece. Again, see the *Base Detail* for dimensions. Cut the notches on the band saw, and sand the cut edges thoroughly.

You now can glue the feet together as you did the chest. After the glue has set, glue the two cleats into the front and back rabbets, and secure them with nails or screws.

Join the chest and base with #8 × 1¼-inch screws driven through slotted pilot holes, allowing for movement in the chest's bottom. Turn the chest upside down, center the base on it, and drive the screws.

8 **Make and install the base moldings.** If you are making your chest from pine, you may be able to purchase the moldings for the base. Otherwise, you must either have it made or make it yourself. Rae cuts his moldings using a Sears molding cutter in his table saw. You also can cut moldings using a router or a shaper. In any case, for safety's sake, shape the edge of a fairly broad board, then rip the molding strip from the board.

The base moldings are mitered and nailed to the chest. Begin with the bullnose molding; butt it against the sides of the chest with glue, but nail it to the feet. This keeps the molding tight to the sides while allowing the sides to expand and contract. Any gaps that develop when it's especially dry—usually during the winter heating season—will appear underneath the bullnose, safe from prying eyes. The ogee molding can be glued and nailed to the chest and the bullnose molding.

9 **Hinge the lid to the chest.** Rae recommends hinging the lid to the chest before adding the lid molding. This allows you to compensate for irregularities or unforeseen glitches—primarily an out-of-square chest. To allow the case to expand without binding the lid, which makes the chest difficult to open, the lid should overhang the case front and sides by ⅛ inch. The back edge of the lid is flush with the chest back.

Rae used special hinges whose range of motion is limited to about 100 degrees. The lid will open just beyond perpendicular, which means it will stay open without being held. Instead of holding the lid with one hand, you can use both hands to root through the chest. The hinges are expensive, however; you may opt to use regular butt hinges and rely on the till lid to hold the chest lid open. (Open the chest, lift the till lid, then settle the chest lid onto the till lid's edge.) Whichever hinges you use, mortise them into the top edge of the chest back and the lid.

10 **Make and apply the lid molding.** With the lid fitted to your satisfaction, remove it from its hinges. Cut the ogee molding to fit. The molding can be glued directly to the lid's front edge, since it is long grain to long grain. But it must be splined to the lid's sides, since these are long grain to short grain. The ideal approach here is to use a biscuit joiner to cut slots in the edge of the lid and in the molding, then to glue up the molding with biscuits. With glue applied only in the slots, considerable wood movement of the lid can occur without

SHOP TIP: Because it is so difficult to clamp the molded edge effectively (clamps tend to slip), do what Rae does: Cut the ogee pattern (he uses a Sears molding cutter in his table saw), glue the molding to the lid, and radius the top edge with a router and a ¾-inch rounding-over bit.

breaking the molding joints. As an alternative, cut a groove in the molding and the lid using the table saw, then cut 2-inch lengths of spline to fit into the grooves. Glue only where the splines are.

11 **Make and install the lid cleats.** If your chest is made from softwood, it's a good idea to reinforce the lid on the underside with hardwood cleats. You already cut the cleats from 2-inch-wide stock. Taper them to 1 inch at each end, leaving a center section of about one-half the overall length at the 2-inch width. You can cut the tapers either on the band saw or with a tapering jig on the table saw.

Mount each cleat with three #10 × 2½-inch screws, driving them through countersunk, oversized pilot holes. Don't glue the cleats to the lid, as this would inhibit the lid's seasonal expansion and contraction.

12 **Apply a finish.** You're ready for the finish of your choice. Rae approached his chest "as a three-dimensional canvas," and he applied three to four contrasting layers of artist's oil

paints to cover the exterior. The inside is painted a neutral color to harmonize with the walnut cleats and till lid, which are finished with tung oil. Rae probably spent more time painting the chest than he did building it.

If your chest is made from a "show wood," finish the outside and leave the inside alone, as any finish on the inside will tend to permeate whatever is eventually stored in the chest. Traditionally, such chests were made entirely from pine, with the outside stained and finished and the inside bare except for the occasional waxing.

13 **(Re)install the lids.** The last step is to install your prefinished till lid. This is accomplished by dropping 1-inch-long springs into the holes in the till lid, then inserting the dowels. Press the dowels into the holes so that they're flush. Maneuver the lid into position so that the dowels spring into the holes in the chest. Should the lid ever need to be removed, just saw through one dowel and lift the lid out.

Reinstall the chest lid, and your project is ready for blankets.

Contributing Craftsmen

Ken Burton, Jr. (Contemporary Quilt Stand)

Ken Burton, Sr. (Early American Settle Table, Bedside Table, Shaker-Style Wall Cabinet)

Jeff Day (Notions Box)

Michael Dunbar (Pipe Box, Splay-Legged Table)

Rodney Gehret (Snake-in-the-Box, Toy Dump Truck)

Bill Hylton (Ned's Crib, Folding Tray Table)

Mitch Mandel (Emmy's Footstool, Vegetable Storage Bins)

Fred Matlack (Rocking Horse, Stilts, New England Pine Cupboard)

Fred Matlack and Phil Gehret of the Rodale Press Design Group (Small Chest, Bunk Beds, Knife Block, Trivets, Baker's Cooling Rack, Folding Stepladder, Walking Duck, Xylophone, Bench/Doll Cradle, Mission Plate Rack, Mudroom Boot Bench, Pine Bookcase)

Kelly Mehler (Walnut Lap Desk)

Walter Morrison (Wall Shelf)

David Page (Piano Bench-Cabinet)

Andy Rae (Six-Board Blanket Chest)

Brad Smith (Youth Chair, Playroom Bookcase, Child's Stool, Child's Coatrack, Toy Chest, Playroom Table and Chairs)

Pat Warner (Display Cabinet)

Rich Weinsteiger (Chopping Tray)

Your Woodworking Projects Can Make You a Winner!

See your project in the next volume of *The Weekend Woodworker* series and win $150 in the bargain. All you have to do is send us a photograph of your project. If the Rodale Press woodworking editors pick your project for inclusion in the next volume, you win $150. See your name in print! Your project on display! *Get the next volume free!*

Enter as many projects as you like.

The main criteria? The project must be something that an intermediate-level woodworker can complete in a weekend or two. Anything you've built in a weekend or two can be entered—furniture, cabinetry, toys, accent pieces. Practical projects and frivolous ones. For the home or shop, the outdoors or in. It can be made from any wood—walnut or plywood, pine or padauk.

So show us what you've built. Send a photo that clearly shows your project to:

Ken Burton
Rodale Press, Inc.
33 East Minor Street
Emmaus, PA 18098-0099

We'll select three projects for inclusion in the next volume and award each project's designer/builder $150.

Submit your projects no later than June 30, 1992.